Dedication

To my husband, Ed Schwartz, who generously supported me,
financially as well as emotionally, as I researched and wrote this book.

Kauai Trails

Walks, Strolls and Treks on the Garden Island

Kathy Morey

WILDERNESS PRESS

BERKELEY

FIRST EDITION January 1991
Second printing May 1992
Third printing May 1995
SECOND EDITION June 1997
Second printing May 1998

Library of Congress Card Number 97-3128
ISBN 0-89997-214-4
Manufactured in the United States of America
Published by **Wilderness Press**
                    2440 Bancroft Way
                    Berkeley, CA 94704
                    (800) 443-7227
                    FAX (510) 548-1355

                    Write or call for free catalog
                    Visit our Web site at www.wildernesspress.com!

Cover photos: Kalalau Valley Overlook, Kokee State Park *(large photo)*
                    Haena Beach *(inset photo)*

Library of Congress Cataloging-in-Publication Data

Morey, Kathy.
    Kauai trails : walks, strolls, and treks on the garden island / Kathy
Morey. -- 2nd ed.
            p.   cm.
    Includes bibliographical references and index.
    ISBN 0-89997-214-4
    1. Kauai (Hawaii)--Guidebooks. 2. Hiking--Hawaii--Kauai--Guide-
books. I. Title
    DU628.K3M67   1997
    919.69'410441--dc21   97-3128
                                                           CIP

Contents

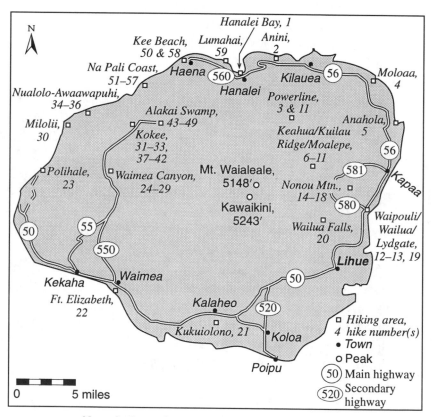

Kauai: Overview of Principal Hiking Areas

Introduction

"Kauai. . . .Oh, it's just a little island. You can fly over it in an hour in a helicopter. Or you can take a half-day bus tour. Or you can rent a car and see everything in a day. It's just a little island."

That became a standing joke in our house, a metaphor for a common misperception about Kauai. Kauai is a little island only from the outside. Kauai is a *big* island on the inside, especially when you see it on foot. True, flying over Kauai or touring it with a guide may give you a different perspective on it or helpful information about it. And even a hasty visit like that will leave you with lasting memories of its beauty. But I'm convinced that if you're at all able, you need to see Kauai on foot, too. It's only when you get out of those metal-and-glass cocoons to touch Kauai with all your senses, to experience it at the slow pace of the walker, that Kauai can really touch *you*. There are rewarding strolls as short as a quarter mile, suitable for just about anyone who's ambulatory; strenuous, multi-day trips like the Kalalau Trail on the Na Pali Coast; and everything in between. How do I know? I walked every trail that's used as a trip in this book at least once in the winter and spring of 1990, for the first edition. I walked many of them again in the spring of 1993, in the wake of Hurricane Iniki (September, 1992), and yet again in the spring of 1995.

When you're on foot, Kauai's rugged landscape seems to be faceted like a diamond, so that with every few steps you take, it reveals a new face to you. The rain may fill one face with rainbows, another with waterfalls flying down sheer cliffs. Where rain is abundant, as on the northern shore, luxuriant vegetation clothes the landscape, softening its lines and muting its colors. Infrequent rain, as on the southwest coast, yields dry golden dunes stretching along the sea for miles and bare red cliffs soaring behind them. Inland, dense banks of ferns dotted with wild orchids set off abandoned roads whose eroded surfaces may display an astonishing array of colors. Cascades barely glimpsed from the highway show themselves to the hiker as immense falls, like Namolokama, the great waterfall that leaps down into Hanalei Valley. Dozens of unnamed waterfalls may be apparent, from broad ribbons of white to stairstep cascades to fragile wisps blowing in the wind. A stroll down a cane road shows you how the clipped, gray-green carpets of the canefields unfold across the plains and stop abruptly at the shaggy, dark green mountains of the forest reserves.

Perhaps I should not have told you this. Perhaps I should have let you go unwarned, let you discover Kauai in your own way. You will have to spend some time on Kauai, walk some time on Kauai, and let me know if I've done the right thing.

Some notes about this Second Edition. . . .

There's more to this new edition than just updated trail details. Former Trips 21–23 are gone; alas, the Lihue Plantation Company no longer gives permission to cross their land.

I've rearranged a few trips to make it easier to use the book—I hope. For example, three closely related trips east of Kokee State Park Headquarters—on the Nualolo, the Awaawapuhi, and Nualolo Cliff trails—that were formerly separated are now together.

Also, I've revised all the maps using better software. I tried to eliminate details that cluttered the maps, detracting from important trail information. To make the trails stand out better, I reshaped many maps so they focused on the trails, making odd-shaped but more usable maps.

Author beginning the Kalalau Trail (Trips 51–57)

Ed Schwartz

Getting Information About Kauai

The search for the perfect trail guide. I wish I could be certain this was a flawless book. However, some things limit an author's ability to produce a perfect, error-free, always up-to-date book. Here are some of the factors, and what you can do to help yourself (and me).

Nature makes constant revisions; so do agencies. Nature constantly reshapes the landscape across which we plan to trek. That's usually a gradual process, but once in a while she makes drastic changes overnight. A landslide can erase a trail in seconds. Erosion can undercut a cliff edge and make last year's safe hike an extremely dangerous one, so that the local authorities close a trail you'd hoped to ramble on. And Kauai's fragile volcanic terrain erodes quite rapidly.

Agencies in charge of hiking areas may close an area because they've realized it's environmentally too sensitive to survive more human visits. An area once open to overnight camping may become a day-use-only area. Trails become impassable from lack of maintenance. Happily, agencies may open new areas because they've been able to acquire new acreage or complete a trail-building project.

Since I first wrote this book, I've seen old trails close and new trails open on Kauai—and then vanish as the rainforest reclaimed them in the wake of a natural disaster. Other trails on public land have become inaccessible because to get to them, you have to cross private land, and the landowner no longer grants permission to cross the land.

Change is the only thing that's constant in this world, so that guidebook authors and publishers always play "catch up" with Nature and with agencies. We want to keep guidebooks up to date, but we are always at least one step behind the latest changes. The day when you'll have constantly-revised books on-line at your wristwatch/computer terminal isn't here yet. So it's possible that a few trail descriptions are becoming obsolete even as this book goes to press.

Write for the latest information. You should use this book in conjunction with the latest trail information from the agency in charge of the areas you plan to hike in (the Division of State Parks or the Division of Forestry and Wildlife). However, this book gives you a much more complete picture of Kauai's principal hiking and backcountry camping opportunities than information available from any single agency can. And it describes those opportunities from a hiker's perspective.

It's a good idea to write to these agencies as soon as you've read this book and decided where you want to hike and camp on Kauai. Ask them for their latest trail and camping maps, regulations, and permit-issuing procedures. Enclose a stamped, self-addressed envelope for *your* convenience in getting the information you need as soon as possible. Their addresses and telephone numbers are in "Getting Permits."

Prepare yourself with general information, too. A generous source of a wide variety of useful information about Hawaii is the Hawaii Visitors Bureau. You'll find it at (800) GO-HAWAI as well as on the World Wide Web at *http://www.visit.hawaii.org*, a site that offers colorful pages including "Vacation Planner" pages for the State of Hawaii and for each major island.

Here are a couple of guidebooks I use. For all the Hawaiian islands, pick up the latest edition of J.D. Bisignani's *Hawaii Handbook* (Moon Publications, Chico, CA). For an outstanding guide to Kauai, get the latest edition of Andrew Doughty and Harriett Friedman's *Ultimate Kauai Guidebook* (Wizard Publications, P.O. Box 991, Lihue, HI 96766-0991, *wizard@aloha.net*).

Let me know what you think and what you find. I hope this book helps make your visit to Kauai even more enjoyable than it would have been otherwise. I plan to keep on updating the book regularly, and you can help me. Let me know what you think of it. Did you find it helpful when you visited Kauai? Was it accurate and complete enough that you enjoyed the walks and hikes you took based on the book? Did you notice any significant discrepancies between this book and what you found when you visited Kauai, discrepancies that you judge are not just the result of two different perceptions of the same thing? What were they? The publisher and I are very concerned about accuracy. We'd appreciate your comments. I'd also like to know about it if you think there are ways in which the book can be improved. Write to me in care of Wilderness Press, 2440 Bancroft Way, Berkeley, CA 94704.

Spoken Hawaiian: An Incomplete and Unauthoritative Guide

What, only 12 letters?! Nineteenth-century American missionaries used only 12 letters to create a written version of the spoken Hawaiian language. Superficially, that might make Hawaiian seem simple. But Hawaiian is a much more complex and subtle language than 12 letters can do justice to. However, we're stuck with those 12 letters, the five English vowels (a, e, i, o, u) and seven of the consonants (h, k, l, m, n, p, w).

Consonants. The consonants have the same sound in Hawaiian as they do in your everyday English except for "w." "W" is sometimes pronounced as "v" when it follows "a," always pronounced as "v" when it follows "e" or "i." (For example, the devastating 1982 hurricane's name is pronounced "I-va," not "I-wa.")

Vowels. The vowels are generally pronounced as they are in Italian, with each vowel sounded separately. Authentic Hawaiian makes further distinctions, but those are of more interest to scholars than to hikers.* The following is a simplified system. Vowel sounds in general are:

a   like "ah" in "<u>a</u>ha."
e   like "ay" in "d<u>ay</u>."
i   like "ee" as in "wh<u>ee</u>!"
o   like "o" in "g<u>o</u>."
u   like "oo" in "f<u>oo</u>d" (or "u" in "r<u>u</u>de")

---

* Remember that Hawaiian evolved as a spoken, not a written, language. Authentic *written* Hawaiian uses two special marks to indicate other variations on pronouncing vowels in *spoken* Hawaiian. Those variations change the meaning of a word. One is the glottal stop, indicated by a single quotation mark ('). It indicates that you should make a complete break in your voice before sounding the vowel that follows it. There really isn't an English equivalent, though the break in "uh-oh!" is close. Another is the macron mark, which is a straight line over a vowel. It indicates that you should pronounce a vowel as a long sound instead of a short sound. For example, the Hawaiian long-a sound is "ah," and the Hawaiian short-a sound is "uh." We have the same sounds in English but don't use special marks to distinguish between them except in dictionaries. Road signs, topographic maps, and this book don't use glottal stops or macron marks.

5

Notice that that means that when you see two or more of the same letter in a row, you pronounce each of them separately:

"Kapaa" is Ka-pa-a.
"Kokee" is Ko-ke-e.
"Iiwi" is I-i-wi.
"Hoolulu" is Ho-o-lu-lu.
"Puu" is Pu-u.

That seems *too* simple, and it is. If you tried to pronounce every vowel, speaking Hawaiian would turn into a nightmare. You wouldn't live long enough to pronounce some words. Fortunately, several pairs of vowels often—but not always—form merged sounds.

Vowel Pairs Whose Sounds Merge. Like every other language, Hawaiian has vowel pairs whose sounds naturally "smooth" into each other. They're similar to Italian or English diphthongs. The degree to which the two sounds are merged in Hawaiian is officially less than occurs in English, but most Hawaiian people I've talked with on Kauai merge them fully. Vowel-pair pronunciation is approximately:

ae   often smoothed to "eye" as in "<u>eye</u>ful" or "i" in "<u>i</u>ce." It's the English long-i sound.
ai   often smoothed as for "ae," above.
ao   often smoothed to sound like "ow" in "c<u>ow</u>."
au   often smoothed to "ow" in "c<u>ow</u>", too.
ei   sometimes smoothed to "ay" as in "d<u>ay</u>." It's the English long-a sound.
eu   smooth the sounds together a *little*, like "ayoo."
oi   usually like "oi" in "<u>oi</u>l"—in other words, just what you're used to.
ou   usually like "oh," the English long-o sound.

Syllables. Every Hawaiian syllable ends in a vowel sound. A Hawaiian syllable never contains more than one consonant. That means every consonant goes with the vowel that *follows* it. Every vowel *not* preceded by a consonant stands alone when you break a *written* word into syllables (you may smooth some of them together when you *speak*). For example:

"Aa" consists of the two syllables a-a (it's a kind of lava flow).
"Kokee" consists of the three syllables Ko-ke-e (a state park I hope you'll visit).
"Kalaheo" consists of the four syllables Ka-la-he-o (a town on Kauai)

"Okolehao" consists of the five syllables O-ko-le-ha-o (a potent liquor once distilled from *ti* plant roots).

"Hanakapiai" consists of the six syllables Ha-na-ka-pi-a-i (a beach and valley on the Na Pali Coast).

"Liliuokalani" consists of the seven syllables Li-li-u-o-ka-la-ni (Hawaii's last monarch and writer of the beloved song "Aloha Oe").

Accent. In general, the accent falls on the next-to-last syllable for words with three or more syllables and on the first syllable for words of two syllables. For words of more than three syllables, you put a little stress on every other syllable preceding the accented one. Don't worry about this; it seems to come naturally.

There are common-usage exceptions, such as *makai* (ma-KAI, with the accent on the last syllable). When you see exceptions such as those, chances are that what has happened is that European usage has fully merged two sounds into one. Proper Hawaiian pronunciation of *makai* would be closer to "ma-KAH-i," a three-syllable word with the last two syllables almost merging.

Hint for Longer Words: Repetition and Rhythm. Have you noticed the tendency in long Hawaiian words for groups of letters to repeat? That kind of repetition is fairly common. When you see a long Hawaiian word, don't panic. Identify its repeating letter groups, figure out how to pronounce them individually, then put the whole word together. Chances are you'll come pretty close to getting it correct.

For example, *Waialeale* throws a lot of people. But look at the repeating letter group *ale* (ah-lay). See the word as "Wai/ale/ale." So, two "a-le"s prefixed with a *wai* (the *ai* merges here) — that makes "wai/a-le/a-le." Once you've identified the repeating groups, the rhythm of the word comes naturally. Try this approach for longer words, including the state fish: *humuhumunukunukuapuaa*: two "hu-mu"s, two "nu-ku"s, and an "a-pu-a-a." Now try it: "hu-mu/hu-mu/nu-ku/nu-ku/a-pu-a-a." ...Very good!

Makai **and** *mauka*. In Hawaii, local people often give directions or describe the location of a place as *makai* (merge the *ai*), which means "toward the sea," or *mauka* (merge the *au*), which means "toward the mountains; inland." I had a terrible time remembering which was which until I came up with this mnemonic:

Go *makai*
Where sea meets sky,

and Tom Winnett came up with:

Mauka is toward the MAUntains.

However, I still think in terms of left, right, north, south, east, and west. I don't often use *mauka* and *makai* in this book.

Do your best, with respect. Approach the language with respect, and give it your best shot. Then be prepared to hear local people pronounce it differently. Learn from them. Maybe it's part of our jobs as visitors to inadvertently provide a little comic relief for those living and working here as opposed to just vacationing here.

Instant Hawaiian (see Bibliography) is a useful booklet that's a lot less frivolous than its title implies. It begins, "So you'd like to learn to speak Hawaiian — you should live so long!" I felt I'd come to the right place. Look for it when you get to Kauai.

Geology and History, Natural and Human

First, the earth

According to the theory of *plate tectonics*, the earth consists of:

A rigid, rocky outer shell, the *lithosphere* ("rocky zone")
Beneath the lithosphere, a hot, semifluid layer, the *asthenosphere* ("weak zone")
A core that doesn't play a part in this oversimplified discussion.

The lithosphere is broken into *plates* that move with respect to each other. Hot, fluid material, possibly from the asthenosphere or melted by contact with the asthenosphere, penetrates up through the lithosphere at three kinds of places:

Mid-oceanic ridges, where plates spread apart
Subduction zones, where plates collide and one dives under the other (subducts)
Hot spots, where a plume of molten material appears in the middle of a plate.

Next, the land

It's believed that the Hawaiian Islands exist where the Pacific Plate, on which they ride, is moving northwest across a hot spot. An undersea volcano is built where the plate is over the hot spot. If the volcano gets big enough, it breaks the ocean's surface to become an island. Eventually, the plate's movement carries the island far enough away from the hot spot that volcanism ceases on that island. Erosion, which began the moment the new island appeared above the sea, tears the land down.

The Hawaiian Islands are successively older toward the northwest and younger toward the southeast. Northwestern islands, like Laysan, are hardly more than bits of volcanic rock now. Southeastern islands,

9

including the major Hawaiian Islands, are still significant chunks of land. In geologically recent times, including today, the big island of Hawaii is the youngest and the farthest southeast of the major islands; Kauai is the oldest and the farthest northwest of the major islands.

The molten material—lava—characteristic of Hawaiian volcanoes is relatively fluid. The fluidity of the lava allows it to spread widely, and repeated eruptions produce broad-based, rounded volcanoes called "shield volcanoes." The volcano expels not only flowing lava but volcanic fragments such as cinder and ash. Alternating layers of these materials build up during periods of volcanic activity. Erosion has sculpted the exotic landscapes we associate with tropical islands. Waves pound the volcano's edges, undercutting them and, where the volcano slopes more steeply, forming cliffs like those of the Na Pali Coast. Streams take material from higher on the volcano, cutting valleys into its flanks and depositing the material they carry as alluvium, like the alluvial apron at the mouth of Kalalau Valley. New episodes of volcanism wholly or partly fill in those landscapes, and erosional forces immediately begin sculpting the new surface as well as the remaining older surface.

Earth began building the great shield volcano of Kauai about 6 million years ago, so Kauai is a mere infant in geological terms, compared to an Earth over 4 billion years old. Kauai's initial period of activity, when the shield volcano was built, apparently ended about 3 million years ago. A quiescent period about 1.5 million years long followed; then a period of renewed volcanic activity began about 1.5 million years ago. New lavas then flowed over the eastern two-thirds of Kauai.

The last lava flow on Kauai is believed to have occurred on its southern shore near Poipu some 40,000 years ago. Erosion reigns now, changing the landscape constantly.

Life arrives

Living organisms colonize new land rapidly. In Hawaii, plants established themselves once there was a little soil for them. Seeds arrived on the air currents, too, or floated in from the sea, or hitched a ride on the feathers or in the guts of birds. Insects and spiders also took advantage of the air currents. Birds were certainly among the first visitors. Living things found little competition and quickly adapted to their new home, evolving into an astonishing variety of species many of which occur naturally only on the Hawaiian islands ("endemic to Hawaii"). The only mammals to arrive were the bat and the seal. Some birds became flightless — a fairly common adaptation on isolated islands with no ground predators.

People arrive

It's unlikely that the site of the very first human colony in the Hawaiian Islands will ever be found. Too much time has passed; too many destructive forces have been at work. However, recent archaeological work has established that people had settled in Hawaii by 300–400 A.D., earlier than had previously been thought. Linguistic studies and cultural artifacts recovered from sites of early colonization point to the Marquesas Islands as the colonizers' home; the Marquesas themselves seem to have been colonized as early as 200 B.C.

The colonizers of Hawaii had to adapt the Marquesan technology to their new home. For example, the Marquesans made distinctive large, one-piece fishhooks from the large, strong pearl shells that abounded in Marquesan waters. There are no such large shells in Hawaiian waters, so the colonists developed two-piece fishhooks made of the weaker materials that were available in Hawaii (such as bone and wood). Over time, a uniquely Hawaiian material culture developed.

At one time, scholars believed that, as related in Hawaii's oral traditions and genealogies, a later wave of colonizers from Tahiti swept in and conquered the earlier Hawaiians. Research does not support that theory. Instead, research has revealed that before European contact, Hawaiian material culture evolved steadily in patterns that suggest gradual and local, not abrupt and external, influences. The archaeologi-

Kauai's "Menehune Fishpond," built, according to legend, by a race of tiny people called Menehunes

Hawaii Visitors Bureau

cal record hints that there may have been some Hawaiian-Tahitian contact in the twelfth century, but its influence was slight.

The Hawaiians profoundly altered the environment of the islands. They had brought with them the plants they had found most useful in the Marquesas Islands: taro, ti , the trees from which they made a bark cloth (*kapa*), sugarcane, ginger, gourd plants, yams, bamboo, turmeric, arrowroot, and the breadfruit tree. They also brought the small pigs of Polynesia, dogs, jungle fowl, and, probably as stowaways, rats. They used slash-and-burn technology to clear the native lowland forests for the crops they brought. Habitat loss together with competition for food with and predation by the newly introduced animals wrought havoc with the native animals, particularly birds. Many species of birds had already become extinct long before Europeans arrived.

On the eve of the Europeans' accidentally stumbling across Hawaii, the major Hawaiian islands held substantial numbers of people of Polynesian descent. They had no written language, but their oral and musical traditions were ancient and rich.

Their technology apparently remained as static as their rigid social system. Commoners, or *makaainana*, lived in self-sufficient family groups and villages, farming and fishing for most necessities and trading for necessities they could not otherwise obtain. The land was divided among hereditary chiefs of the noble class (*alii*). Commoners paid part of their crops or catches as taxes to the chief who ruled the land-division they lived on; commoners served their chief as soldiers. Higher chiefs ruled over lower chiefs; the higher chiefs received taxes and commoners to serve as soldiers from the lower chiefs in turn. People especially gifted in healing, divination, or important crafts served the populace in those capacities (for example, as priests). There was also a class of untouchables, the *kauwa*. Most people were at death what they were at birth.

Strict laws defined what was forbidden, or *kapu*, and governed the conduct of *kauwa* toward everyone else, of commoners toward *alii*, of *alii* of a lower rank to *alii* of higher rank, and of men and

Hawaii's native goose and state bird, the nene

women toward each other. Some of the laws seem irrationally harsh. For example, a commoner could be put to death if his shadow fell on an *alii*. Chiefs frequently made war on each other. If the chiefs of one island were united under a high chief or a king, often that island would make war on the other islands.

The people of Kauai, like other Hawaiians, worshipped many gods and goddesses. The principal ones were Ku, Kane, Kanaloa, and Lono. Ku represented the male aspect of the natural world. Ku was also the god of war and demanded human sacrifice. Kane was the god of life, a benevolent god who was regarded as the Creator and the ancestor of all Hawaiians. The Kauaians worshipped Kane at many places. The high *alii* of Kauai, both men and women, made a difficult annual pilgrimage from Wailua to worship at Kane's altar on the forbidding, stormy summit plateau of Kauai's sacred mountain, Waialeale. Kanaloa ruled the dead and the dark aspects of life, and he was often linked with Kane in worship.

Lono was another benevolent god; he ruled clouds, rain, and harvests. The annual winter festival in Lono's honor, *Makahiki*, ran from October to February. *Makahiki* was a time of harvest, celebration, fewer *kapu*, and sporting events. Images of Lono were carried around each island atop tall poles with crosspieces from which banners of white *kapa* flew. (Legend said Lono had sailed away from Hawaii long ago and would return in a floating *heiau* (temple) decked with poles flying long white banners from their crosspieces.) Chiefs and chiefesses met the image of Lono with ceremonies and gifts, and commoners came forward to pay their taxes.

Systems like that can last for hundreds and even thousands of years in the absence of compelling internal problems or changes and of external forces, as the Hawaiian system did. But change eventually comes.

The Europeans arrive by accident

Christopher Columbus had sailed from Spain to what he thought was the Orient, hoping to find a sea route to replace the long, hazardous land route. But in fact he discovered an obstacle called North America. With a direct sea route between Europe and the Orient blocked, people sought other sea routes. The southern routes around the Cape of Good Hope at the tip of Africa and Cape Horn at the tip of South America proved to be very long and very treacherous. Still, the trade was lucrative. The European demand for Oriental goods such as spices, Chinese porcelain, and silk was insatiable. By trading their way around the world, a captain, his crew, and the government or the tradesmen that financed them might become very wealthy in just one voyage.

All over Europe, people came to believe that a good, navigable route *must* exist in northern waters that would allow them to sail west from Europe around the northern end of North America to the Orient. (It doesn't exist.) Captain James Cook sailed from England on July 12, 1776, to try to find the Northwest Passage from the Pacific side.

In December of 1777, Cook left Tahiti sailing northeast, not expecting to see land again until he reached North America. Instead, he sighted land on January 18, 1778, and reached the southeast shore of Kauai on January 19th. In Hawaii, it was the time of *Makahiki*, the festival honoring the god Lono. The Hawaiians mistook the masts and sails of Cook's ships for the poles and *kapa* banners of the floating *heiau* on which Lono was to return. They received Cook as if he were Lono.

Cook was an intelligent and compassionate man who respected the native societies he found and who tried to deal with their people fairly and decently. He tried to keep crewmen who he knew had venereal diseases from infecting the natives, but he failed. Cook did not stay long in Hawaii. He spent most of 1778 searching for the Northwest Passage; unsuccessful, he returned to Hawaii in early 1779 to make repairs and resupply. It was *Makahiki* again. All went well at first, but the Hawaiians stole an auxiliary boat from one of his ships. When he tried to retrieve it, there was a brief skirmish, in which Cook and four of his crew were killed.

Cook's ships survived a second futile search for the Northwest Passage, after which the crew sailed westward for England, stopping in China. There the crew learned the astonishing value of another of the expedition's great discoveries: the furs of the sea otters and seals of the Pacific Northwest. Trade with the Orient suddenly became even more profitable, and Hawaii was to become not an isolated curiosity but an important point on a major world trade route.

In Hawaii, the young chief Kamehameha began his conquest of the islands in 1790. Kamehameha actively sought Western allies, weapons, and advice. He conquered all the islands but Kauai and Niihau; his two attempts to invade Kauai failed.

Kamehameha's wars, Western diseases, and the sandalwood trade decimated the native Hawaiians. Chiefs indebted themselves to foreign merchants for weapons and other goods. New England merchants discovered that Hawaii had abundant sandalwood for which the Chinese would pay huge prices. Merchants demanded payment in sandalwood. The heartwood nearest the roots was the best part; the whole tree had to be destroyed to get it. The mountains were stripped of their sandalwood trees. Those ordered into the mountains often died of exposure and starvation. Communities that had depended on their labor for food also starved.

Kamehameha I died in 1819, leaving the monarchy to his son Liholiho and a regency in Liholiho's behalf to his favorite wife, Kaahumanu. Liholiho was an amiable, weak-willed alcoholic. Kaahumanu was strong-willed, intelligent, capable, and ambitious. She believed that the old Hawaiian *kapu* system was obsolete: no gods struck down the Westerners, who daily did things that were *kapu* for Hawaiians. Six months after Kamehameha I's death, she persuaded Liholiho to join her in breaking several ancient *kapu*. The *kapu* system, discredited, crumbled; the old order was dead.

The missionaries arrive

Congregationalist missionaries from New England reached Hawaii in 1820, Kauai in 1821. Liholiho grudgingly gave them a year's trial, but the king of Kauai welcomed them: one of his sons had been traveling abroad and had returned with the missionaries. The end of the *kapu* system had left a religious vacuum into which the missionaries moved remarkably easily. To their credit, they came with a sincere desire to commit their lives to bettering those of the people of Hawaii. Liholiho's mother converted to Christianity and made it acceptable for other ali*i* to follow her example. Kaahumanu became a convert, too, and set about remodeling Hawaii socially and politically, based on the Ten Commandments.

An ecosystem passes

Cook and those who came after him gave cattle, goats, and large European pigs as gifts to the Hawaiian chiefs, and the animals overran the islands. They ate everything. Rainwater sluiced off the bare hillsides without replenishing the aquifers. Areas that had

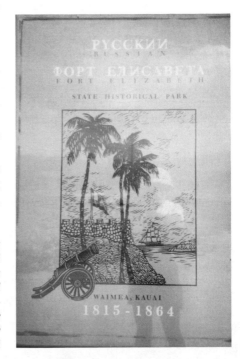

At the ruins of Russian Fort Elizabeth (Trip 22), signs tell the story of Imperial Russia's attempts in the late 18th and early 19th centuries to establish colonies in and around the Pacific, including a colony on Kauai

been blessed with an abundance of water suffered drought now. Native plants could not reestablish themselves because the unrestrained animals ate them as soon as they sent up a shoot. People wrongly concluded that native plants were inherently unable to reestablish themselves, and they imported non-native trees like the eucalyptuses and ironwoods that you see so often today.

The native habitat area and diversity shrank still more before the new sugar plantations. Planters drained wetlands for the commercially valuable crop and erected dams, ditches, and sluices to divert the natural water supply into a controllable water supply. What they did was not so very different from what the Polynesians had done when they had cleared the native lowland forests in order to plant their taro, but the scale was far vaster. In one particularly terrible mistake, growers imported the mongoose to prey on the rats that damaged their crops. But the rat forages at night, while the mongoose hunts by day: they seldom met. What the mongooses preyed on instead were the eggs of native ground-nesting birds.

Few of Hawaii's native plants put forth showy flowers or set palatable fruit, so the new settlers imported ornamental and fruiting plants to brighten their gardens and tables. Many shrubs and trees did so well in Hawaii's favorable climate that they escaped into the wild to become pest plants, crowding out native species and interrupting the food chain.

Birds brought over as pets escaped to compete with native species. More species of native birds have become extinct in Hawaii than anywhere else in the world, and most of the birds you see will be introduced species like the zebra dove and the myna.

It is tragic but true that when you visit Hawaii, you will probably see very few of its native plants and animals. Kauai's upland forests offer some of the best remaining opportunities to see species that are truly unique to Hawaii.

A culture passes

Literacy replaced the rich Hawaiian oral tradition, and many legends and stories were forgotten before someone thought to write them down. The significance of many place names, apart from their literal meaning, has been lost forever. Zealous missionaries and converts believed that the native traditions were evil, and they nearly succeeded in eradicating all traces of the native culture.

A nation passes

Hawaiians saw that their only hope of surviving as an independent nation in the modern world was to secure the protection and guarantees of freedom of one of the major powers. The Hawaiian monarchs would have preferred the British, but British influence was ultimately inadequate to withstand American influence. American missionaries doled out God's grace. American entrepreneurs established plantations and businesses. American ships filled the harbors. Economic and cultural domination of Hawaii eventually passed into American hands, particularly after the new land laws of 1850 made it possible for foreigners to own land in Hawaii. The Hawaiian monarchy lasted until 1893, but most of its economic and therefore its political power was gone. Hawaii as an independent nation disappeared soon after.

A race passes

The native Hawaiian people lost much of their importance in the changing, Westernized economy early in the nineteenth century. The burgeoning sugar and pineapple plantations needed laborers, and the Hawaiians were diligent, capable hired hands when they wanted to be. But they did not comprehend the idea of hiring themselves out as day laborers for wages. Planters began to import laborers from other parts of the world: China, Japan, the Philippines, Portugal. Many imported laborers stayed, married, raised families, and went on to establish their own successful businesses. The Hawaiians were soon a minority in their own land.

The numbers of full-blooded Hawaiians declined precipitously throughout the nineteenth century. Beginning with the tragic introduction of venereal disease by Cook's men, venereal diseases swept through the native population who, particularly at *Makahiki*, exchanged partners freely. Venereal disease often leaves its victims sterile, and many who had survived Western diseases, wars, and the sandalwood trade were unable to reproduce. Others married foreigners, so their children only were part Hawaiian. Today most authorities believe that there are no full-blooded Hawaiians left, not even on Niihau, the only island where Hawaiian is still the language of everyday life.

Hawaii becomes American

In the late nineteenth century, the Hawaiian monarchy seemed to some powerful businessmen and civic leaders of American descent to get in the way of the smooth conduct of business. They thought Hawaii would be better off as an American territory. Queen Liliuokalani did not agree. She wanted to assert Hawaii's independence and the authority of its monarchs.

The business community plotted a coup, deposed Liliuokalani in 1893, formed a new government, and petitioned the United States for territorial status. The United States formally annexed Hawaii in 1898. Military projects and mass travel brought mainland Americans flooding into Hawaii. Many stayed, and so the majority of people in Hawaii came to see themselves as Americans, though a minority disagreed (some still do). After many years as a territory, Hawaii became the fiftieth state in 1959.

On November 23, 1993, the United States belatedly apologized to the Native Hawaiian people (Public Law 103-150). Today, several groups seek to restore some measure of self-rule to Hawaii. Models advocated range from that enjoyed by the recognized Native American tribes versus the rest of the United States' citizens and lands, to that of Liechtenstein and Switzerland. To learn more, visit the Hawaiian Sovereignty Elections Council web site at *http://planet-hawaii.com/hsec/index.html.*

Things to come

The huge tourist industry is both a blessing and a curse. Massive development pushes the Hawaii-born off the land to make way for hotels. Displaced Hawaiians, whatever their ethnic background, find themselves having to survive as waiters, chambermaids, clerks—in essence, as the servants of those who have displaced them. Many also fear that tourism will result in the Hawaiian paradise being paved over and lost forever; others feel that it already has been. The story of Hawaii's evolution is far from over.

Kauai Museum

Don't miss the Kauai Museum, 4428 Rice St., Lihue, Kauai, HI 96766, telephone (808) 245-6931. Its fine exhibits on Hawaii's natural and human history more than justify its modest admission fee.

Getting Around on Kauai

Public transportation

Kauai now has bus service; the fare as of July 1996 is $1/regular fare, $0.50 for seniors, students, and disabled people (drivers have the authority to ask for identification). Call the County of Kauai Transportation Agency at (808) 241-6410 from 7 A.M. to 5 P.M. Monday through Saturday to get more information, including a copy of the bus schedule. The bus will get you to the island's major communities but, alas, not to most of the trailheads in this book. Consider using the bus to explore the island's settled areas and renting a car only on those days you want to hike from trailheads that are far from your lodgings or any bus stop. Some rules for the bus are: carryons limited to 9 x 14 x 22 inches; no oversized backpacks and baggage; no boogie boards; no food or drink, no smoking, and no profanity on buses; no drop-offs at undesignated bus stops.

Driving and driving maps

If your plans include hikes that public transportation can't get you to, you should arrange for a rental car well in advance of your visit. Ask for a modest vehicle in a drab color so it's inconspicuous when parked at trailheads. Get a road map of Kauai in advance, perhaps from one of the national automobile clubs if you belong to one. It's good to be able to study the map in advance and have some notion of the island's roads before you tackle them. Some of the maps provided by tourist bureaus are so cute they're useless.

An excellent map covering the entire island and especially good for driving is James A. Bier's *Map of Kaua'i* from University of Hawaii Press. This is one in a series of similar, outstanding, color maps for all the major islands. They're inexpensive and updated frequently. They include street maps of major towns and indexes to streets and points of interest. If you can't find them on the mainland, you'll find them in abundance in Hawaii, at nearly every grocery store, drugstore, and souvenir stand.

Driving on Kauai is generally slower than on the mainland, thank goodness. The major highways are two-lane roads except for a few stretches near Lihue, the county seat. The speed limit is as high as 50 miles an hour on some stretches, but they are exceptions. Count on an average speed of 30 miles an hour around the island. Look out for morning and evening traffic jams around Lihue. Driving time can make serious inroads in your hiking time.

Hiking and hiking maps

Road maps are useless for hiking trails. For trail maps, I recommend the maps in this book—there are maps for all the trips. If you want more detail, get the United States Geological Survey (USGS) 7½' series of topographic ("topo") maps for Kauai. Topos show elevation details as well as roads and trails. However, topos are not updated as often as you'd like. That's why you should use them in conjunction with the maps in this book and maps from the agencies in charge of the island's hiking areas, the Division of State Parks, Kauai District, and the Division of Forestry and Wildlife, Kauai District. If you do not write for the latter in advance, you will need to go into Lihue to get them. See their addresses in "Getting Permits or Permission" in this book.

Kauai is covered by 11 topos, as shown in the illustration below. It's also nice to have the USGS *Kauai County* topo map. If your mainland backpacking store does not carry the Kauai topos, you may get them in person or by mail from:

>   Western Distribution Branch
>   U.S. Geological Survey
>   Box 25286, Federal Center
>   Denver, CO 80225

or

>   Western Mapping Center
>   (NCIC-W)
>   U.S. Geological Survey
>   345 Middlefield Road
>   Menlo Park, CA 94025

Write first for catalogs and prices. When you order the maps, enclose your check for the required amount, made out to the U.S. Geological Survey.

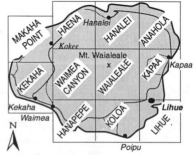

**USGS 7½' Topographic Maps of Kauai
(Names Uppercase)**

Or there may be a store near you that specializes in maps. Look in your telephone directory under "Maps."

The Division of Land and Natural Resources on Kauai now publishes an excellent topographic map of Kauai showing all the trails maintained by the State of Hawaii. This two-sided, color map also includes summaries of the forest reserves, trails, and camping and hunting regulations on Kauai. You can get the map by sending a 10 x 13-inch stamped, self-addressed envelope to the Department of Land and Natural Resources, Division of Forestry and Wildlife; see their address in "Getting Permits" in this book. The map is big—2 feet wide and almost 3 feet long!—so either call to find out the exact postage required or put at least four first-class stamps on your stamped, self-addressed envelope.

Another useful map is Earthwalk Press's *Recreation Map of Northwestern Kaua'i*. Earthwalk Press's maps include topographic data, trail descriptions, and a wealth of other information. If you can't find their maps in your travel store, call them at (800) 828-MAPS.

Getting Permits

The trip descriptions in this book include information about what permits you need (if any) and to whom you should apply for them. All wilderness camping trips require permits. Arrange for them well in advance if possible—*at least one and a half months, longer for Na Pali Coast (Kalalau Trail) permits*—to avoid disappointment.

State Parks

You can apply for Division of State Parks permits in advance by mail. Your application must be accompanied by a photocopy of acceptable identification (such as a driver's license) for each person 18 years old or older. The Division of State Parks is at:

Department of Land and Natural Resources
Division of State Parks, Kauai District
3060 Eiwa Street, Room 306
Lihue, Kauai, HI 96766
(808) 274-3444

If you need to see them in person, Eiwa Street branches off of Rice Street, the main thoroughfare of Lihue. The counters for the Division of State Parks and the Division of Forestry and Wildlife are next to each other in Room 306, but they act independently. You should address inquiries to each separately.

Division of Forestry and Wildlife

You may also apply for Division of Forestry and Wildlife permits in advance by mail; they do not require identification. The Division of Forestry and Wildlife is at:

Department of Land and Natural Resources
Division of Forestry and Wildlife, Kauai District
3060 Eiwa Street, Room 306
Lihue, Kauai, HI 96766
(808) 245-3433

See also the note on actually going into Lihue to see them in person in the paragraph above.

If you put off getting agency permits until you get to Kauai, you will have to go into Lihue to get them.

Weather

The short of it. Let's face it: Kauai is a rainy place. You need to know that it's:

- Rainier on the north shore, which gets up to 45 inches of rain a year
- Less rainy on the east side, which gets up to 30 inches of rain a year
- Driest on the south and west, which get as little as 5 inches a year at Polihale and up to 20 inches a year at Poipu.
- Rainy in the mountains, like Kokee State Park, especially the nearer you get to Mt. Waialeale, the rainiest spot on Earth.

If you want to get away from the rain, head for the south and west coasts. The figure below summarizes the situation:

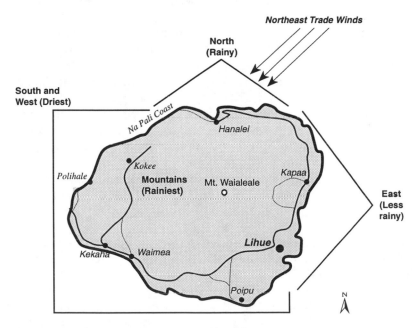

The long of it. Hawaii's weather is temperate to a degree that puts the so-called "temperate" zones of the world to shame. The humidity is moderate, too: 50–60%, not the sweltering horror of some other tropical lands. You are still in the northern hemisphere, so it is warmer in the summer and cooler in the winter, but nothing like the sweltering/freezing mainland.

Hawaii's mild climate is determined largely by its tropical location and also by the northeast trade winds that sweep across it. The northeast trade winds—so-called because sea captains took advantage of them on their trade routes—are dependable, steady winds that blow from the northeast west across the thousands of miles of open sea that separate the Hawaiian Islands from the continents. They are responsible for keeping the temperature and the humidity moderate. Since they are the prevailing winds in this area, the side of the island that faces them is called the "windward" side. The opposite side of the island is the opposite of windward; in nautical terms, "leeward."

Sometimes the trade winds fail and are replaced by "kona" winds from the south. "Kona" means "leeward," because it's the leeward side of the island that more or less faces these occasional winds. Kona winds bring hot, sticky air. Fortunately, they are rare in summer, when they would be really unpleasant, and occur mostly in winter, when the lower overall temperatures moderate their effect. Kona storms are subtropical low-pressure systems that occur in winter, move in from the south, and can cause serious damage. There is apparently no pattern to them; in some years, they do not occur at all, but in others they occur every few weeks.

On Kauai, average temperatures along the coast range from highs of 79–84° F to lows of 60–68° F. The "cooler" ones are winter temperatures, the warmer ones summer. It's rainier from November through March than it is the rest of the year. Expect colder temperatures, more wind, and considerably more rain if you are in a mountainous region, like Kokee State Park.

You may have read that Mt. Waialeale, Kauai's second highest peak, is the wettest place on earth. What that means is that over many years, Waialeale has had the highest average annual rainfall (I've seen figures ranging from 450 to 480 inches annually). Other places may have a year or two of torrential rains that exceed that figure. But on Mt. Waialeale, every year is that rainy. The trade winds pick up a great deal of moisture on their long sweep across the open ocean to Kauai. The first serious obstacle they encounter on Kauai is Waialeale, and there they unburden themselves. Rain clouds enshroud both Waialeale and Kawaikini, Kauai's highest peak and Waialeale's neighbor, almost constantly; it's a rare moment when you can see them. The huge amount of rain they get nourishes all of Kauai. West of Waialeale and Kawaikini lies an immense, forbidding swamp, the Alakai Swamp, maintained by the constant rains and home to some of earth's rarest plants and animals. However, Waialeale's constant rain need not concern you much, as there are no trails to Waialeale.

The driest sections of Kauai are along the southern and western coasts approximately from the big resort area at Poipu to desertlike Polihale and on up the Na Pali Coast almost to Hanakoa Valley. The east coast gets more rain; the north coast still more; and the mountain interior the most. At any given time, it is almost certainly raining somewhere on Kauai, but in the coastal regions, it's seldom prolonged or unpleasant. The passing showers offer you a chance to enjoy rainbows with your hikes. But if you'd rather not be rained on, head for the southern or the western coast.

If it's rainy on the coast, you can be pretty sure it will be even rainier in the mountains. You may want to postpone your visit to Kokee State Park or Waimea Canyon State Park for a drier day. Or walk mountain roads instead of mountain trails; see the trips for suggestions.

You can't expect resort-quality weather in hiking areas! The relatively dry, sunny weather advertised for Hawaii is typical only of a few coastal resort areas, like Kauai's Poipu and Polihale areas. That's why Kauai's biggest and busiest resorts are in the Poipu area. Much of Hawaii, including most of Kauai, is covered with rainforests and is very wet. That's where the most beautiful and interesting hikes are! Be prepared for rain when you hit the trail, and consequently for weather markedly cooler than that of the resort you've left behind, especially if the trail is in the mountains.

Equipment Suggestions and Miscellaneous Hints

Let no one say
And say it to your shame
That all was beauty here
Until you came.

—— Sign, Lake Manyara National Park, Tanzania

This book isn't intended to teach you *how* to hike or backpack. If you can walk, you can hike, especially the "very easy" hikes. You can learn about backpacking in *Backpacking Basics* by Thomas Winnett and Melanie Findling (see Bibliography). Just be sure the trip you pick is within *your* hiking limits.

This book is intended specifically to let you know *where* you can hike on Kauai, *what* to expect when you hike there, and *how* to get to the trailhead for each hike. And that, I hope, will help you decide *which* hikes to take.

This section contains suggestions which I hope will make your hikes even more pleasant, and perhaps better protect you and the environment. Of course, you're the only person who lives in your body, so you'll have to judge what's really appropriate for you. But there are a few things you might want to know before you go—things that may be very different from the hiking you've done at home on the mainland. (Maybe you already know them, but it's hard to shut me up when I think I have some good advice.)

It's up to you. No book can substitute for, or give you, five things only you can supply: physical fitness, preparedness, experience, caution, and common sense. Don't leave the trailhead without them.

Minimum equipment for very easy and easy dayhikes. Wear or carry these items as a minimum:

- Sunglasses
- Coach's whistle. You can blow a whistle for help longer and louder than you can shout
- Appropriate footwear
- Strong sunblock applied before you set out
- Insect repellent if you are attractive to mosquitoes and deerflies
- Food. Recommended minimum for easy hikes: high-energy,

concentrated-nutrition snack bars
- Water. No open source of water in the U.S. is safe to drink untreated, so fill water bottles from treated sources (e.g., the bathroom tap at your hotel). Recommended minimum: 1 pint for very easy and easy hikes, 1–2 quarts for moderate hikes, 2 quarts for strenuous hikes
- Lightweight "space blanket"—a couple of ounces of metallized mylar film usable for temporary shelter or rain protection
- Appropriate clothing so you can keep warm when the temperature drops, when it rains, and when it gets windy. Even in Hawaii, and especially in the mountains, the weather can turn nasty quickly. Be prepared with extra, appropriate clothing—especially a warm cap—when it does so. See **Hypothermia**, below.
- If you wear corrective lenses and/or require special medications, take extra lenses and carry a small supply of your medications

Minimum equipment for moderate and strenuous dayhikes. Start with the minimum equipment for easy hikes, above. Add—
- Extra food and water. For moderate and strenuous hikes, carry lunch and some snack bars
- Extra appropriate clothing. See **Hypothermia**, below
- Map (and compass if you can use it)
- Flashlight with extra bulbs and batteries
- Means to dig a hole 6–8 inches deep and at least 100 feet from water, in order to bury solid body wastes; tissue that you will also bury (or pack out)
- Pocket knife
- First-aid kit—backed by first-aid training
- Waterproof matches and something you can keep a flame going with (such as a candle) *only when necessary to start a fire in order to save a life*

Equipment for backpacks. The following is a minimal checklist for backpacking equipment.

Minimal Backpacking Equipment List

Backpack	Tent	Sleeping pad
Sleeping bag	Permit	Everything listed above for dayhikes
Boots	Socks	Shirts
Hat	Rain gear	Shorts or long pants
Underwear	Toiletries	Personal medication
Stove and fuel*	Eating utensils	Cookware and clean-up stuff

*You cannot take stove fuel on a plane. You must buy it at your destination.

Tennis shoes? I've noted in the hike descriptions whether tennis shoes—that is, lightweight oxford-type shoes—are okay to wear or whether I think you should wear boots. I base that recommendation on the length of the hike and the difficulty of the terrain. What tennis shoes lack that boots can provide are ankle support and soles that grip. Only you can really decide how important those are to you.

Boot care. If you're going to hike a lot, be sure your boot seams are freshly sealed and you've freshly waterproofed the entire boot, including the cloth portion, if any. Use a heavy-duty waterproofing compound like a wax, and bring some of it along in order to renew the coating if necessary. Chances are your boots will get wet, especially in the winter. And they'll stay wet, because things dry slowly in the tropical humidity. It's pretty tough on the boots and, together with the abrasion of mud particles, could cause boot seams to fail.

Hiking stick. Take your hiking stick if you usually hike with one. The flight attendants can put it in the closet where they hang the carry-on suits and dresses or in the overhead compartments. Kauai's terrain can be very slippery when wet, and a hiking stick can be a big help in maintaining your footing. And it can double as a spider stick (see below).

Spider stick. There are a very few brushy trails where you and some orb spiders may meet unexpectedly, head-on. You probably don't like collecting spiders with your face, but these critters make it hard not to do so. Here's one way to avoid them without killing them. Pick up and use a "spider stick"—a long, strong stick that you carefully wave up and down in front of you as you hike. You can feel the tug when the stick connects with a web. Detach the anchor strands that hold the web in your way, and lay them aside on the adjacent shrubbery. An orb spider normally rebuilds most or all of her web daily, so you've caused her only minor inconvenience. Your hiking stick can probably double as a spider stick.

Sleeping bag. It should be able to tolerate wet conditions. For example, it could have a Gore-Tex shell or it could have a synthetic fill. You are almost certain to get rained on a bit while camping.

Tent. You'll need one for protection from the rain and the various campsite critters. None of the critters is particularly dangerous. They're probably not what you'd choose to bed down with, though (for example, toads, centipedes, ants, cockroaches).

Clothes while backpacking. On the one hand, it's best to go as light as possible, especially on a difficult trail like the Kalalau Trail. On the other hand, almost nothing—not even synthetics—dries overnight in Kauai's humid climate under camping conditions. You can't expect to rinse a shirt out in the evening and find it dry in the morning. Socks wet from soggy trails or stream crossings will probably stay wet for a while. Consider what things you can stand to wear damp and what you can't stand unless they're dry. Pack just one or two of the "okay if damp" things. Pack a set of the "gotta be dry!" things for each day plus one or more extras, just in case. (For me, it's socks.)

At the end of a soggy day of backpacking. On those occasional rainy days, you may wonder how you're going to get reasonably clean without getting any wetter than you already are. Well, the socks you've worn all day are "goners" for the time being, wet and muddy on the outside but relatively clean on the inside. While you're changing into dry clothes, turn your "used" socks inside out and mop yourself off with them.

Hypothermia? On Kauai? It's possible if you go into the mountains. Remember that going higher is equivalent to going north into colder climates, Kauai's mountains are very wet, and mountains are often very windy. Please be prepared as you would be for going into any mountainous region.

Biodegradable? Ha, ha, ha! The following things are popularly supposed to be biodegradable if you bury them: toilet tissue; facial tissues; sanitary napkins; tampons; disposable diapers. That must be a joke. They often last long enough for either running water to exhume them or animals to dig them up. It's actually pretty easy to carry them out if you put them in a heavy-duty self-sealing bag.

Getting hiking and backpacking food. If you are planning to backpack on Kauai, consider shopping for your hiking and backpacking chow on Kauai. Food prices *are* higher in Hawaii, but you have enough stuff to put in your luggage without bringing your food, too. There are several well-stocked supermarkets on the island, particularly around Kapaa and Lihue, and some camping stores. You can buy almost anything from the "raw ingredients" (oatmeal, bread, crackers, peanut butter, cheese, . . .) to dehydrated and freeze-dried chow.

Companions. The standard advice is: never hike alone; never camp alone.

Water. Take your own drinking water for the day. Plan on treating water while backpacking. No open source of water anywhere in the U.S. is safe to drink untreated. Treat water by boiling (1–5 minutes at a rolling boil) or filtering (note that filters clog relatively quickly in Kauai's sediment-rich water).

Don't spread pest plants: wash off your shoes or boots. As I mentioned in the chapter on geology and history, Hawaii has been overrun by introduced plants. It's important to try to control the spread of these plants. One thing you can do to help is to wash the soil, and with it the seeds of any pest plants, you hope, off of your shoes or boots *before you leave* a hiking area.

Avoiding leptospirosis. Fresh water on Kauai may be contaminated with the bacterium that causes leptospirosis. There's a pamphlet about leptospirosis that's available from the Kauai Department of Health (3040 Umi Street, Lihue, HI 96766, (808) 245-4495). The following summarizes some of its contents: Muddy and clear water are both suspect. The bacterium invades through broken skin or the nose, mouth, or eyes. It enters the bloodstream and infects different organs, particularly the kidneys. Precautions that would especially apply to you here are not to go into streams if you have open cuts or abrasions and not to drink [untreated] stream water.

If you do swim in fresh water on Kauai, you should know that the incubation period of leptospirosis is 2–20 days. The onset is sudden and is characterized by "high fever, with chills and sweats, severe headache, muscle pains, weakness, and sometimes vomiting and diarrhea." You should see a physician immediately if you suspect leptospirosis. A "best" course of treatment hasn't been established, but it's believed that administering certain antibiotics early in the course of the disease will shorten the disease and make symptoms less severe. The pamphlet says that most cases are mild and that people [with mild cases] recover in a week or two without treatment. However, severe leptospirosis infections may damage kidneys, liver, or heart and may even cause death.

Using This Book

How this book organizes the trips

Kauai is closer to being round than any of the other major Hawaiian islands. And Mt. Waialeale sits almost in the middle of it. So imagine the hour hand of a clock pinned to Mt. Waialeale, and I'll use the clock analogy for describing where the trip is on Kauai's circumference. At 12 o'clock, for example, the imaginary Kauai clock hand points to Hanalei. At 6 o'clock, the hand points a little past Poipu. Here's the Kauai clock pointing to Nonou Mountain, which is at 3 o'clock:

The trips start, of course, at 12 o'clock at Hanalei and move clockwise around Kauai past Kapaa, Lihue, Poipu, Waimea, Kekaha, Waimea Canyon State Park, Polihale, Kokee State Park, the Na Pali Coast on the northwestern edge of the island, and finally, at about 11 o'clock, to Haena at the end of the highway past Hanalei.

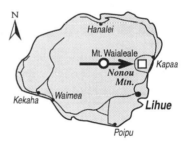

And that's pretty much the order in which you'll find them in this book. One exception is the trips that begin on Mohihi Road in the Kokee area. First, the book covers the trips whose trailheads are on the main road that passes through Kokee State Park, Highway 550. Mohihi Road branches off Highway 550, and I've put hikes whose trailheads are on Mohihi Road after the hikes whose trailheads are on 550. Mohihi Road starts out going west to east but eventually turns south. Trips starting from Mohihi Road appear in the order you'd find their trailheads as you traveled farther away from Kokee State Park on Mohihi Road. Another exception is the Awaawapuhi Trail, which follows the Nualolo Trail even though the Awaawapuhi trailhead is much farther up Highway 550 than the Nualolo trailhead, and the two trailheads are separated by other trailheads. But I want to keep them together because you can link the Nualolo and Awaawapuhi trails together in a wonderful shuttle or loop trip, and the description of that trip follows the Nualolo and Awaawapuhi trail descriptions. (Those of you who have this book's first edition will recognize that I've reorganized the hikes in this area, as some readers suggested.)

If several trips are located at the same "hour" on the Kauai clock, I've tried to organize them so that the trips that start nearer the coast come before those that are farther inland.

Look for the Kauai clock with each trip.

How to read the trip descriptions

The trip descriptions are in the following format, and here is what the information in each description means:

Title (self-explanatory).

Location: The Kauai clock illustrates the trip's general location relative to the rest of Kauai.

Type: There are four types of trips; icons show which type a trip is:

Loop trips: You follow trails that form a closed loop; you don't retrace your steps, or you retrace them for only a proportionally short distance.

Semiloop trips: The trip consists of a loop portion and an out-and-back portion.

Out-and-back trips: This is by far the most common type of trip in this book. You follow trails to a specified destination and then retrace your steps to your starting point.

Shuttle trips: You start at one trailhead and finish at another, "destination" trailhead. They are far enough apart (or walking between them is sufficiently impractical) that you need to have a car waiting for you at your "destination" trailhead or to have someone pick you up there.

Difficulty: A trip's difficulty is based first on total distance and second on cumulative elevation gain and rate of gain. Let's say that the elevation gain is negligible to moderate (it's never steeper than about 500 feet/mile for any significant distance). Block letters code for a trip's difficulty:

V   A **very easy** trip is 1 mile or less.

E   An **easy** trip is more than 1 mile but not more than 2 miles.

M   A **moderate** trip is more than 2 miles but not more than 5 miles.

S   A **strenuous** trip is more than 5 miles.

If the trip has a section of, say, a half-mile or more where it's steeper than 500 feet/mile, or if the trail is hard to follow, then I've given it the next higher difficulty rating.

Shoes: Some trips just aren't safe if you're not wearing boots with soles that grip and which will give you some ankle support. However, only *you* live in your body, so you will have to be the final judge of what you can safely wear. Bare feet are never safe, in my opinion, except perhaps on a less-used beach. Icons show the minimum safe shoe type:

 Tennis shoe

 Hiking boots strongly recommended

 Hiking boots mandatory—route is very rough

Terrain type: Icons give you a general idea of the kind of terrain you'll be walking. Some hikes offer mixed terrain; for them, I've tried to indicate the terrain type where you'll spend the most walking time:

 Inland; hilly or mountainous

Near or at the ocean, such as along a beach or on cliffs above the sea

Distance: The distance is the total distance you have to walk.

Elevation gain: This figure is the approximate cumulative elevation gain, and counts all the significant "ups" you have to walk, not just the simple elevation difference between the trailhead and the destination. It's the cumulative gain that your muscles will complain about. Some trips are **upside-down:** you go *downhill* on your way out to the destination, *uphill* on your return.

Hiking time: This is based on my normal hiking speed, which is a blazing 2 miles/hour.

"Icon box": Location (the Kauai clock for this trip), trip type, trip difficulty, shoe type, distance, elevation gain, and average hiking time are organized into an "icon box" like this:

Distance: 7 miles

Elevation gain: 1500' (upside-down)

Hiking time: 3½ hours

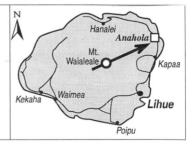

Topos: The topo or topos listed here are the ones that cover the area you'll be hiking in on this particular trip. All the listed topos are 7½' topos. Topos are strictly optional for the very easy and easy trips but are strongly recommended for the other trips.

Trail map: Tells you where this book's trail map for this trip is (usually at the end of this trip or of another trip in the same area—e.g., "At the end of Trip 20"). See the end of this chapter for the trail map conventions.

Highlights: This gives you an idea of what I think the best features of the trip are. Usually, it's the scenery—that's one of the principal things you came to Kauai for!

Driving instructions: This gives you instructions for driving to the trailhead, usually in terms of driving from Lihue. You may be staying anywhere on Kauai, but Lihue is a convenient reference point. Be sure you have a good road map of Kauai to supplement these instructions.

Permit required: A few trips require you to have someone's permission to camp. This section will tell you what you need permission for, if anything, and whom to apply to. See "Getting Permits" for addresses.

Description: This is the detailed description of the trip as I perceived it. I've tried to give you an idea of the more obvious plants and other features you'll find, where the rough spots are, when you'll be ascending or descending, where viewpoints are, and what you'll see from those viewpoints. On some trips, the trail is faint to nonexistent, and the agency in charge has marked the route by tying tags of colored plastic ribbon to the plants along the route. You navigate by moving from tag to tag.

Supplemental information.... At the bottom of most of the trips, there's some extra information about the historical significance of places you'll see along the route. Or maybe there's a story—a Kauai myth, for example—related to the trip which I hope will add to your enjoyment of the trip. Perhaps there'll be a bit more information about the plants or the geology in the area. I put most of the supplemental information at the end so that it wouldn't interfere too much with the description of the trip itself. I think safety dictates that you give your attention first to the trip and only secondarily to the supplemental information. That is not a problem with very easy hikes, so the supplemental information is often part of the main description in those hikes.

Trail map conventions. The legend on the following page shows this book's trail map conventions.

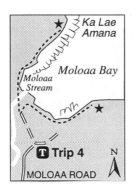

Map Legend

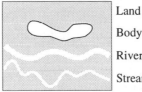 Highway number

RIVER NAME   Self-explanatory

Stream Name   Self-explanatory

T **Trip 1**   Trailhead for numbered trip(s)

– – – – – – –   Trail

- - - - - - - - - - - -   Use trail or route where there is no trail as such (e.g., along a beach)

ROCK TRAIL   Trail name (if any)

★   Destination of trip

★ **Trip 1**   Destination of trip on trail with more than one destination

════════   Highway

════════   Paved road

= = = = =:   Unpaved road

Land

Body of water, ocean

River, large stream

Stream

Mileage scale

0   ¼   ½   1 mile

Hiking in the backcountry entails unavoidable risk that every hiker assumes and must be aware of and respect. The fact that a trail is described in this book is not a representation that it will be safe for you. Trails vary greatly in difficulty and in the degree of conditioning and agility one needs to enjoy them safely. On some hikes routes may have changed or conditions may have deteriorated since the descriptions were written. Also, trail conditions can change even from day to day, owing to weather and other factors. A trail that is safe on a dry day or for a highly conditioned, agile, properly equipped hiker may be completely unsafe for someone else or unsafe under adverse weather conditions.

You can minimize your risks on the trail by being knowledgeable, prepared, and alert. There is not space in this book for a general treatise on safety in the mountains, but there are a number of good books and public courses on the subject, and you should take advantage of them to increase your knowledge. Just as important, you should always be aware of your own limitations and of conditions existing when and where you are hiking. If conditions are dangerous, or if you are not prepared to deal with them safely, choose a different hike! It's better to have wasted a drive than to be the subject of a mountain rescue.

These warnings are not intended to scare you off the trails. Millions of people have safe and enjoyable hikes every year. However, one element of the beauty, freedom, and excitement of the wilderness is the presence of risks that do not confront us at home. When you hike you assume those risks. They can be met safely, but only if you exercise your own independent judgment and common sense.

Hiking Table

The following hiking table* summarizes all the trips in this book. It will help you quickly decide which trips interest you and which are within your party's abilities.

Trip Number and Name	Best As...	Type	Difficulty	Miles
1 Hanalei Bay Walk	Dayhike	O&B	Easy	2⅔
2 Anini Beach Walk	Dayhike	O&B	Very easy	1
3 Powerline to "N. View"	Dayhike	O&B	Easy	2
4 Moloaa Bay	Dayhike	O&B	Easy	2
5 Anahola Beach Walk	Dayhike	O&B	Easy	2
6 Moalepe Trail	Dayhike	O&B	Moderate	5
7 Keahua Arboretum	Dayhike	O&B	Very easy	—
8 Kuilau Ridge	Dayhike	O&B	Moderate	4½
9 Kuilau-Moalepe	Dayhike	Shuttle	Moderate	4¾
10 Powerline to "S. View"	Dayhike	O&B	Moderate	5
11 Powerline Shuttle	Dayhike	Shuttle	Strenuous	9
12 Waipouli Stroll	Dayhike	O&B	Very easy	⅔
13 Waipouli-Lydgate	Dayhike	O&B	Moderate	4¾
14 Nonou Mtn. East	Dayhike	O&B	Moderate	3½
15 Nonou Mtn. Shuttle	Dayhike	Shuttle	Moderate	3¼
16 Valley Vista Hale	Dayhike	O&B	Easy	1½
17 Kuamoo-Nonou	Dayhike	O&B	Strenuous	6
18 Nonou Mtn. West	Dayhike	O&B	Moderate	3
19 Lydgate-Wailua	Dayhike	O&B	Moderate	3
20 Wailua Falls	Dayhike	O&B	Very easy	—
21 Kukuiolono Park	Dayhike	O&B	Very easy	1
22 Russian Fort Elizabeth	Dayhike	O&B	Very easy	⅔
23 Polihale State Park	Dayhike	O&B	Moderate	5
24 Iliau Nature Loop	Dayhike	Loop	Very easy	¼
25 Kukui Trail to View	Dayhike	O&B	Moderate	2
26 Kukui Trail to Wiliwili	Dayhike	O&B	Strenuous	5
	2-day b'pk	O&B	Moderate	5
27 Waimea River	Side trip	O&B	Strenuous	<15
	Dayhike	Shuttle	Strenuous	10
28 Koaie Canyon	Side trip	O&B	Strenuous	7
29 Northern Dam	Side trip	O&B	Moderate	2
30 Milolii Ridge	Dayhike	O&B	Strenuous	9½

* Abbreviations: b'pk = backpack; O&B = out-and-back trip; — = negligible. Terms: side trip = dayhike from a destination to which you've backpacked.

Hiking Table* (continued)

Trip Number and Name	Best As...	Type	Difficulty	Miles
31 Halemanu-Cliff Trail	Dayhike	O&B	Easy	1¾
32 Halemanu-Black Pipe	Dayhike	Semiloop	Moderate	4
33 Canyon Adventure	Dayhike	Loop	Strenuous	8
34 Nualolo Trail	Dayhike	O&B	Strenuous	7½
35 Awaawapuhi Trail	Dayhike	O&B	Strenuous	6½
36 Nualolo-Awaawapuhi	Dayhike	Shuttle	Strenuous	9¼
		Loop	Strenuous	10¾
37 Kokee Nature Trail	Dayhike	Loop	Very easy	⅛
38 Halemanu-Kokee	Dayhike	Loop	Moderate	3
39 Kumuwela-Waininiua	Dayhike	Semiloop	Moderate	4
40 Mystery Trail	Dayhike	Loop	Moderate	2
41 Puu Kaohelo-Berry Flat	Dayhike	Semiloop	Moderate	3½
42 Kaluapuhi Trail	Dayhike	O&B	Moderate	3½
43 Pihea Trail	Dayhike	O&B	Moderate	3⅓
44 Kawaikoi-Sugi Grove	2-day b'pk	O&B	Moderate	3⅔
45 Pihea-Alakai	Side trip	Loop	Moderate	3⅔
46 Kawaikoi Stream	Side trip	Semiloop	Moderate	2⅔
47 Poomau Canyon	Side trip	O&B	Moderate	2¼
48 Kohua Ridge	Side trip	O&B	Strenuous	8
49 Mohihi-Waialae	Side trip	O&B	Strenuous	8½
50 Kee Beach Stroll	Dayhike	O&B	Very easy	⅓
51 Kee Beach to Viewpoint	Dayhike	O&B	Moderate	1
52 Hanakapiai Beach	Dayhike	O&B	Moderate	4
	2-day b'pk	O&B	Moderate	4
53 Hanakapiai Falls	Dayhike	O&B	Strenuous	8
	Side trip	O&B	Moderate	4
54 Hanakoa Valley	4-day b'pk	O&B	Moderate	12
55 Hanakoa Falls	Side trip	O&B	Moderate	1
56 Kalalau Beach	6-day b'pk	O&B	Moderate	22
57 Kalalau Valley	Side trip	O&B	Moderate	4
58 Haena Beach Park	Dayhike	Loop	Moderate	2⅓
59 Lumahai Beach	Dayhike	O&B	Easy	1½

* Abbreviations: b'pk = backpack; O&B = out-and-back trip; — = negligible. Terms: side trip = dayhike from a destination to which you've backpacked.

The Trips

Trip 1. Hanalei Bay Beach Walk

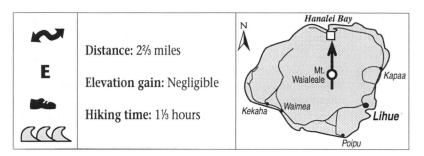

Distance: 2⅔ miles

Elevation gain: Negligible

Hiking time: 1⅓ hours

Topos: Optional: *Hanalei*

Trail map: At the end of this trip.

Highlights: Most visitors to Kauai agree that Hanalei Bay—indeed, the entire Hanalei region—is one of the loveliest places in the world. Why not enjoy a stroll on the bay's sands, from the Hanalei River to Waioli Stream? If the weather is fair, stay a while. If it's misty, you're in luck: you'll probably see spectacular waterfalls inland!

Note that this walk, like any beach walk, can be hazardous on a stormy day with high surf. Also, Hanalei Bay's waters are polluted by agricultural runoff; consider that as well as the height of the surf when deciding whether to swim here.

Driving instructions: Drive north and west from Lihue on Highway 56, past the Hanalei National Wildlife Refuge Billboard. There's a wonderful viewpoint here; stop and enjoy it. Now continue toward Hanalei, down a switchback, and across the Hanalei River on a one-lane bridge. The rule for these one-lane bridges is that you yield to any traffic that's already on the bridge; if there's none, you may proceed with caution.

In Hanalei town, where Hanalei Center is on the left side of the highway, you turn right onto Aku and follow it a short distance to a beachfront road. Turn right again and follow the beachfront road north to a parking lot by the Hanalei River. Park here, a little more than 34¾ miles from Lihue.

Permit required: None.

Description: The first thing you'll want to do here is to stroll north very briefly to the riverbank in order to take in the view upstream and inland, where steep cliffs richly clothed in greenery rise skyward. After the rain, the fluted cliffs boast long, sheer waterfalls; be sure to look closely for the tiny ones as well as for the obvious ones. Pause often during this walk to gaze from sea to cliffs and to enjoy the contrast.

Now walk out and turn south, roughly paralleling the water's edge. You'll probably want to swing inland around the old pier ("Hanalei Landing" on the topo). The beach is backed by tropical almond and ironwood trees; tree heliotrope with its short stature, broad crown of gray-green leaves, and wonderfully twisted form; and beach naupaka. Streamers of beach morning glory and beach vitex extend down onto your broad, sandy "trail."

Fishermen cast their nets into the nearer waters, while surfers play farther out. People and dogs stroll, splash, and romp along the strand. The beach's sands may harbor—ah—*contributions* from the local dogs as well as the occasional shell. Oh, well, a close-up examination is seldom as romantic as a view from a distance! On the quieter, wave-washed sections, you're likely to spot a scuttling ghost crab (see Trip 12 for more on ghost crabs).

You follow the curve of the bay as it gradually turns west. Some 1⅓ miles from the parking lot, you reach the east bank of the mouth of beautiful Waioli Stream—more about Waioli below. Here, purple water hyacinth blooms a little upstream and snowy-white cattle egrets wade through the limpid water on their stilt-like legs. Of all the scenes immediately along the bay, this one is, I think, the prettiest.

Hanalei Bay as seen from the south

There's private property on Waioli Stream's west bank, and it's posted NO TRESPASSING. So take a splash in the stream, enjoy the scene from the east bank, and then retrace your steps.

On your way back, if the weather is sunny, look for a good spot to settle down for a few restful hours. After all, there's more to a beach walk than just *walking*!

Namolokama and Waioli....Waioli Stream begins as a waterfall from Namolokama Mountain, some four miles south of Hanalei Bay. When swollen by recent rains, this waterfall is a spectacular sight from many points along Kauai's northeast shore.

In his charming book *Kauai Tales*, a retelling of traditional Kauai stories, Frederick B. Wichman applies the name "Namolokama" to the waterfall. Characters in the stories liken the cascading long hair of a young woman to Namolokama Falls—for example, Na-iwi's daughter's hair in the story of Na-keiki-o-na-iwi (see Trip 59, the side trip into Kalalau Valley).

Here's a story that's about Waioli Stream and Namolokama, but it has a more serious purpose, according to Mr. Wichman, and illustrates an important way in which oral traditions convey information down the generations. Can you guess that purpose as I try to paraphrase the story?

It's about the search of a young man for the woman he loves but whom he has never seen. He has heard her from a great distance as she sang to him, calling to him to seek her along Waioli. Starting perhaps from Tahiti, he sails into Hanalei Bay and begins his search where Waioli Stream meets the sea. At several different places along Waioli, he meets women whose appearance and demeanor illustrate that place's characteristics. For example, at Maha-moku, near the mouth of Waioli's valley, the story says the stream forms a pond over which a hau tree hangs, its fallen yellow blossoms drifting on the glassy water as they turn a deep red-yellow. The woman there wears a *lei* of *hau* flowers. She is resting as the stream rests at Maha-moku after its long journey down mountain and valley.

Each time the young man thinks perhaps he has found the hidden singer, then realizes the woman is not she, and continues to search along Waioli. As he leaves, each woman gives him a sheet of *kapa*, the bark cloth of Polynesia, of a different color, a color characteristic of that place, for his wife-to-be. For example, the tapa of Maha-moku is the red-yellow of the drifting *hau* blossoms.

At last he comes to the pool at the foot of the great waterfall of Namolokama, where swirling clouds and darkness hide everything. He can go no farther along Waioli Stream. But there is no one there, not the singer, not even the song. He places the *kapa* sheets one by one upon the water as gifts. The clouds clear, revealing Namolokama, and the *kapa*s, which are the colors of the rainbow, dissolve into Namolokama's mists. Through the rainbow mist he sees a woman and understands that she is not only the one he has sought and found at last but is Anuenue, the goddess of the rainbow. She welcomes him with the song he has followed for so long.

What a lovely story the ancient Kauaians devised to help people remember the ancient route up Waioli Stream!

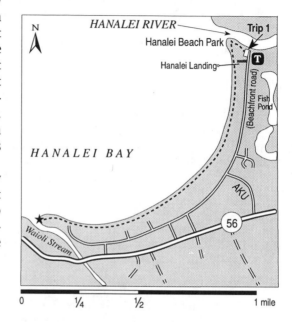

Trip 2. Anini Beach Walk

	Distance: Just under 1 mile Elevation gain: Negligible Hiking time: About ½ hour—but allow more time for beachcombing	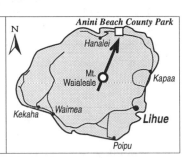

Topos: Optional: *Hanalei*
Trail map: See below.
Highlights: Anini Beach County Park offers not only its pretty beach and large fringing reef but amenities that help make your visit enjoyable. There are other attractive beaches in this area, but I recommend this beach for a relaxing visit because none of the others is as well equipped for visitors. Beachcombers should try their luck here!

Note that this walk, like any beach walk, and the waters themselves, can be hazardous on a stormy day with high surf.

Driving instructions: Drive north and west from Lihue on Highway 56, past Kilauea. There are two turnoffs to Kalihiwai Bay, one east and the other west of the Kalihiwai River. You want the second turnoff, west of the Kalihiwai River. After you dip inland (south) to cross the Kalihiwai River, the road curves seaward (north). As the road begins to curve west, you reach the junction with the second road to Kalihiwai Bay—and to Anini Beach County Park. Turn right here and follow the descending road to a **Y** junction. Take the left fork, which continues downward and curves around a rocky headland, Ka Lae o Kowali, and then straightens out as it passes west along what the topo calls "Kalihikai Beach" but which is your destination. . . .Say what?! You thought you were going to Anini Beach!

Not exactly. You're going to Anini Beach County Park. This is very confusing: what the topo calls "Anini Beach" is farther west, around Honono Point. But Anini Beach County Park is *here*, east of Honono Point, at what the topo calls "Kalihikai Beach."

(The University of Hawaii *Kaua'i* map shows this more clearly than the topo does. Maybe what the topo labels as "Kalihikai Park" is now called Anini Beach County Park.)

Park here, a little over 2 miles from the highway and 28¼ miles from Lihue.

Permit required: None unless you want to camp; for camping permits, see Appendix A.

Description: Exactly where you start your walk will depend on where you park. Wherever you start from, you'll probably be glad after your long drive to see that this park offers restrooms, tables, and picnic pavilions! Camping is allowed at the west end of the beach (see Appendix A).

Let's assume you park at the east end. Walk out to the beach proper past the structures, across the grassy strip, and through ironwood and tropical almond trees. These trees took a terrible beating from Hurricane Iniki (September 1992)—most of them had been shattered—and may still be recovering when you visit. Turn west-southwest and stroll along the sand until you reach the campground; then retrace your steps. Inland, across the road, there's a peaceful scene of pastures and low green hills.

Black mynas with their yellow eye stripes and jaunty gait, and zebra doves with their faces and breasts dusted with a metallic pale-blue, patrol the strand, foraging for who-knows-what and mooching from picnickers like you and me if given half a chance. You know you shouldn't feed them, but. . . .

The water offshore is often quite calm, thanks to a large offshore reef. In spite of the reef, sturdy shells may reach the strand. Keep your eyes peeled if you enjoy shell-hunting.

I happened upon a large heap of small, mostly intact shells and of other sea-treasures next to one of the buildings—an odd location, almost hidden from casual strollers, for such rich pickings. Perhaps a recent storm had swept them up there. There was nothing rare or remarkable, but so what? There were *lots* of shells, and that was even better! As I knelt there sorting through them, I heard a woman say, "I'm *so* disappointed. I thought there was supposed to be good shelling here." I stood up and hailed her, and pretty soon the two of us were completely absorbed in our respective hunts. It wasn't long before I had more shells than I could carry, so I kept a couple and slipped the rest back into the heap where someone else—maybe my shell-hunting acquaintance— might have the fun of finding them.

I hope your beachcombing luck at Anini Beach County Park is as good as ours was.

Trip 3. Powerline Trail to "North View"

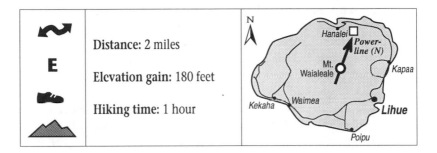

Distance: 2 miles

Elevation gain: 180 feet

Hiking time: 1 hour

Topos: *Hanalei*
Trail map: At the end of this trip.
Highlights: Views of the Hanalei River and Hanalei National Wildlife Refuge; views of lots of waterfalls, especially if it's been raining.
Driving instructions: From Lihue, drive north on Highway 56 for 29½ miles, past the Princeville Airport. In 1 mile more, turn left onto Pooku Road. If the Pooku Road sign is missing, look for a long white fence on the inland side of the highway. Pooku Road is just north of where the fence stops. Continue past the stables 1¾ miles to the end of the pavement. Park in the wide area just beyond the pavement's end A water tank is visible from here.
Permit required: None.

Description. The Powerline Trail is just too good to be reserved for *macho* hikers, so here's a short, very scenic walk from its northern end. (See Trips 10 and 11 for trips from its southern end.)
Walk south on the dirt road past the water tank. On this very gentle grade, you soon pass a postal-box-type hunter's check station on your left (east). The shrubbery along the road is fairly dense: guava, strawberry guava, sword fern, *uluhe* (another kind of fern), and *hau* (a wide shrub with very round leaves and clear yellow, hibiscus-like flowers). Exercise caution if you decide to go guava-hunting; the dense, matted vegetation may conceal abrupt and dangerous dropoffs.
Near the ½-mile point, be sure to turn around to enjoy the view seaward over the Hanalei Valley. The Hanalei National Wildlife Refuge stretches out below you; sunshine glints off its watery taro patches. This view is another perspective of the one you get from the observation point along Highway 56, but here you can enjoy it in peace—no cars whizzing along the highway just a few feet from you.
Nearing the 1-mile point, you pass a huge, fern-draped mango tree and presently make a very gentle descent. Keep your eyes peeled for

openings in the shrubbery as you approach the 1-mile point, just about opposite Hihimanu, the massive triangular peak on the ridge across the Hanalei River. Make sure you're on solid ground, and then take a look at the waterfalls around you. Just south-southwest of you, look for a cascade tucked into a small ridge extending from the ridge you're on; the cascade's water rushes off to join the Hanalei River. There may be another small waterfall from a bench on Hihimanu. To the southwest, mighty Namolokama Falls plunges off the north face of Namolokama Mountain; it is the headwaters of Waioli Stream, which enters Hanalei Bay near the bottom of the bay's crescent. West-southwest, look for a chain of three—no, four—no, five—who can count them all?—cascades from the north face of Hihimanu. The longer you stand here, the more waterfalls you'll see. This is what I've called "the northern falls viewpoint," and it's your destination for this hike.

There's a lot more to the Powerline Trail. But for this trip, after you've enjoyed the views here, it's time to retrace your steps to your car.

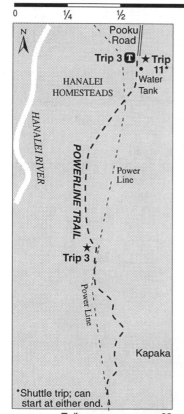

To/from map on page 63

Who's (or what's) that on the trail?....Besides the true wildlife, company you may have on most trails can include other hikers, hunters and their dogs, feral animals (goats and pigs), and lost hunting dogs. Be alert for vehicles when your trail is actually a road. Many trails on Kauai pass through areas where hunting is legal. (The occasional terrible stench from some unidentifiable source may be a carcass rotting in the forest.)

You'll have to use your own judgement about how to handle what you meet. Here are some things that worked for me. You should always stay on established routes, trails, or roads in order to avoid being mistaken for a game animal. If you meet lost hunting dogs, try what one hunter advised me: tell them firmly, "Go home." Wild goats are very alert and shy; you can't get close to them. It's possible you'll surprise wild pigs rooting along the trail. Slow your pace to give them time to get away. Give vehicles the right-of-way.

Trip 4. Moloaa Bay Walk

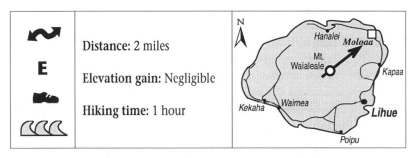

Distance: 2 miles

Elevation gain: Negligible

Hiking time: 1 hour

Topos: *Anahola*
Trail map: See below.
Highlights: A rugged, scenic bay with lots of no company!

Driving instructions: Drive north from Lihue on Highway 56 past Anahola. At 20 miles, just as you begin to curve westward around Kauai's north shore, look for Koolau Road off to your right (seaward). There may be a fruit stand at the junction to help you identify Koolau Road. (If you miss Koolau Road here, it comes around and rejoins the highway in 3 miles.) Follow Koolau Road down into the valley of Moloaa Stream 1¼ miles to the junction with Moloaa Road. Turn right (seaward) onto Moloaa Road and take it down through lovely, rural scenery to a fork— actually, it's more like a T—just before the bay. There's no point in driving any farther, so park off the road here.

Permit required: None.

Description. The fork in the road is just a few steps from the beach-access points, which are off the left fork. One beach access is through a gate next to the last house at the very end of the road. If you open the gate, please close it; you may also be able to just step through it. The other beach access is between that house and the one next door; it's marked by a painted pole that says BEACH ACCESS. Please respect the privacy of homeowners along the bay, and conduct yourself in keeping with a family setting, which this is.

Let's assume you go through the gate and start with the more northerly part of the bay first.

Northerly part. Beyond the gate, you pick up a sandy track that quickly descends to Moloaa

Stream, which you ford. You walk along the beach past ironwood trees, beach *naupaka*, and morning-glory vines. Few seashells survive the pounding of the surf on the rocky shelves you'll see out in the bay. The beach ends at a field of black boulders, but you can pick up a path either inland or under some beach heliotrope trees and continue a short distance northeast through surprisingly well-trimmed grass. You may see the "gardeners"—horses—grazing on the bluffs above you. In a little less than half a mile from the gate, boulders block your way again, and this time there's no easy way around them. Stop here to watch the breakers running into the bay. When you're ready, retrace your steps across Moloaa Stream to the southerly part of the bay.

Southerly part. Past Moloaa Stream, you cross rocky shelves and a slab of concrete sticking out of the sand in order to continue your walk. The fallen leaves of false almond trees litter the beach along here, adding a touch of color, because they typically turn red before they fall. Look for little holes near the wave line with streaks of sand tossed out of them. Ghost crabs have been at work here! In about half a mile, another boulder field blocks your way. If you're here late in the day, these boulders are a fine spot to relax and enjoy the colors of the sunset. As the light fades, it's time to return to your car.

On your way back to your car, if it's dusk, look for fragrant white trumpet flowers in the vines on the inland side of the road and for the spectacle of hundreds of white cattle egrets coming to roost for the night in the trees across Moloaa Stream.

Eager to get the word.... Edward Joesting, in his *Kauai, the Separate Kingdom*, notes that the community of Moloaa was where Catholic missionaries enjoyed their first substantial success with converts and first substantial trouble with officialdom on Kauai. The Catholic missionary Father Arsenius Walsh arrived on Kauai at Koloa in December of 1841, some 21 years after the Protestant missionaries. On a journey around Kauai, he "stopped at Moloaa where he made a list of thirty-four persons who wanted religious instruction." Walsh found an assistant, Father Barnabe Castan, waiting for him when he returned to Koloa. The people at Moloaa heard about the assistant and sent a delegation to Walsh to beg that Castan be stationed in their village. Walsh finally gave in to their requests, and soon there was a Catholic school at Moloaa.

The then-governor of Kauai, the chiefess Kekauonohi, and the chief at Moloaa were staunch Protestants. The chief was particularly annoyed that some of Moloaa's children were attending the new school, so he ordered that the parents of those children could not "cut wood in the mountains, fish in the sea, or take taro from their own lands." That, in effect, cut those families off from all of the necessities of life, and it reflects some of the hardships faced by converts from the established faith, whatever they both are. The governor, Kekauonohi, relaxed those restrictions eventually, but Joesting observes that she was in no hurry to do so.

In the meantime, the Protestant missionaries referred to Walsh as a man of low character (he smoked a pipe and took an occasional drink), and Walsh "proclaimed that the textbooks used in Protestant schools were composed of lies."

A scene from the Powerline Trail (Trips 3, 10, and 11)

Trip 5. Anahola Beach Walk

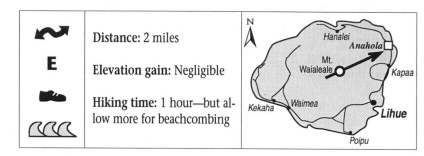

Distance: 2 miles

Elevation gain: Negligible

Hiking time: 1 hour—but allow more for beachcombing

Topos: Optional: *Anahola*

Trail map: At the end of this trip.

Highlights: A lovely drive, a long, strollable strand, and the possibility of beachcombing recommend Anahola Beach, where reefs provide partial shelter from the sometimes-rough seas. Anahola Beach County Park offers tables, restrooms, and camping (see Appendix A).

Note that this walk, like any beach walk, and the waters themselves, can be hazardous on a stormy day with high surf.

Driving instructions: Drive north and west from Lihue on Highway 56, through Kapaa and Kealia. As you leave the towns behind and as the road curves along Kauai's northeast coast, the scenery seems to grow in loveliness. *Such beautiful cliffs inland! Such splendid bluffs and beaches seaward!* If this is your first visit to Kauai's northeast coast, you'll quickly realize why the north side of the island is so beloved for its scenery—which gets better and better the farther you go. Continue on the highway to the turnoff at Anahola Road for Anahola Beach County Park. Turn right and follow the road to a **Y** junction; take the right fork. Follow the road east to a parking lot at the extreme east end of Anahola Beach; at an obscure **Y** junction, which you may not notice, take the left fork. Park here, a little over 1 mile from the highway and about 12½ miles from Lihue.

Permit required: None unless you want to camp; for camping permits, see Appendix A.

Description: The east end of Anahola Bay, near where you park, soon trails off into black rocks and low bluffs dotted with ironwood and *hau* trees.

So, from the parking lot, turn westward along the beach, where trees like tropical almond, ironwood, and tree heliotrope provide the backdrop, and where beach *naupaka* and beach morning-glory grace the fine sand. A reef keeps the surf in check along this eastern segment of the strand.

You stroll past the huge concrete-and-iron supports of what appears to be a ruined pier. Just a little over ½ mile from your start, you meet the mouth of the Anahola River. Approach quietly so as not to scare away the sanderlings that feed at this food-rich meetingplace of river and sea. You may have to struggle to suppress a laugh at the sanderlings' antics. These lively shorebirds chase the retreating waves frantically, as if catching the waves were all the birds lived for. Actually, they're hunting tiny mudflat invertebrates exposed by the waves' action. And then, when the waves roll in again, the birds race just as frantically away from them, as if to say, "Yikes, we'll die if we get our feet wet!"

If it's shallow enough, wade across the Anahola River and continue your walk on the west side of the beach. Near the beach's western end, about 1 mile from your start, you find a jumble of black boulders just before a small sandy point on which there's a house. Looking back the way you came, you'll see the tall supports of the light on Kahala Point, which marks the east end of Anahola Bay.

It was near the west end of Anahola Bay that I found a treasure-trove, mostly of coral, but with some shells, too. Corals are fascinating! How are the living animals, which seem hardly more than brainless little bits of protoplasm, able to form colonies, build reefs, and leave behind these beautiful, intricate homes? A study of corals can leave you with the uneasy feeling that most mall-developers, for example, lack even the instinctive aesthetic sensibility of a coral polyp.

When your pockets are full of sea treasures, turn east toward the Kahala Point light and head back to your car.

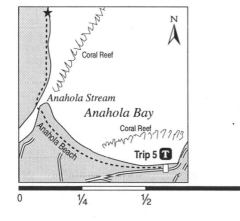

Trip 6. Moalepe Trail

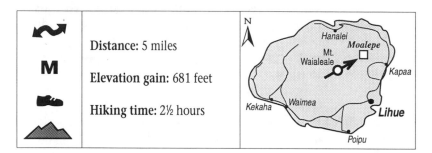

Distance: 5 miles

M

Elevation gain: 681 feet

Hiking time: 2½ hours

Topos: *Kapaa, Waialeale*
Trail map: On these facing pages.
Highlights: Watching the dramatic, jagged Makaleha Mountains with their luxuriant cloak of tropical vegetation that rise on your right (north) as you climb toward a delightful viewpoint/picnic spot—what more could a person ask for!

Driving instructions: From Lihue, drive north on Highway 56 well past The Marketplace at Coconut Plantation and into downtown Kapaa, 11 miles. Keep your eyes peeled for Highway 581, which leaves Highway 56 headed inland at a sharp left turn if you're going north (a shallow right turn if you're going south). Follow Highway 581 3½ miles to Olohena Road. (On some maps, most of the north part of Highway 581 *is* Olohena Road. If you're using one of those maps, continuing following Olohena Road after Highway 581 turns south.) Take Olohena Road inland (northwest) 1½ miles to a three-way junction with a dirt road and paved Waipouli Road (coming in on the right at a very sharp angle). There's no trailhead sign, but there is a hunter's check station, like a big silver postal box, which is marked WAILUA GAME MANAGEMENT AREA. Park just off the road here.

Permit required: None.

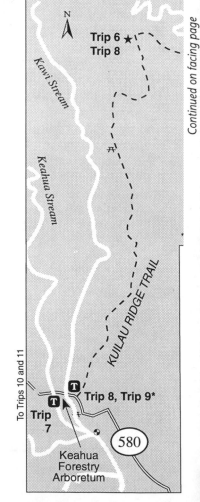

Description. The first part of this trail is on the dirt road just ahead of you where Olohena Road ends. It's a right-of-way across private property, from which you're fenced off on both sides. You quickly pass a clump of eucalyptuses and another of *hala* trees. Soon you're ascending gently northwest between pastures edged with guava trees, Philippine orchids—small purple blossoms on foot-long bare stems—and an occasional *uluhe* ("false staghorn fern"). The valley of Moalepe Stream drops away on your right (north). Beyond it, Kamalii Ridge begins its impressive rise to the summits of the Makaleha Mountains. Be careful if you're tempted to reach for fruit that's just beyond the edge of the road. The dense grasses may disguise abrupt dropoffs, and your calculated swipe at

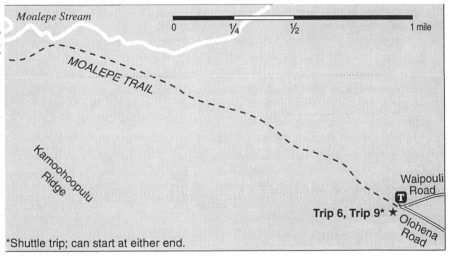

a guava can turn into an ankle-twisting slide down a concealed bluff.

The Moalepe Trail tends throughout its length to be more of a disused road than a footpath. Go straight ahead (continue northwest) at an unmarked road junction (not shown on the map) where the other road goes uphill and south. You continue to enjoy an easy ascent until you reach a steep switchback. Past the switchback, you climb to another unmarked road junction (also not shown on the map), where you'll go left (continue northwest). The road becomes steeper and deeply rutted, then levels out briefly under guavas and ferny-foliaged trees.

Nearing the end now, the trail ascends steeply, makes a hard turn west, and comes to an open, grassy area on Kamoohoopulu Ridge above Moalepe Stream and below the squared-off southwest face of Kapehuaala. The Moalepe and Kuilau Ridge trails meet here. Spend some time picnicking and enjoying the view here, and then retrace your steps to your car.

Trip 7. Keahua Forestry Arboretum

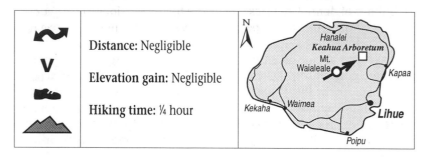

Distance: Negligible	
Elevation gain: Negligible	
Hiking time: ¼ hour	

Topos: Optional: *Waialeale*
Trail map: See Trip 6.
Highlights: Keahua Arboretum is lovely, peaceful spot, well-suited to picnicking (three picnic shelters).
Driving instructions: Drive north from Lihue on Highway 56, cross the Wailua River, and almost immediately turn left onto Highway 580 (at the traffic light), 8 miles. You pass the turnout for Opaekaa Falls and continue past the junction with Highway 581, which you reach in 3 more miles. The road passes through some residential areas and becomes narrower, more winding, and full of big potholes. At 7 miles from Highway 56, you pass the Kuilau Ridge trailhead just before reaching a pair of parking areas on the north (right) side of the road on either side of a stream that flows across the road. Don't cross the stream if the water is high. Otherwise, park in either lot.
Permit required: None.

Description. There are two different paths for two different areas in the Arboretum, one on each side of the stream and both on the south side of the road. The area on the east side of the stream is the one you pass first as you drive up to the Arboretum. The one on the west side of the stream has the official Arboretum sign. Let's take the one by the official Arboretum sign first.

West side (about 10 minutes; one picnic shelter). Unfortunately, none of the plants are marked so that you can identify them. The Arboretum pamphlet says that the tall trees with the beautiful pinkish-brown and green bark are a kind of eucalyptus, the painted gum. Rose gums with less colorful bark share this swath of lawn with them. Both are introduced trees; the painted gum is a native of New Guinea and the Philippines, the rose gum of Australia. They were introduced for reforestation and for lumber. A cinder path leads south through them, climbs a little slope, and descends past a *hau* thicket on the other side to the west-side picnic shelter near the stream. Most of the Arboretum was hacked out of dense *hau* thickets. (At the top of the slope, another cinder path leads down to an open area where nothing much is going on; don't bother with it.)

East side (about 5 minutes; two picnic shelters). Again, none of the plants are marked so that you can identify them. A short cinder path leads south past some African tulip trees and soon ends at the first of the two east-side picnic shelters. Farther on, across the grass, there's a second picnic shelter by a big mango tree that overhangs the stream. You'll notice ginger, *ti*, and *hala* on both banks of the stream. *Hau* thickets wall in the Arboretum on the east. You get the feeling they're just waiting for their chance to take over again, and when they're ready, it'll happen overnight—*pow!*—no more Arboretum.

Either side is great for a picnic and for just relaxing, dozing, and sunning on the grass.

Where to see marked plants.... As of this writing, places you *can* visit for free and see marked plants are the Iliau Nature Loop (Trip 24) and the Awaawapuhi Trail (Trip 35; ask for the trail guide to its plants at Kokee Museum).

The stream at Keahua Forestry Arboretum

Trip 8. Kuilau Ridge Trail

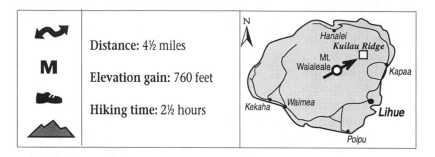

Distance: 4½ miles

M

Elevation gain: 760 feet

Hiking time: 2½ hours

Topos: *Waialeale, Kapaa*
Trail map: See Trip 6.
Highlights: A gentle grade on an old road gives you almost continuous good views and brings you first to a picnic shelter, then to a scenic open area just below the Makaleha Mountains. If you're short on time, try at least to make the two-mile round trip to the picnic shelter.
Driving instructions: Follow the driving directions to Keahua Arboretum, where you'll want to park. The marked Kuilau Ridge trailhead is an easy stroll east on the road (back the way you came), about 100 yards, and it's on the north side of the road (on your left as you walk east).
Permit required: None.

Description. Heading uphill, you quickly leave behind the valley where the Arboretum is located. Like the Moalepe Trail, the Kuilau Ridge Trail tends to be more like a retired road than a footpath. The footing is generally good, but watch out for the occasional deep rut in the road. The view opens west to Kawaikini and Mt. Waialeale; the Makaleha Mountains rise sharply to the north. The ridge you're traveling along cuts off views to the east, but on its slope you'll see red-fruited thimbleberry, *uluhe, ti,* guava, eucalyptus, *hala,* lantana, and blue-flowered cayenne vervain. Twining yam vines embrace other plants. Look for small purple Philippine orchids nodding atop one- to two-foot stems, their green fruit capsules hanging below the blossoms.

The fact that you're skirting a ridge becomes more apparent the higher you go: Kawi Stream's valley falls away to your left, luxuriant vegetation softening its sharp contours. The forest cover is light along this old road. *Kukui* trees with their lobed, light-green leaves join the astonishing variety of plant life around you as your trail winds its way up the ridge. Ignore what may seem like spur trails; stay on the main road.

At about the one-mile point, you reach an open, grassy knoll and a picnic shelter. A few *ohia lehua* trees dot this little plateau. If they're blooming, you'll know them by their hemispherical, pompom-like flowers of an intense red color (see also *ohia lehua* **tree**, below).

The trail leaves the picnic-shelter area on the east edge, making a slight descent and a switchback. It then climbs via a few more switchbacks to a stretch where you have an excellent view of Nonou Mountain (The Sleeping Giant, Trips 14–18). Now you descend a bit, walk the little ridge between Kawi and Opaekaa streams, and presently cross Opaekaa Stream on a wooden footbridge. As you resume gently climbing northeast, the plains around Lihue come into view.

At an unmarked junction past the bridge, take the north (lefthand) fork through an avenue of young paperbark eucalyptuses, ferns, and downy rose myrtle (introduced from Asia and the Philippines; a noxious pest plant here). You gradually climb to a small open area on Kamoohoopulu Ridge, where it almost seems as if you could reach out and touch the squared-off southwest face of Kapehuaala, a high point of the Makaleha Mountains. This delightful spot is the end of both the Kuilau Ridge and Moalepe trails. Retrace your steps from here.

Ohia lehua **tree....**If the *ohia lehua* trees aren't blooming, you may be able to identify them anyway by their mottled, light bark; open, rounded crown; small, dark-green leaves; and slightly awkward appearance. It's one of the most widespread and variable of the remaining native Hawaiian trees. When I mention *"ohia"* in this book, I mean *ohia lehua*.

Their height is that of a medium-size tree here, but under other conditions they may be no higher than shrubs or be 80-foot giants. The brilliant red (rarely yellow) pompoms of *ohia lehua* blossoms aren't really the flowers. They're the flowers' stamens, springing from fluted, greenish "cups" of nectar that attract native birds to these widespread, adaptable trees.

Ohia blossoms are sacred to Pele, the volcano goddess. *Ohia* wood was used for canoes, houses, *poi* boards, bowls, temple idols, and oracle towers (see Trip 19).

Monkeypod tree on the
Kuilau Ridge Trail

Trip 9. Kuilau Ridge-Moalepe Shuttle

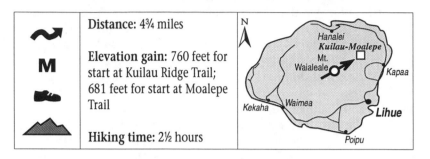

Distance: 4¾ miles

Elevation gain: 760 feet for start at Kuilau Ridge Trail; 681 feet for start at Moalepe Trail

Hiking time: 2½ hours

M

Topos: *Kapaa, Waialeale*
Trail map: See Trip 6.
Highlights: You get the best of both the Kuilau Ridge Trail and Moalepe Trail trips by combining them into this shuttle trip. That's saying a lot, because both of these trails are perfectly beautiful!
Driving instructions: Refer to the Kuilau Ridge Trail (Trip 8) and Moalepe Trail (Trip 6) for driving instructions. All you need to do is decide at which trailhead to start.
Permit required: None.

Description. If you decide to start at the Kuilau Ridge Trail, follow the directions for that trail (Trip 8) to the open, grassy area below Kapehuaala. After enjoying this lovely spot, look for a road cut that makes a hard turn east (on your right as you face Kapehuaala). Follow it, reversing the directions for the Moalepe Trail, to its end at Olohena Road.

You can just as easily start at the Moalepe Trail and finish on the Kuilau Ridge Trail near the Arboretum. If you do so, follow the directions for the Moalepe Trail (Trip 6) to the open, grassy area below Kapehuaala. When you're ready to leave, follow the trail that goes south, soon passing through an avenue of paperbark eucalyptuses, downy rose myrtle, and ferns. Continue, reversing the directions for the Kuilau Ridge Trail, to its end near Keahua Forestry Arboretum. Be sure to allow time to stop and enjoy the view at the picnic shelter 1 mile from the end of the trail.

Trip 10. Powerline Trail to "South View"

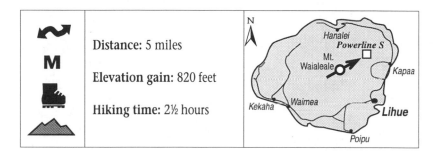

Distance: 5 miles

Elevation gain: 820 feet

Hiking time: 2½ hours

Topos: *Waialeale*
Trail map: See next page.
Highlights: Good walking on an abandoned road; excellent views of the adjacent stream valleys and mountains if cloud cover permits; vivid soil colors: some painter went mad here and threw buckets of reds, oranges, and blacks—too many colors to count—on this trail.
Driving instructions: Follow the driving directions of Trip 7 to Keahua Forestry Arboretum. Continue across the stream a little over ¼ mile farther to a couple of turnouts on the north (right) side of the road. The turnouts are the starting points of a couple of rough 4WD roads that shortly meet; you can start out on either road. Look for a hunter's check station—a very large, silver postal box—at one of the turnouts. Park off the road in one of the turnouts.
Permit required: None.

Description. The Powerline Trail is too good to be reserved for those who are up for strenuous hikes, as Trip 3 points out. This trip offers you a chance to enjoy part of it from its southern end.

The Powerline Trail leaves either turnout going uphill north-northwest. Whichever fork you take, it's very deeply rutted and overgrown for the first 100 yards or so, so watch your step. *Hau* may threaten to choke the road off but won't succeed. You'll soon meet the other fork of the road near an open area where you have an excellent view toward Kawaikini. You continue northwest between banks smothered by *uluhe*; at about ¼ mile from the start, you pass a powerline tower. The road dips, rises, and passes more towers. *Ohia lehua* trees and an occasional guava tree appear along the roadside, and the winding road gives you wonderful views now west toward Kawaikini, now northeast toward the Makaleha Mountains.

Near the half-mile point, there's an open area that offers great views

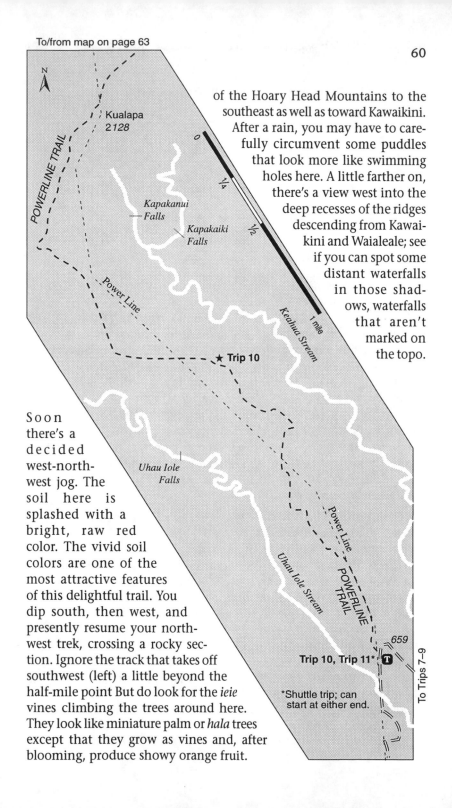

N

Kualapa
2128

POWERLINE TRAIL

Kapakanui
Falls

Kapakaiki
Falls

Power Line

0

1/4

1/2

1 mile

Keahua Stream

★ Trip 10

Uhau Iole
Falls

Power Line

Uhau Iole Stream

POWERLINE TRAIL

659

Trip 10, Trip 11* 🚏

*Shuttle trip; can
start at either end.

To Trips 7–9

of the Hoary Head Mountains to the southeast as well as toward Kawaikini. After a rain, you may have to carefully circumvent some puddles that look more like swimming holes here. A little farther on, there's a view west into the deep recesses of the ridges descending from Kawaikini and Waialeale; see if you can spot some distant waterfalls in those shadows, waterfalls that aren't marked on the topo.

Soon there's a decided west-northwest jog. The soil here is splashed with a bright, raw red color. The vivid soil colors are one of the most attractive features of this delightful trail. You dip south, then west, and presently resume your northwest trek, crossing a rocky section. Ignore the track that takes off southwest (left) a little beyond the half-mile point But do look for the *ieie* vines climbing the trees around here. They look like miniature palm or *hala* trees except that they grow as vines and, after blooming, produce showy orange fruit.

You continue generally northwest for another 2 miles. More bright colors streak the soil, and you have glimpses over the green depths of Keahua Stream to the east and Uhau Iole Stream to the west. Wild purple Philippine orchids occasionally nod "hello" from the fern-clad roadside.

At about 2½ miles from the start, you find an opening in the roadside shrubbery that offers you an excellent view to the north of two lovely waterfalls: higher Kapakanui Falls to the left, lower Kapakaiki Falls to the right. Ahead, you can see the road you're on winding far up the ridge to the northwest. But this "southern falls viewpoint" is your goal for this hike, so rest here, enjoy the view, and then retrace your steps to your car when you're ready.

Ieie....According to one source, those handsome *ieie* plants you saw near the half-mile point were sacred to the god Ku and had many uses in old Hawaii. The stems and roots were used in building houses and outrigger canoes, to make fish traps and sandals, and to weave the frameworks for feathered helmets and for idols. The fruit is edible and was eaten as a famine food, which probably means it tastes so bad you wouldn't eat it unless you were absolutely desperate.

Trip 11. Powerline Trail Shuttle

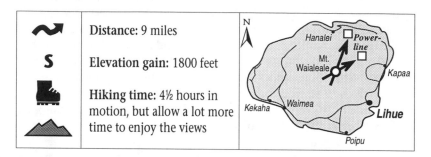

Distance: 9 miles

Elevation gain: 1800 feet

Hiking time: 4½ hours in motion, but allow a lot more time to enjoy the views

Topos: *Waialeale, Hanalei*

Trail map: Begins on the map at the end of Trip 6, continues on the map at the end of this trip, and concludes on the map at the end of Trip 3.

Highlights: Every good feature of Trips 3 and 10 plus the thrill of walking across a good chunk of the northeast quadrant of the island. This is my favorite low-mountain trail, and it was while admiring the waterfalls streaming from the cliffs above the Hanalei River that I realized just how big Kauai really is.

Driving instructions: This trip is written for a start at the south end, but there's no reason why you shouldn't start at the north end if you wish. To start at the south end, shuttle one car to the north trailhead near Hanalei (see Trip 3) and then drive around to the start of Trip 10.

Permit required: None.

Description. Starting from the south end, follow Trip 10 to its end at the "southern falls viewpoint." From there, you continue northwest, descend 70 feet, and then begin climbing again. What an incredible palette of soil colors you see here: blue-gray, vermilion, brick red, soft brown, veins of orange, a splash of black, an ochre color that's formed by a yellow-green mossy covering over brown soil, tans, reds so deep and dark they're almost purples, even a touch of lavender! A large eroded area provides crumbly soil on which fluffy gray lichens form mounds. The view is tremendous: Nonou Mountain to the east-southeast, Kalepa Ridge to the southeast, the Hoary Head Mountains to the south, and the flat Lihue Basin spreading out toward the sea.

Similar views greet you at another large, eroded area near the 3-mile point. To the east, there's a sweeping view of the valley of Keahua Stream. Wailua Reservoir gleams in the distance. A short way on, you seem to be at a 3-way junction, but keep going ahead (north) across the ridge, where

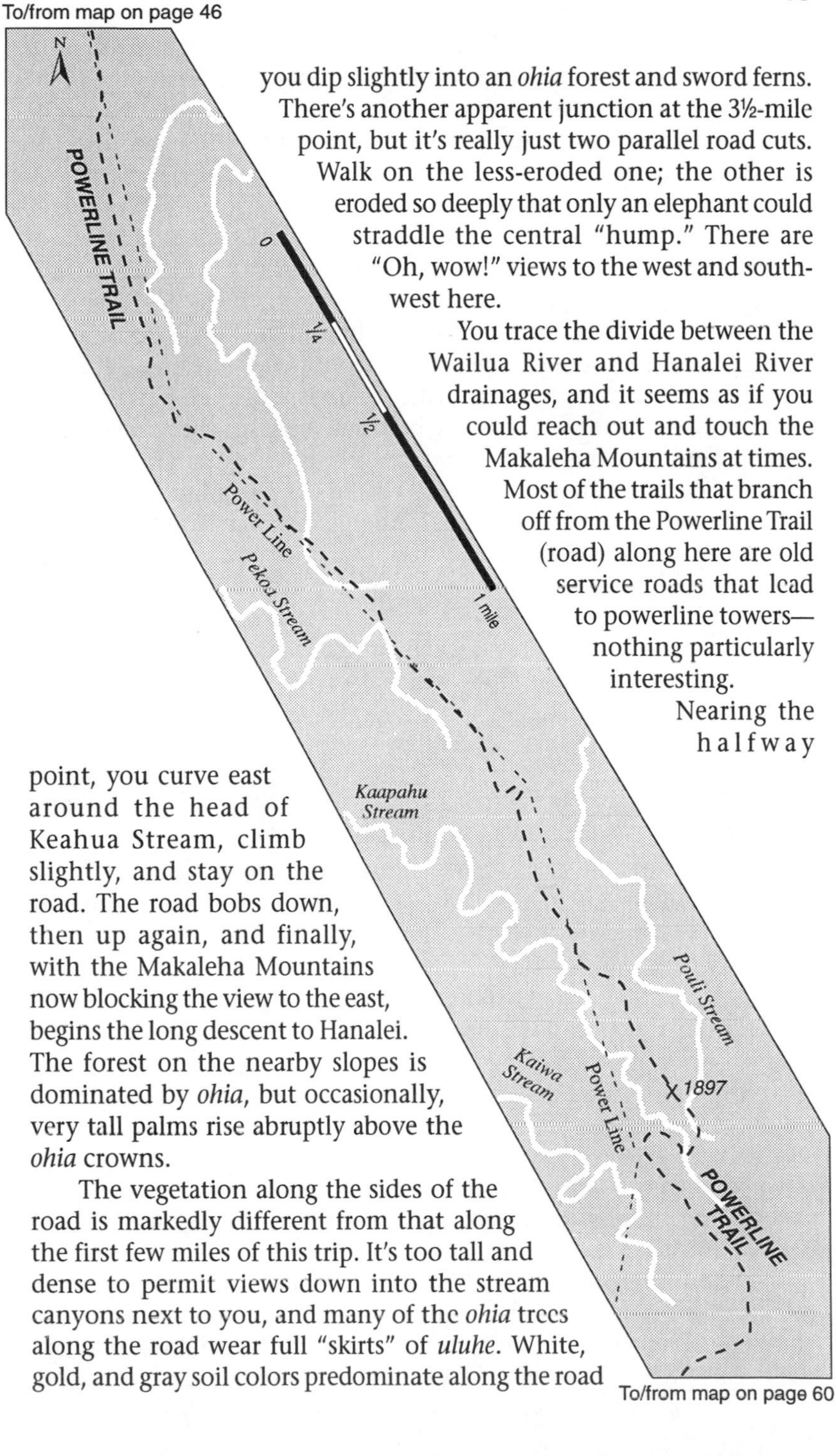

To/from map on page 46

N

POWERLINE TRAIL

0

¼

½

1 mile

Power Line

Pekou Stream

Kaapahu Stream

Kaiwa Stream

Power Line

Pouli Stream

X 1897

POWERLINE TRAIL

you dip slightly into an *ohia* forest and sword ferns. There's another apparent junction at the 3½-mile point, but it's really just two parallel road cuts. Walk on the less-eroded one; the other is eroded so deeply that only an elephant could straddle the central "hump." There are "Oh, wow!" views to the west and southwest here.

You trace the divide between the Wailua River and Hanalei River drainages, and it seems as if you could reach out and touch the Makaleha Mountains at times. Most of the trails that branch off from the Powerline Trail (road) along here are old service roads that lead to powerline towers—nothing particularly interesting.

Nearing the halfway

point, you curve east around the head of Keahua Stream, climb slightly, and stay on the road. The road bobs down, then up again, and finally, with the Makaleha Mountains now blocking the view to the east, begins the long descent to Hanalei. The forest on the nearby slopes is dominated by *ohia*, but occasionally, very tall palms rise abruptly above the *ohia* crowns.

The vegetation along the sides of the road is markedly different from that along the first few miles of this trip. It's too tall and dense to permit views down into the stream canyons next to you, and many of the *ohia* trees along the road wear full "skirts" of *uluhe*. White, gold, and gray soil colors predominate along the road

To/from map on page 60

now, and Kekoiki peak is prominent to the east-northeast.

As you head northwest down a switchback a little past the 5-mile point, you'll catch a dramatic view of Namolokama Mountain to the west. Can you see any waterfalls streaking its steep cliffs? They may be little more than long, slender, white ribbons. Many are intermittent, but it's worth your while to go "waterfall hunting" here for a few minutes, especially if it's rained recently (as it almost certainly has). Unfortunately, you can't see the many streams that rush down the slopes next to the Powerline Trail, but you can often hear them if you stop to listen.

On the topo, the trail appears to intersect a few streams, but don't look for actual stream crossings. This region is more like a swamp, the road being slightly higher than the bogs and pools on either side. Occasionally you may see tiny, single white orchids with a purple lower lip.

The Powerline Trail bears briefly toward the low point on the ridge that runs north-northeast from Namolokama Mountain and then straightens out to parallel the ridge. That infamous pest plant, the melastoma, forms dense hedges a short distance back from the roadside (see below).

Near the 7-mile point, you reach an area where large, broken pipes litter the road. Beyond the pipes, you make a quick descent to the familiar reddish soil of Kauai, and you may begin to see a few road apples. The Powerline Trail is a popular equestrian route, and you'll be coming out 1¾ miles from Pooku Stables. A stream gurgles loudly as it crosses under the road here, and strawberry guava thickets line the roadsides now. Side trails continue to lead to uninteresting powerline towers, so stay on the main trail. Guava trees reappear, and you may be tempted to forage off-trail. Be careful: the dense grasses often conceal steep dropoffs. There is no guarantee of solid ground underneath all that vegetation just off the trail.

Soon you get your first really good view of the beautiful green coastal plains of Hanalei. Occasional openings in the roadside shrubbery at last offer you some glimpses of the Hanalei River, whose course and tributaries you've been hiking above since you crossed the Wailua-Hanalei divide.

At the 8-mile point, you reach what I've called "the northern falls viewpoint" of the Powerline Trail, as described in Trip 3. Take in the view, try to count the waterfalls, and then reverse the steps of Trip 3 to your shuttle car.

That infamous pest plant, the melastoma.... Look for wide, rounded shrubs five to six feet high, narrow leaves with prominent longitudinal veins, pink to purple flowers, woody fruit, and hairy, rough stems. This is one of the many "bad guys" you're trying to avoid spreading when you wash off your boots before leaving a hiking area.

Looking for a longer hike in this area? Consider a shuttle between the northern end of the Powerline Trail and the start of the Moalepe Trail! With only about ¼ mile separating the southern end of the Powerline Trail and the start of the Kuilau Trail, you can link all three trails into a single, very long, but simply wonderful dayhike.

White hibiscus blossoms

Trip 12. Waipouli Sunrise Beach Stroll

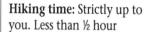	**Distance:** Less than ⅔ mile maximum (how far you go is up to you) **Elevation gain:** Negligible **Hiking time:** Strictly up to you. Less than ½ hour

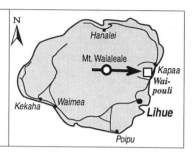

Topos: Optional: *Kapaa*

Trail map: See next page.

Highlights: Sunrise; rainbows in miniature; the Morning Crab Show and the Morning People Show (read on!).

Driving instructions: This is a stroll you shouldn't have to drive to. *The time of day and the mood are really more important than a specific place.* Chances are you're staying within walking distance of a beach. If it's an east-facing beach, you can adapt this stroll to that beach: walk over to the nearest east-facing beach *just before sunrise.*

If you have your heart set on Waipouli Beach, drive north from Lihue on Highway 56, across the Wailua River, and turn in at The Marketplace at Coconut Plantation, 9 miles. Park wherever it's convenient. This stroll starts from the paved walkway through the big, open, grassy area that's between a couple of the hotels. Some maps show it as Waipouli Beach Park.

Permit required: None.

Description. Fill your teacup or coffee mug, and sip as you stroll east to the beach. You'll probably see birds sorting through the damp grass for breakfast. Look for long-legged, long-necked white cattle egrets and black mynas with yellow feet and a racy-looking yellow stripe around their eyes.

When you reach the beach, you can walk in the sand, follow the trail-of-use through the ironwood trees, or walk on the grass. You can even just pick a place on the sand—maybe on a nice big piece of driftwood—and stay there till the sun has risen.

If you want to keep walking, turn left and head north. We liked walking near the ironwood trees. If it's rained during the night or there's been a heavy dew, each long, floppy needle on the ironwood trees has a drop of water hanging from it. Each drop fills with dazzling colors as the sun rises—a rainbow momentarily trapped in the universe of that drop.

You'll notice that the sand is pocked with hundreds of holes ranging from ones smaller than your little finger to ones that look as if they could hold a squirrel. Smaller holes have streaks of thrown sand radiating from them. Some larger ones have a heap of sand on one side. You'll have to stop and sit for a while to enjoy what's going on here: The Morning Crab Show (see below).

If you keep walking north, you'll pass through a couple of grassy areas in front of hotels and reach the fence at the north end of the beach. Turn around and head south. Strolling south, you'll notice that the Morning People Show is in progress. You're part of it, so smile: it's showtime! Beyond the big grassy area from which you started, you pass in front of a couple more hotels. Soon you reach an area defined by black boulders which overlooks picturesque Wailua Bay; this is Alakukui Point. Fragrant spider lilies grow here. The number of spiders who've spun their webs between the leaves suggests another reason why the plants are called "spider" lilies. Your nose will tell you that there are restaurants around here which are serving breakfast. Why resist? It's the beginning of a lovely new day on Kauai, and you need to keep up your strength in order to enjoy it!

Retrace your steps to your car whenever you're ready.

The Morning Crab Show. Sit still, and don't look hard at any par-

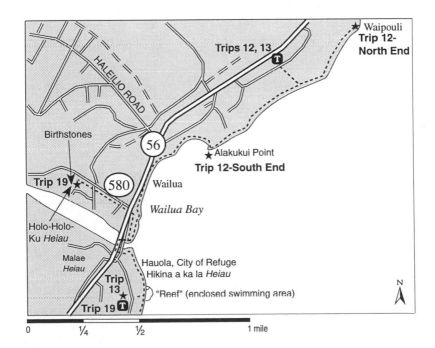

ticular hole. Be alert for movement within your field of vision. Ghost crabs are like faint stars: easier to pick out when you don't look at them directly. Soon you'll notice tiny scurrying movements. Minutes or just seconds may elapse between them. Pick out the area where they're occurring, and when you've got it, look directly. A little crab, almost translucent and mottled like the sand, will dart out of the hole and—*whap!*—suddenly there's a new sand streak. It's thrown a clawful of sand away, sometimes as much as a foot. (At least, I think that's what it was doing.)

The Morning People Show. As you return southward, you'll notice that lots of other people are out, performing their morning rituals: running, jogging, walking, meditating, sitting on driftwood drinking coffee, and practicing *tai chi chuan*. (At least, I think that's what they were doing.)

Trip 13. Waipouli-Lydgate Beach Trek

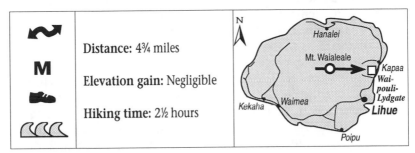

Distance: 4¾ miles

Elevation gain: Negligible

Hiking time: 2½ hours

Topos: Optional: *Kapaa*
Trail map: See Trip 12.
Highlights: You'll enjoy beachcombing all the way around Wailua Bay, the visit to Lydgate State Park, which is a gem, and beachcombing and snorkeling at Lydgate.
Driving instructions: Follow the driving instructions for Trip 12.
Permit required: None.

Description. Walk out to Waipouli Beach as described in Trip 12, and walk south to Alakukui Point. Then descend to the beach and continue south on the sand. You're walking around Wailua Bay now. It's not a good swimming beach, but it certainly is pretty! You'll encounter a barrier of volcanic boulders under some beach heliotrope trees partway around the bay. Climb over them; some of them are loose and slippery, so watch your footing. Boulders that are under water at least part of the time are "home" for marine animals. Carefully look under them to see who's home (often, a colony of snails).

Back on the sand, you reach the Wailua River in ¾ mile from Alakukui Point. It's too deep to ford safely, and the currents where the river meets the sea are said to be very treacherous. No problem: turn inland and climb the boulders to get to the roadway (it's easier than you think). The first bridge is a cane road that may be open to vehicles, so you can't use it. The next bridge inland, Highway 56, has narrow pedestrian walkways on either side. Cross the Wailua River on it and then turn seaward through some widely spaced boulders, across a grassy area and a cane road, and down some low dunes to the beach. Continue your walk along the beach as it follows the riverbank past Hauola and Hikina a ka la (see Trip 19), curves south away from the mouth of the Wailua River, and reaches the protected swimming area described in Trip 19 in ⅓ mile. (You may wish to continue your beachcombing a little farther south to the line of boulders described in Trip 19.)

Return to your car the way you came.

Maui's mischief.... Few of the gods and goddesses of ancient Hawaii "survived" Christianity. Two who did and whose adventures are still widely told and enjoyed are Pele, the volcano goddess, and Maui. The demigod Maui is best known for having cleverly forced the sun to spend more time in the sky above the earth so that people could enjoy days and nights of approximately equal length. Before that, legend says, the lazy sun rose from his resting place, hurried across the sky, and returned to his rest, leaving people with very short days and very long nights. Haleakala Crater on Maui is the site of that exploit. But that's just one of Maui's escapades. Here, at the mouth of the Wailua River, legend says he turned his eight brothers into stone and sank them in the river's mouth. Here's one version of what happened.

Maui wanted to draw all the Hawaiian islands into one land mass. To do so, he needed the great strength of a giant fish called Luehu—but first he had to catch Luehu. Repeatedly he put to sea from Wailua in a canoe with his eight brothers to hunt Luehu, but Luehu evaded him. How did Luehu know when Maui was hunting for him? Maui's mother told him that the nine mudhens living in Wailua would warn Luehu that Maui was looking for him by building a great fire.

So Maui put an image of himself in his canoe, sent his brothers out with the image in order to make the mudhens think he had gone hunting Luehu, and hid along the Wailua River to spy on the birds. When the mudhens started the fire to warn Luehu, Maui jumped out, forced them to tell him how to make fire, and used the knowledge to confuse Luehu about what he (Maui) was really up to.

The next time he and his brothers hunted Luehu, their mother warned Maui not to pick up a gourd canoe-bailer that he would find floating at sea. Maui, in the stern of the canoe, disobeyed her, picked up the gourd, and put it behind him in the canoe. Maui ordered his brothers not to look back at him. This time they caught Luehu, who pulled the canoe around the islands, wrapping the fishing line around them and drawing them closer together.

Suddenly they heard a great shouting from shore in admiration of a beautiful woman in their canoe. Surprised, Maui's brothers looked back and saw that the gourd canoe-bailer had changed into a beautiful woman! In that moment of inattention, Luehu escaped, and the islands drifted apart again. When Maui got back to the Wailua River, he turned his eight disobedient brothers into stones that he sank in the mouth of the river.

When Luehu was drawing the islands together, only Kauai and Oahu actually touched, near Nawiliwili Bay on Kauai and at Kaena Point on Oahu. Today, it's said that there's a rock called Pohaku o Kauai, or Stone of Kauai, at Kaena Point. The legends say it's a little piece of Kauai that remained stuck to Oahu when they drifted apart.

Trip 14. Nonou Mountain East Side

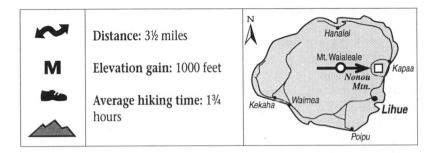

Distance: 3½ miles

Elevation gain: 1000 feet

Average hiking time: 1¾ hours

Topos: *Kapaa*
Trail map: At the end of this trip.
Highlights: When was the last time you walked across a giant? Nonou Mountain is also known as The Sleeping Giant. He's perfectly placed to offer you, from the picnic shelter on his "chest," Alii Vista Hale, wonderful views of the sparkling Pacific, of the Lihue Basin, and of the spectacular mountains inland from Kapaa.
Driving instructions: Drive north from Lihue on Highway 56 for 8 miles and turn inland (west) off Highway 56 onto Haleilio Road. This turn is a little north of the turnoff for Highway 580 and has a traffic light. Drive to where the road begins to curve to the left. On your right, near telephone pole #38, there's a marked trailhead and a short road that leads to a Department of Water pump. There's room to park across the road on the shoulder.
Permit required: None.

Description. This is my favorite of the three official Nonou Mountain trails (Nonou East, Nonou West, and Kuamoo-Nonou). It's more open—offering much better views along the trail itself—than Nonou West and Kuamoo-Nonou. It's slightly longer than Nonou West, but its elevation gain is more gradual, which translates as "easier" if you want to get to the top.

Walk a few feet up the road toward the pump, and then take the trail that bears left off the road. Follow this pleasant, relatively open trail up several switchbacks through ironwood, swamp mahogany, Christmas berry, koa *haole*, guava, and silk oak. Cayenne vervain adds its distinctive blue flowers to the understory, and you may notice the white flowers of bindweed twining through the shrubs.

You make a rather long northward traverse between the ½- and ¾-mile markers, during which you give up a little elevation. There are lots of good views eastward over Kapaa and Waipouli to the ocean. Soon you're making an easy to moderate ascent with an occasional scramble over volcanic boulders. After passing a big volcanic outcrop, you round Nonou Mountain's north ridge and are briefly on its western (inland) side. For a while you're in dense guava and eucalyptus forest as you switch back and forth over the ridge.

You pass through a stretch of *ti, hau,* and *hala,* which reminds you you're in the tropics. As you crisscross the ridge, good views of the Makaleha Mountains greet you, soon followed by views of Kalepa Ridge, Wailua Bay, and the Hoary Head Mountains. It's easy to lose the trail at a couple of very bare, eroded, steep places. These are places where the trail makes a switchback, turning sharply right to avoid most of the bare spots.

Near the top, you reach a three-way junction guarded by some *hala* trees whose root systems have to be seen to be believed. Take the left fork through a forest of *ti* and dense strawberry guava. (The right fork is the Nonou Mountain West Trail.) You soon come to another fork, from which both paths lead to the Alii Vista Hale Picnic Shelter on the Sleeping Giant's "chest." The path on the right is a little easier.

This level, grassy spot is just made for picnicking and loafing. The shelter offers a roof and a table with benches; on the seaward side, there's a little bench with a great view. You don't have a 360-degree view here because of the trees and the Giant's "head," but all you have to do is walk around to enjoy panoramic views inland and seaward. If you're lucky, there'll be some light showers, and you can enjoy the sight of rainbows appearing and disappearing as the silvery threads of rain sweep across Kauai. (Look for rainbows away from the sun, not into it.)

Retrace your steps when you feel ready to do so—it's hard to leave this lovely place.*

The Sleeping Giant.... Before you set off on this delightful trip, you'll probably want to know something about The Sleeping Giant you're going to walk on. You can see his profile from practically anywhere in Kapaa. But what is he doing there? I've read at least three Sleeping Giant legends. My favorite is the one our friend Dan Masaki, who's a native of Kauai, told us:

Once upon a time, a little boy who lived in the village where Kapaa now stands caught a fish and took it home to his mother. When they were

---

*There's a trail of use that leads south, away from the shelter and toward an antenna on the Giant's "head." It even has a mileage stake. It soon degenerates into a rock scramble requiring some bouldering skills and having considerable exposure on either side. I understand it leads out to the Giant's "nose," from which there is said to be a sheer dropoff of hundreds of feet on three sides. Because of that, I can neither recommend it to you nor get all the way out there myself—I'm slightly acrophobic. But a few readers have written me that they've tried it and enjoyed it.

getting ready to eat the fish, it begged for mercy and pleaded, "Feed me, feed me." They were astonished, but they thought the fish was a very powerful spirit whom they dared not offend. So they fed the fish some *poi*.

At once the fish began to grow very rapidly. The family kept feeding the fish more *poi,* and as the fish grew, it began taking on human characteristics. It wasn't a fish any more. It was a boy. He kept growing and demanding more food. In no time at all, he was a giant. He had the whole village enslaved, feeding him.

The villagers were desperate, but no one knew how to get rid of the giant. Then a beautiful maiden had an idea. "Let me try to free us from the giant," she said. Of course, the villagers agreed. The maiden took out her ukelele and played it as she sang the giant to sleep. The village was free! She must have played and sung superbly, for the giant still sleeps today. Let's hope he doesn't wake up while you're walking on him!

(The ancient Hawaiians didn't have ukeleles, you say? Well, legends are bigger than mere facts, just as the Sleeping Giant is bigger than we are.)

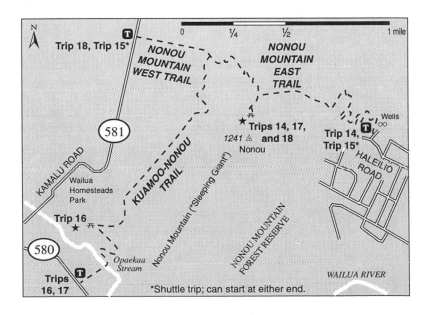

Trip 15. Nonou Mountain Shuttle

M

Distance: 3¼ miles

Elevation gain: 1000 feet for start from east side, 800 feet for start from west side

Hiking time: 1¾ hours (allows extra time for steepness of west side)

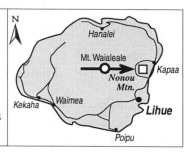

Topos: *Kapaa*
Trail map: At the end of Trip 14.
Highlights: Views, of course! The wonderful views from the picnic shelter at the top as well as the fine views from the Nonou Mountain East Trail—you get the best of both trails with this shuttle.
Driving instructions: Decide which way you want to go—east to west or west to east. Then shuttle a car to one trailhead, and drive around to start your hike at the other trailhead. See the driving instructions for Trips 14 and 18 for details.
Permit required: None.

Description. Follow the hiking description of Trip 14 or Trip 18 to the Alii Vista Hale Picnic Shelter. Then reverse the hiking description from the picnic shelter for the other trail (Trip 18 or Trip 14, respectively).

If you hike up on the Nonou Mountain West Trail and go down on the Nonou Mountain East Trail, staying on the Nonou Mountain East Trail at the big, bare areas is a little tricky. At each bare area the trail is making a switchback, so descend just a few steps and then go sharply left. The tread of the trail is obvious again and leads away from the bare area.

If you hike up on the Nonou Mountain East Trail and go down on the Nonou Mountain West Trail, note where the two rows of Norfolk pines end and look for the stakes. You bear right here (left is the Kuamoo-Nonou Trail).

Enjoy!

Trip 16. Valley Vista Hale Picnic Shelter

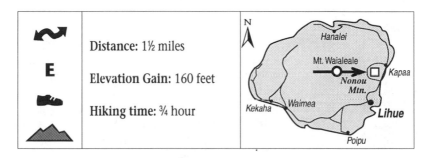

Distance: 1½ miles

Elevation Gain: 160 feet

Hiking time: ¾ hour

Topos: *Kapaa*
Trail map: At the end of Trip 14.
Highlights: This is a delightful short hike that takes you through a densely forested area out to a picnic shelter with surprisingly good views considering how little elevation you gain. Bring your lunch and stay for a while!

Driving instructions: Drive north on Highway 56 from Lihue 8 miles, and turn inland (west) on Highway 580 just north of the Wailua River. Pass the turnout for the Opaekaa Falls viewpoint and continue toward the steep, bare, stone "pillars" on Nonou Mountain's south face (they'll be on your right). There's a trailhead sign on a gate, which is on the right (north) side of the highway.

Permit required: None.

Description. Follow the path northeast along a row of trees to Opaekaa Stream. You descend slightly to cross the stream on a wooden bridge, then follow the trail as it curves along a *hau* thicket on one side, a fenced-off area on the other. Blue-flowered vervain brightens the edges of your trail as you ascend into a dense forest of *hau* and strawberry guava. Large ferns dominate the understory here.

You climb gently through this dense cover, making a few long switchbacks, to an open spot that overlooks the Lihue Basin. The Valley Vista Hale Picnic Shelter welcomes you here. Sit down and enjoy the view of Aahoaka, the small, sharp-peaked hill to the southwest; Kalepa Ridge to the southeast; Wailua Homesteads Park just below you; the cliffs of Kawaikini and Mt. Waialeale to the west; the Makaleha Mountains to the north; and the jagged spires of Kalalea Mountain near Anahola far to the north.

After taking in this beautiful scene, retrace your steps to your car.

Rolling shrimp.... Opaekaa ("rolling shrimp") Stream is named for the *opae*, a kind of freshwater shrimp native to Hawaiian waters. *Opae* were a favorite food of the ancient Hawaiians. They hatch in fresh water, are swept out to sea, where they continue their life cycle, and then migrate back to the streams to reproduce, climbing upstream with specially adapted appendages. In the past, the *opae* could be seen rolling and tumbling in the water at the base of Opaekaa Falls, where the stream plunges over a steep cliff into a narrow canyon. They are no longer found in Opaekaa Stream but can be found in other places on Kauai. Freshwater shrimp with similar adaptations are found throughout Polynesia. Unfortunately, habitat destruction and predation by an introduced Tahitian freshwater prawn have reduced the *opae*'s numbers on Kauai.

Mouth of Waioli Stream at Hanalei Bay (Trip 1)

Trip 17. Alii Vista Hale Picnic Shelter

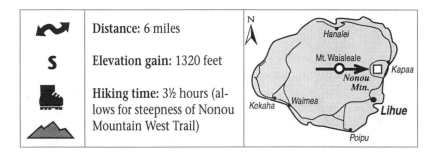

⤳	Distance: 6 miles
S	Elevation gain: 1320 feet
👢	Hiking time: 3½ hours (allows for steepness of Nonou Mountain West Trail)
⛰	

Topos: *Kapaa*
Trail map: At the end of Trip 14.
Highlights: Double the viewing pleasure: you get to enjoy first the views from Valley Vista Hale Picnic Shelter and second, by climbing the Nonou Mountain West Trail, those from Alii Vista Hale Picnic Shelter atop Nonou Mountain.
Driving instructions: Follow the driving directions for Trip 16.
Permit required: None.

Description. Follow Trip 16 to the Valley Vista Hale Picnic Shelter.

Continue northeast along Nonou Mountain's west side on a gently rolling trail under cover so dense it may be hard to identify the trees around you. Instead, you can try identifying them by the leaves and the fruit that have fallen to the trail. Take the quiz that follows this trail description! There's usually a rich scent of decomposing vegetation. But do you notice the almost-medicinal scent in areas where the yellow cattley guava fruits are mashed onto the trail?

At an obscure junction just past the one-mile marker, bear right (east), climb a little, and pass one thing you won't have to identify from leaves on the trail: a striking clump of giant bamboo. Avoid false trails leading downhill in this vicinity. You descend a little now and pass through a stand of towering Norfolk pines. A long up-and-down stretch through more Norfolk pines lets you know you're approaching the junction with the Nonou Mountain West Trail. Keep your eyes open for those two metal markers described in Trip 18, the Nonou Mountain West trip, and for the very regular "avenue" of Norfolk pines that bracket the Nonou Mountain West Trail.

Turn right (uphill) at the junction and follow Trip 18's directions from that junction to the top of Nonou Mountain.

Return the way you came.

Name that tree! Remember, you're looking at leaves that have fallen to the ground, so their color will generally be "dead"—that is, some shade of brown. What tree goes with the:

- Very round leaf with abrupt, sharp point opposite the stem? (*Hau.*)
- Lobed leaf, a little like a maple or a sycamore; black, walnut-shell-like fruit capsule? (*Kukui.*) (Young *kukui* leaves may not be lobed, however.)
- Very slender, sickle-shaped leaf, four or five inches long? (*Koa.*)
- Very long, narrow leaf ending in a point, with sawtoothed edges; fruits are squarish, tapering capsules with brush-like ends? (*Hala.*)
- Two- to three-inch leaf, leathery and oval; round red or cylindrical yellow fruit? (*Strawberry guava or yellow cattley guava—there are more of the latter along this trail.*)
- Four- to seven-inch leaf, leathery and tapering; fruit a ⅜-inch cylindrical woody capsule with three tiny chambers? (*Swamp mahogany.*)
- Large leaf composed of many leaflets that are smaller at the top, much longer at the bottom, lower ones deeply divided, giving the whole leaf a fern- or feather-like appearance? (*Silk oak.*)

Trip 18. Nonou Mountain West Side

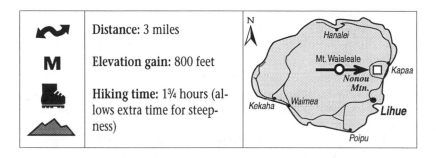

Distance: 3 miles

Elevation gain: 800 feet

Hiking time: 1¾ hours (allows extra time for steepness)

Topos: *Kapaa*

Trail map: At the end of Trip 14.

Highlights: As for Nonou Mountain East Side, the big reward is the wonderful view from the top.

Driving instructions: Following the driving instructions of Trip 17, but continue past the Kuamoo-Nonou trailhead. At the junction with Highway 581, turn right (northeast) on Highway 581. Start looking at the numbers on the telephone poles. The Nonou Mountain West trailhead is on your right (east) by telephone pole #11. Please park so you don't block the gate.

Permit required: None.

Description. Step over the low sill in the gate that bars vehicle access to this trail and walk east up a fenced avenue of trees for about ⅓ mile. At the top of this avenue, where the forest begins, there's a lovely view of the pastoral countryside and the Makaleha Mountains to the west and northwest. A few lemon-scented gums—my favorite tree—grow in the pasture south of this avenue.

Follow the trail into the forest a short distance to a poorly marked junction with the Kuamoo-Nonou Trail. Look for two small metal stakes, one on each side of the trail. The downhill stake has START marked on it. The nearly level trail that leads southwest from there is the Kuamoo-Nonou Trail. The Nonou West Trail—your trail for this trip—marches straight uphill on your left, almost southeast, between two very straight, parallel rows of Norfolk pines. (If for some reason the stakes are not there, look for that very regular planting of two rows of Norfolk pines going straight uphill.)

Hike uphill between the pines to the first of many switchbacks, some gentle, some steep, which you'll take through a dense forest of strawberry guava, silk oak, and *ti*. The trail grows steeper until you pass an immense *koa* tree whose roots you clamber over.

Now there's a brief level stretch before you climb steeply to the three-way junction by the *hala* trees. The trail to the shelter is the right fork. (The left fork is the Nonou Mountain East Trail.) Follow the right fork to the next fork and to the shelter as described for the Nonou Mountain East Trail. Enjoy the excellent views!

Return the way you came when you can finally tear yourself away from the scenery. Take your time, especially if the trail is muddy—it would be easy to slip and fall here.

Koa....*Koa* leaves, as you know by now, are sickle-shaped—usually. But there's an entirely different shape of *koa* leaf that you'll also encounter: a leaf consisting of many very tiny leaflets and having an airy, ferny appearance. Young *koa* trees sport the ferny leaves, sometimes even when they've grown quite large. You'll sometimes see those "juvenile" leaves on a mature tree most of whose leaves are sickle-shaped. The tiny *koa* flower, a white powderpuff, and the juvenile leaves are what *koa haole* (or *haole koa*) is named for.

Amazing, stilt-like roots of hala *trees on* **Nonou Mountain**

Trip 19. Lydgate State Park-Great Sacred Wailua Walk

Distance: 3 miles

M

Elevation gain: Negligible

Hiking time: 1½ hours

Topos: Optional: *Kapaa*
Trail map: See Trip 12, page 67.
Highlights: Picnicking, beachcombing, and snorkeling at Lydgate State Park and a visit to some of the most ancient and sacred sites on Kauai.

If you're hiking with children, I recommend you drive rather than walk on Highway 580's narrow-to-nonexistent shoulders to get to the sites along that highway.

Driving instructions: This trip begins at Lydgate State Park. As you are coming north from Lihue on Highway 56, at about the 8-mile point but before you cross the Wailua River, look for a sign that says LYDGATE AREA a little beyond the golf course. Rely on the road sign rather than the mileage marker. Turn right off the highway, bear right where the hotel parking road branches left, turn left past the sewage disposal facility, and continue to Lydgate, where there are two parking areas. The more southerly parking area is by a very large pavilion; the more northerly overlooks the sea. Note that "Lydgate State Park" isn't shown by that name on the *Kapaa* topo. It's where the topo shows a semicircular protected swimming area out in the water (just under the words "Hikina o ka la Heiau," a misspelling of Hikina a ka la, as you'll see).

Permit required: None.

Description:

Lydgate State Park. This description assumes you'll park at the more northerly of the parking areas. Walk out to the beach and turn south for a short walk to where tree heliotrope, ironwood trees, beach *naupaka*, and *hala* grow around a heap of black boulders. Turn around here to begin a leisurely beachcombing walk back toward the protected swimming area. Beachcombing is a state of mind, and it really doesn't matter whether you find anything as long as you're enjoying the hunt. Most shells are pounded to bits on the rough trip to this beach, so the only ones you're likely to find are those that are very tiny or very sturdy or both—treasures nonetheless if *you* find them.

Soon you're back in the vicinity of the parking area, where there are also some picnic shelters, restrooms, and Lydgate's chief delight, the protected swimming area. It's a semicircular artificial "reef" built out into the ocean with black volcanic boulders. It's divided by more boulders into two parts: a tiny, shallow enclosure on the left for the little children, and a deeper, much larger enclosure for the bigger children (including those over 21). The snorkeling here is wonderful, and the "reef" makes it safe in most weather.

Through Lydgate/Wailua River State Park on The Way of the Chiefs. As you approach the mouth of the Wailua River, you begin your journey along Wailua Nui Hoano ("Great Sacred Wailua"), following "The Way of the Chiefs." Great Sacred Wailua, which includes the area around the river's mouth and which extends inland along the river some two miles on the south bank and three miles on the north bank, was one of the two most sacred spots in all the islands. The kings and high chiefs of Kauai dwelt here and made their annual pilgrimage to Mt. Waialeale from here. Many voyages to and from Tahiti began and ended here before such voyages ceased altogether some time in the thirteenth century. Details about the sites shown in boldface type are given after the end of this trip description.

As the beach begins curving inland to eventually become a riverbank, look left toward the hotel for a big boulder surrounded by beach *naupaka*. The plaque on it identifies the site as **Hauola**, a City of Refuge, where those who had committed crimes or fled from the horrors of war might come for safety. As you visit these *heiau*, or temples, remember that they were places of worship, and treat them with respect. Hauola is part of a larger temple complex the rest of which lies a little up the bluff behind the stone with the plaque. This thirteenth-century complex was called **Hikina a ka la**, the Rising of the Sun, because the rays of the morning sun struck it as the sun rose.

Continue your walk on The Way of the Chiefs to Highway 56. A *heiau* that you can't see or get to from here lies across the highway in the cane fields. It was called **Malae**, and its remains are the largest *heiau* remains on Kauai. You may be able to see it from the ruins of **Poliahu**, which you need to drive to.

Walk north on the shoulder of Highway 56 (carefully!), and cross the Wailua River. As you cross, pause to enjoy the panorama: the luxuriant *hau* thickets line the wide river's banks as it flows from those jagged peaks to the west.

Up Highway 580 on The Way of the Chiefs. It's ½ mile from Hikina a ka la to the junction of Highways 56 and 580. Highway 580 runs along the north side of the Wailua River. Cross Highway 56 and start up Highway 580 at the traffic light that controls their junction. The shoulders of Highway 580 are almost nonexistent until you cross a ditch. After that, the Coco Palms side (north) is wider, but the site you're heading for is on the river (south) side, about ¼ mile from the junction. Please use your best judgement.

On the south side of the road, you come first to **Holo-Holo-Ku** *heiau*, a very small *heiau* which was a place of human sacrifice. Just behind Holo-Holo-Ku, around some shrubbery, there is a site of immense importance: the **Birthstones**. All Kauaians of chiefly rank had to have been born at the Birthstones, and therefore at Holo-Holo-Ku; if born elsewhere, they were considered commoners regardless of their ancestry.

Ignore the modern stairway leading uphill from here. It goes to a little cemetery so hemmed in by *hau* that there are no river views. It would be very peaceful there if it weren't full of people like us who are milling about, feeling a little silly because they ran up here assuming there was another *heiau* or a viewpoint.

Return to your car the way you came.

Along the way....

Hauola, City of Refuge....A criminal would stay at a City of Refuge for several days, performing rites prescribed by the priests, after which that person was free to leave without punishment. Remember, Hauola functioned in the times when a commoner could be put to death if his shadow fell on an *alii*. Cities of Refuge provided one means of escape. Persons fleeing the horrors of the frequent wars might also come to Cities of Refuge for safety. (According to Edward Joesting (see Bibliography), it is not certain that this was actually a City of Refuge.)

Hikina a ka la.... Hikina a ka la was a massive structure whose enclosing walls were eight to eleven feet thick and six feet high. Edward Joesting notes that Hikina a ka la was divided into three sections and that in the middle section there were reported to be the graves of "an entire family who had desecrated the structure by living and cultivating land within the walls."

Holo-Holo-Ku.... The god Ku dominated worship at Holo-Holo-Ku, although all the gods were represented here. Once a month on a designated night, the priest's executioner strangled the chosen sacrificial victim, who was often a prisoner of war. But if no prisoners of war were available, the victim would be some unlucky Kauaian whom the priest had secretly selected.

The ancient Kauaians would build an "oracle tower," a tall structure of *ohia* poles, over the sacrificial stone. The oracle tower had at least two uses: the priest would commune with the gods from the tower, and the corpse of the victim would hang from the tower until the flesh fell from the bones.

Holo-Holo-Ku is said to be the oldest *heiau* on Kauai and to be of Tahitian design. It lies just below a ridge called Ka Lae o ka Manu, the Crest of the Bird. Edward Joesting notes that the "Crest of the Bird" image may have recalled the crest of a fighting cock (also echoed in the crest on a warrior's helmet) and thus emphasized the importance and dominance of this location.

The Birthstones.....An ancient chant records that the site, not the child's parentage, conferred nobility: a child born at Holo-Holo-Ku was a chief whether its parents were chiefs or commoners. The child of chiefs if *not* born at Holo-Holo-Ku was not of chiefly rank. The mother supported her back on one of the Birthstones and her legs on the other as she delivered her child. The child's umbilical cord had to be wrapped in *tapa* and hidden in the rock cliff behind the Birthstones.

The flat slab of stone you'll see next to the Birthstones is set over the remains of a sacrificed dog. That is the sign that place is *kapu* for commoners. Edward Joesting notes that while the Birthstones were normally *kapu* for commoners, the king of Kauai would choose women of common ancestry to give birth here when the chiefly ranks became depleted for some reason.

Bellstone and Poliahu.....Please do not try to walk to the Bellstone or to Poliahu, which lie farther up Highway 580 on the riverbank. The highway shoulders don't permit safe walking. Drive to Poliahu, which is an impressive ruin with excellent views over the Wailua River. Legend says that Menehunes, the "little people" of Kauai mythology, built Poliahu and Malae *heiau*. Malae is across the river nearer the river's mouth; look for it if you visit Poliahu. According to legend, deities gathered at Poliahu once a month, on the night of Kane. Mere mortals dared not go there!

On your way you'll pass (but not actually see) the site of the Bellstone. Another legend says that after a child had been born at Holo-Holo-Ku, the priests carried it up to the Bellstone. The priests struck the Bellstone with a rock in a certain way so that it gave off a sound that announced up and down the Wailua Valley that a new chief had been born.

Defunct? Maybe not.....It is customary to think of the *heiaus* as being defunct as places of worship, but you'll often see fresh offerings at them. At Hikina a ka la I saw a very traditional offering: a fresh fish wrapped in *ti* leaves and tucked into a stone mound. An offering you'll frequently see is a stone wrapped in a *ti* leaf. At Poliahu I once saw a very contemporary offering: a bar of Hershey's Supreme Chocolate with Almonds—wrapped in a *ti* leaf, of course. That offering was to give me an idea years later. . . .

In early 1993 my husband and I were having no luck finding a home in the new town we wanted to move to—I'll call it Fairview—and I had to go to Kauai to do my post-Iniki re-scouting. Every other day we would talk: "Found anything yet?" I'd say. "No," he'd reply. We were getting desperate. Then I decided to ask for help. I'm not much on Western religions, but I respect the gods of old Hawaii, and I hoped they wouldn't mind hearing from a *haole*. So on my way to a trailhead one morning, I bought a big chocolate bar, plucked an especially fine *ti* leaf from the many plants around the place where I was staying, and drove to Poliahu to leave my offering with a petition for a new home. When I got back to my lodgings that evening, there was a message from my husband: "Congratulations, you're now a resident of Fairview!"

Please don't disturb the offerings.

Boulder and marker for Hauola, City of Refuge

Trip 20. Wailua Falls Non-hike

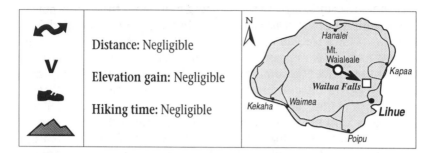

Distance: Negligible

Elevation gain: Negligible

Hiking time: Negligible

N
Hanalei
Mt. Waialeale
Kapaa
Wailua Falls □
Kekaha   Waimea
Lihue
Poipu

Topos: Optional: *Kapaa*
Trail map: At the end of this trip.
Highlights: This is one of the easiest hikes in this book because you can't really hike here. Don't take it personally. The trail to the base of Wailua Falls—seen on *Fantasy Island*—is closed because it's so dangerous. People have been hurt trying to hike it, and I don't want you to be one of them. There are too many other wonderful things for you to enjoy on Kauai. So read the story below, then drive to the viewpoint, get an eyeful of the falls, and remember the wedding I'm going to tell you about.
Driving instructions: Drive north from Lihue on Highway 56 2 miles to the junction with Highway 583. Turn left (inland) on Highway 583 (Maalo Road), which seems more like a glorified cane road. Maalo Road doodles its way northward for 4 miles to end at a large turnout that overlooks Wailua Falls. Park there and walk a few steps to the railing.
Permit required: None.

Description. From the turnout, you can get several views of the double cascade of Wailua Falls and of the large pool at its base. Every few minutes a new wave of tourists washes over the turnout. Watching them is as much fun as looking at the falls. Some of them will, in turn, watch you. (After all, you're a tourist, too.)
A Perfect Wedding.... Just a year ago, they had vacationed on Kauai and had fallen in love with each other all over again. Today would be the wedding of their dreams: at the base of idyllic Wailua Falls, she radiantly happy in her pretty new dress and flower-decked hat, he tall and handsome in his white slacks and silk sportshirt, their family and friends surrounding them, as an authentic Hawaiian *kahuna* married them.
Their friend "Hawaii Sam" had arranged everything. It had cost a fortune. True, the *kahuna* seemed semi-comatose. But they'd written and

memorized their own vows and could recite them to each other if they had to. This was *their* day, and it was a gorgeous one.

The limousines carrying the wedding party from the airport pulled to the side of the road where the trail to the base of the falls started. The place was full of tourists. But where was the trailhead? What was that big, ugly fence blocking the way, that sign saying DANGER DO NOT GO BEYOND GUARDRAIL? "Didn't I tell you folks?" said Hawaii Sam. "They closed the trail. Too dangerous. We'll hold the ceremony here." *Here,* they thought, *at this wretched roadside? Surrounded by screaming kids, jostled by yelling parents, scrutinized by a dozen senior citizens?* The wedding party stood there, feeling conspicuous, ridiculous, and angry. Where was the *Fantasy Island* setting, the serenity, the dignity? Where the hell was the *romance?!* They were so furious they couldn't speak, couldn't move.

And then they started to laugh and couldn't stop. Hawaii Sam pulled out a cassette deck and drowned out the tourists with Hawaiian music. The *kahuna* came to life and began a chant they couldn't understand. The happy couple exchanged the vows they'd composed. Hawaii Sam dashed around videotaping everything for posterity. It was over in a few minutes, and the limousines whisked them away to a splendid wedding reception that lived up to their hopes and Hawaii Sam's advertising.

The videotape of the ceremony is a work of genius. *It* is very nearly the wedding they dreamed of. My friend Kelly Poor, who was in the wedding party with her husband Joel and who told me this story, says there is no hint of the scruffy roadside or the milling tourists—just the joyful faces of the wedding party against the glorious landscape of Kauai. And I'll bet that after a while, that's how they'll remember it—the wedding as it should have been, not as it was.

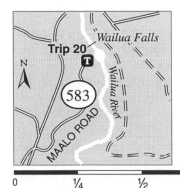

0   ¼   ½   1 mile

Trip 21. Kukuiolono Park

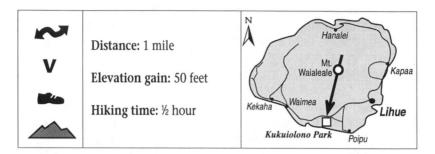

	Distance: 1 mile
	Elevation gain: 50 feet
	Hiking time: ½ hour

Topos: Optional: *Koloa*
Trail map: At the end of this trip.
Highlights: A tiny Japanese garden where fibrous begonias bloom so lavishly that the flowering stems bend almost horizontally over the path, and lovely views from a pavilion on a quiet hill, both part of a golf course so pretty that non-golfers may consider taking up the game.
Driving instructions: From Lihue, drive south and west on Highway 50 to Kalaheo town, 13 miles. At the intersection with Papalina Road, a sign points seaward to Kukuiolono Park. Turn left (south) toward the ocean onto Papalina Road. Follow Papalina Road as it goes uphill and curves around a new housing project on the downhill side. You pass the walls of Kukuiolono Park on the right. It's a sharp right turn into the park itself.

You may park just inside the gate on the right and walk from there, as described in this hike. Or, if you arrive late and want to avoid getting locked in, park just *outside* the gate. Park hours are 6:30 A.M. to 6:30 P.M., but if things on the golf course are slow, they may lock up by 6:00 P.M. *You* can come and go after the gate is locked, but your car can't.
Permit required: None.

Description. From the the gate, walk up the road south and then west on an easy grade through a natural colonnade of huge trees covered with pothos and wood rose vines. There's a lovely, cathedral-like air to the shady avenue formed by these columnar giants. Too soon, you reach the open area at the end of the avenue. Next to a bronze deer on your right, a plaque dated 24 January 1919 commemorates Walter D. McBryde's gift of this park to Kauai; there's a parking lot on the left, and the road forks here (the left fork includes the parking lot). Look for big mango trees draped with orange trumpet vines to the left of the parking lot—quite a sight when the vines are in bloom! You go straight ahead across the parking lot toward the Japanese garden. Most of Kukuiolono Park is a golf course. Jungle fowl and domestic chickens roam freely on the wide-open fairways. Watch out for golf carts and—*whack!*—flying golf balls.

Japanese garden. On the far side of the parking lot, there's a sign advising you that there's an exhibit of Hawaiiana near here. It's at the end of a paved walkway that leads seaward from the parking lot. You curve right at the walkway's end to find the exhibit just beyond a stone wall.

More interesting is the charming little Japanese garden here. None of its paths go directly to the parking lot, so cross the grass to pick them up. The paths form sort of a double loop around the garden, where a "dry stream" of carefully-raked cinders "flows" under a tiny stone bridge and around containers of *bonsai* plants. A *bonsai* bougainvillea, covered with purple blossoms, particularly caught my eye. I hope it's there, blooming, when you visit. It's hard to avoid bumping into the flower-laden stems of the fibrous begonias which fall over the paths. Ornamental red and green *ti* make a colorful display here, and your nose will tell you that there's sweet fern around.

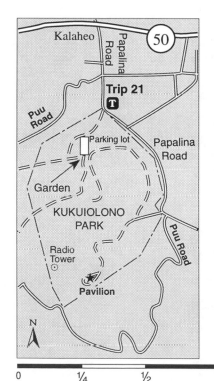

Pavilion viewpoint. Now take the chained-off road on the far left side of the parking lot south-southwest past a grove of fragrant plumeria trees and then past the fifth green. There's some pretty impressive microwave equipment around here (antennas, towers, and so on, probably part of a telephone satellite ground station). The road forks beyond the green, but both forks loop around your next destination, a pavilion—in ruins, "thanks" to Hurricane Iniki, unless it's been rebuilt—overlooking the gently rolling green countryside below, an omnirange station, and the ocean. Whether the pavilion is there or not, it's the view you've come for, and what a fine view it is!

Retrace your steps when you're ready to leave.

Birdie on the volcano.... Geologically, the island of Kauai is the top of a single huge shield volcano that last erupted about 3 million years ago, as you may have read elsewhere in this book. Subsequent episodes of volcanic activity beginning about 1.5 million years ago built newer volcanoes on top of the original shield volcano. Kukuiolono Park with its golf course lies at the summit of a small shield volcano of that later period of volcanism. Talk about a hazard on the course!

Wailua Falls (Trip 20)

Trip 22. Russian Fort Elizabeth State Park

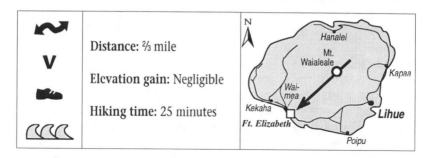

Distance: ⅔ mile

Elevation gain: Negligible

Hiking time: 25 minutes

Topos: Optional: *Hanapepe, Kekaha*
Trail map: At the end of this trip.
Highlights: In the 1700s and 1800s, Imperial Russia joined other European nations in the scramble for wealth in the Pacific. There are few traces of Russia's presence left; this fort is one of them.
Driving instructions: Drive south and west from Lihue on Highway 50 23½ miles almost to Waimea town. Just before you cross the river going west, look on the seaward side for the driveway into Ft. Elizabeth. Signs along the highway point it out. Park in the lot; there are restrooms adjacent.
Permit required: None.

Description. From the parking lot, walk west, past a junction with a path that goes south to the shore, and go to the information sign, where you can read about Ft. Elizabeth's history.

The fort's ruined walls, which are off to your right, are quite impressive. The walls are very thick and look sturdy but are now quite fragile. Don't climb on them! Follow the path toward the fort and around its west wall to its entrance. Inside the entrance, numbered and labeled (though hard to read) stakes lead you counterclockwise in a loop around the interior to over a dozen different sites where the fort's architect had planned for different activities or kinds of storage. However, as the information sign says, there has not been any archeological excavation yet to confirm or correct that information. Still, it's fun to stretch your imagination and try to picture the fort completed and in use, perhaps with the Russian representative, the colorful and deluded Georg Scheffer (below), bustling around giving orders. Today, the fort is filled with graceful *kiawe* trees lifting their airy crowns over patches of nodding, yellow composite flowers.

When you've seen the interior, return to the fort's entrance and (unless the trail segment on the west has been completed) turn right and retrace your steps back to the junction beyond the information sign— almost to the parking lot, but not quite. At this junction, take the path that goes south to the shore and a view of Waimea Bay. To the south, Waimea Bay glitters in the sunlight; to the west, the Waimea River rolls toward the sea.

When you're ready, return to your car.

What might have been.... In the late eighteenth century, when Europeans discovered Hawaii, the Russians were active on the Pacific coast of North America, hunting the fur seal and the sea otter. The furs were immensely valuable, and the Russian American Company held the imperial Russian monopoly on the trade. The company's headquarters were in St. Petersburg, from which it had to resupply its North American headquarters in Sitka, Alaska. It took nine months to a year for a ship from St. Petersburg, sailing out of the Baltic Sea, to resupply the people stationed in Sitka. Supplies arrived irregularly if at all; the people at Sitka sometimes faced the challenge of how to survive till the next supply ship. Naturally, the company was eager to find a closer source of supplies.

The company initially tried to establish an outpost in California at Ft. Ross on what is now the Sonoma coast, but the California enterprise developed too slowly. The company became interested in Hawaii and in 1815 dispatched a representative, Georg Scheffer, to gain a foothold for them in Hawaii. Scheffer was German but was chosen for the role because he was well-educated (he was a physician) and spoke English (next to Hawaiian the most common language in the Islands because of the British and American presence there). Unfortunately, Scheffer had chronic delusions of grandeur, tended to be quarrelsome, and regularly fell out with the people around him.

Scheffer arrived in Hawaii in time to cure Kamehameha I and his favorite wife, Kaahumanu, of an illness. Grateful, Kamehameha promised Scheffer he could establish an outpost in Hawaii for the Russian American Company. While Scheffer waited for that promise to be fulfilled, Kamehameha's British and American advisers convinced him the Russians would usurp his kingdom if given a chance. Scheffer was lucky to escape Kamehameha with his life.

He escaped to Kauai in 1816, where the king of Kauai, Kaumualii, chafed under Kamehameha's rule. Kaumualii and one his wives fell ill, and Scheffer cured them both. The grateful Kaumualii promised his help to the Russians—help that Kaumualii hoped they would reciprocate by freeing him of Kamehameha. They made a secret agreement whereby the Russians would help Kaumualii throw off Kamehameha's yoke and

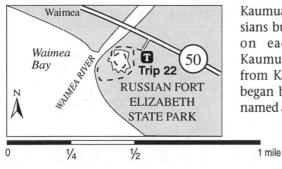

Kaumualii would let the Russians build a fort and man it on each of the islands Kaumualii planned to seize from Kamehameha. Scheffer began building Ft. Elizabeth, named after the consort of the then-Czar of Russia, and setting himself up in a princely manner in Hanalei, which Kaumualii had given him.

The Americans were anxious to prevent Russian competition, and they spread a story: there were serious disagreements between Russia and America; now the Russian minister had left the United States; now Russia and America were at war! In May 1817, they seized Scheffer and hustled him aboard a ship, telling him that all Russians had to leave the island because of the "war." Ft. Elizabeth was completed and and used by Hawaiian troops but was dismantled in 1864.

Trip 23. Polihale State Park

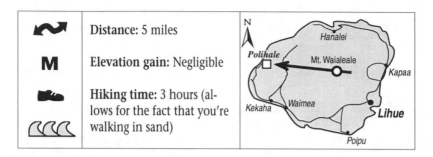

Distance: 5 miles	
Elevation gain: Negligible	
Hiking time: 3 hours (allows for the fact that you're walking in sand)	

Topos: *Makaha Point*
Trail map: At the end of this trip.
Highlights: A visit to the extreme southern end of the Na Pali Coast; an opportunity to walk for miles on a long, nearly empty beach; sunlight and space that go on forever.
Driving instructions: From Lihue, drive south and west on Highway 50 past Kekaha town. About 7 miles north of Kekaha, you reach a fork: the fork you want goes east (right); the other veers west onto the Barking Sands facility of the Pacific Missile Range. Take the east (right) fork through cane fields a very short distance and then in ½ mile turn north (left) where a sign directs you to Polihale. Follow this light-duty dirt road. In about 3½ miles, you pass a junction shaded by a very large tree, the "ghost tree" junction, where a shuttle ride, if you arrange it, can pick you up. In another mile, you pass a junction with the southern end of the road that serves the camping area. In another ½ mile, you reach an often-dry streambed. There's a parking area on your left. This is where the day-use area of Polihale begins. The stream, though intermittent, may have washed part of the road out, making it impossible for you to drive farther.
Permit required: None for day use; apply for permission to camp from the Division of State Parks, Kauai District. Call the Division to be sure the road to Polihale is open.

Description. This description assumes you start from the day-use parking area by the streambed. Begin by crossing the streambed and walking north toward the southernmost cliffs of the Na Pali Coast.
North toward the cliffs. There's a feeling of great openness here and a special quality to the light that reminds me of the vast mainland deserts. You stroll through beach *naupaka*, morning glory, and Indian pluchea. On your right, valleys between the cliffs are inaccessible on

account of dense thickets of *koa haole* and thorny *kiawe*. Polihale *heiau*, which you may have noticed on the topo, lies up on those slopes, hidden by the dense growth.

Picnic pavilions, some shaded by tree heliotrope, dot the sand and hide in the low dunes. Your way is soon blocked by a boulder field. Polihale Spring is said to be hidden under the sand here, but I'm told you have to dig to find it. It's ½ mile from the parking area to the boulder field.

South along the beach. Turning south, you retrace your steps and cross the bed of the stream that flows past the day-use parking area. You'll probably want to walk closer to the water than to the dunes. The dunes to your left hold scattered campsites, which you can occasionally see. Swimming is not safe here except in summer, and then only when the water is very calm. But strolling along the empty beach with just the wind and waves for company is delightful. Polihale seems made for long, contemplative walks. You can walk for almost 2 miles beyond the streambed before the looming parking-lot lights and antennas of the Barking Sands facility tell you it's time to think about turning around. Another clue that it's time to turn around lies out in the sea: a small crescent of coral that encloses a green pool. Near the south end of the crescent, you may see the rusted remains of a tracked vehicle sticking out of the sand.

Of course, you'll want to see whether the sands of the dunes really "bark", and I wish you luck. I tried sliding down them, plunge-stepping down them, and squeezing the sand between my hands, without getting a *yip!*, much less a *woof!*, out of them. A chance acquaintance provided two explanations you'll read about below.

Retrace your steps from here if you want to return on the beach. If you've set up a shuttle, about 50 yards south of the coral is the last good point at which to turn inland. You'll soon pick up tire tracks and then a sandy road which you can follow north to the huge monkeypod "ghost" tree. You can't just turn inland anywhere because of the *kiawe* and *koa haole* thickets which cover the dunes. The growth is sometimes low, which may make you think you can just walk through it. But *kiawe* sports some of the nastiest thorns you've ever accidentally stepped on, so think again.

Ghosts and silent dunes.... Polihale is a very sacred area. In Kauai mythology, the souls of the dead leave the world of the living at Polihale to dwell in the depths of the ocean in Milu, the land of the dead.

Well, not quite all of the dead leave. The huge monkeypod tree at the junction with the dirt road to the southern end of the beach has a resident ghost, according to Sonny, who was a native of Kauai. "I've seen him lots of times," he told me. "Why is the ghost there?" I asked.

"He died there." "What happened to him?" "I don't know; he just died."
I couldn't learn any more about the ghost.

But then, Sonny didn't owe me any information. We'd met only a
few minutes earlier. I'd made the mistake I hope to spare you: I walked
too far past the unmarked end of Polihale State Park and found myself
on Barking Sands without permission. I trudged forever along a paved
road bordered by mowed grass strips—very boring terrain—feeling
dumber and dumber, looking for a way to cut through the thickets of
kiawe and *koa haole* and get back to the road where I would meet my
shuttle ride. Fat chance. The thickets never opened up. I was sure I was
going to be scooped up by the military police.

Then along came a faded blue pickup truck with Sonny—sixty-some
years' worth of the brightest smiles I'd ever seen. He must have recognized the genus *hikerus lostus*, and he helped me get back—a very long,
roundabout way back—to the day-use area at Polihale. Sonny had been
born and raised in Kekaha. Nope, he'd never been interested in moving
anywhere else, though a lot of his school friends had gone to the mainland. What they had to tell of the mainland hadn't sounded so good to
him, so he'd stayed in Kekaha.

I asked Sonny why the dunes didn't "bark" anymore. He grinned.
"The dog died. Naw, not really. There's not enough moisture left in them."
And that's the official explanation from other sources, but I didn't really
need confirmation. Anyone smart enough to avoid the mainland and
stay on Kauai is smart enough to know why the dunes don't bark.

Strolling north from Polihale parking area

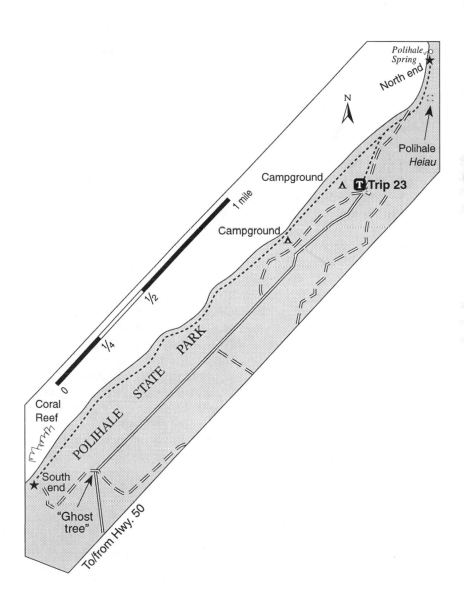

Polihale
Spring

North end

N

Polihale
Heiau

Campground ▲ 🅣 Trip 23

1 mile

Campground ▲

½

¼

POLIHALE STATE PARK

0

Coral
Reef

★ South
  end

"Ghost
tree"

To/from Hwy. 50

Trip 24. Iliau Nature Loop

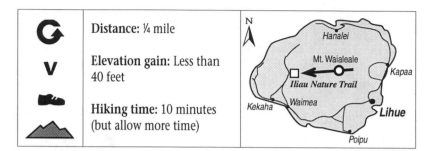

Distance: ¼ mile

Elevation gain: Less than 40 feet

Hiking time: 10 minutes (but allow more time)

Topos: Optional: *Waimea Canyon*
Trail map: At the end of this trip.
Highlights: Stunning views of Waimea Canyon and a chance to learn to identify some of Kauai's mountain plants, including the rare *iliau*, on a very brief stroll.
Driving instructions: There are two highways into Waimea Canyon, Highway 550 (Waimea Canyon Road) from Waimea and Highway 55 (Kokee Road) from Kekaha. You should be aware that different Kauai maps mark these highways differently, but on the ground, the highway from Kekaha is marked 55 and the highway out of Waimea is hardly marked at all. Highway 55 is easier to find because its junction with the road you'll take from Lihue, Highway 50, is better marked. Highway 550 is shorter, narrower, and steeper, but it's also more scenic and is the route I prefer (I took the bigger cover photo from Highway 550).
To take Highway 550, drive south and west from Lihue on Highway 50 to Waimea town, 24 miles. Look for Waimea Baptist Church on the right (inland) side of the road as you're going through the town. Turn right onto the road that's on the west side of Waimea Baptist Church. That road is Highway 550 (Waimea Canyon Road). Follow it for 7 miles uphill to its junction with Highway 55. From here to its end at Puu o Kila (see Trip 43), the road is considered to be Highway 550. Continue as described below (". . .Continue up the hill for 2 more miles to the trailhead. . . .").
To take Highway 55, drive south and west from Lihue on Highway 50 to Kekaha town, 27 miles. Turn right onto signed Highway 55 (Kokee Road) and follow it for 8 miles, through a gully and then uphill to its junction with Highway 550. Continue up the hill for 2 more miles to the trailhead for the Iliau and Kukui trails. The trailhead is on the right (east) side of the road, and there's a small, dirt turnout/parking lot on the left (west) side of the road. Park here to start your hike.

Permit required: None.

Description. The trail begins with a little climb to a bench, and you may have to duck under the overhanging limb of a big *koa* tree. Then you descend to a fork and proceed straight ahead; this segment is part of both the Iliau and Kukui trails. It's likely that the first group of plants that will catch your eye are the *iliau* plants. There's a big patch of them, off to your left, soon after your initial descent. They look rather like miniature *hala* trees with their slender stems and heads of drooping fronds. The *iliau* is related to the silversword and, like that more famous plant and like the mainland's century plants, it grows without flowering for many years, then produces a tall stalk of showy flowers and dies in that blaze of glory.

Follow the loop by going left (north) at a brown post about 100 feet before a hunter's check station for the Kukui Trail. Along the nature trail, you'll notice fluffy mounds of gray-green lichens carpeting the ground. There are numerous, precipitous canyon overlooks just off the trail on your right; follow the beaten track if you wish, but watch your step! It's a long way down.

At a sign that says *moa*, you may do a double-take. Isn't that a giant, extinct, flightless bird of New Zealand? Or the colorful jungle fowl that rules the meadow in front of Kokee Lodge up the road? Yes and no. Here, it's a curious little green-stemmed plant about a foot high with yellow knobs at the top. It's said to be a very primitive plant, "a living link to earth's earliest plants." The *moa* has leaves, but they're barely noticeable; the plant seems to be all stems and knobs.

Soon you reach a junction from which you can go right and up to a bench that overlooks the canyon or you can continue on the trail (left and down). On the trail, after passing under several *ohia* and *koa* trees, you turn back up the slope and retrace your steps to the highway. Or, if you'd like to stay for a picnic, there's a pretty picnic shelter on a grassy rise a few steps beyond the hunter's check station and on the opposite side of the trail from that station.

Life of signs.... Signs are ephemeral. Weather destroys many and is already attacking those on the Iliau Nature Trail. Don't be disappointed if some are gone when you visit. Try to learn from those that remain.

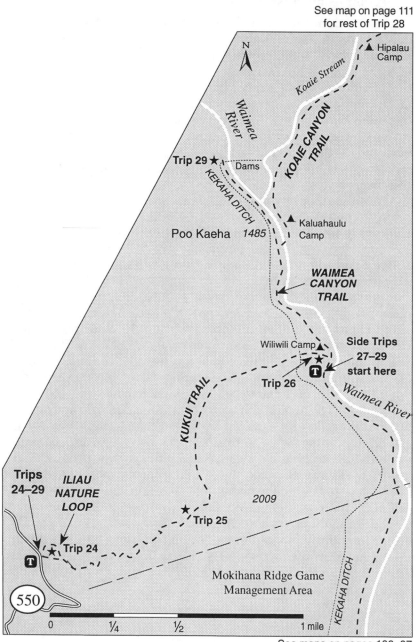

See map on page 111
for rest of Trip 28

Hipalau
Camp

Koaie Stream

Waimea River

KOAIE CANYON TRAIL

Trip 29 ★

Dams

KEKAHA DITCH

Poo Kaeha   *1485*

Kaluahaulu
Camp

**WAIMEA
CANYON
TRAIL**

Wiliwili Camp

**Side Trips
27–29
start here**

Trip 26

Waimea River

KUKUI TRAIL

**Trips
24–29**

*ILIAU
NATURE
LOOP*

2009

★ Trip 25

★ Trip 24

T

550

Mokihana Ridge Game
Management Area

KEKAHA DITCH

0   ¼   ½   1 mile

See maps on pages 106–07
for rest of Trip 27

Trip 25. Kukui Trail to Viewpoint

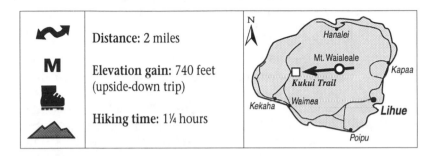

Distance: 2 miles

Elevation gain: 740 feet
(upside-down trip)

Hiking time: 1¼ hours

Topos: *Waimea Canyon*
Trail map: At the end of Trip 24.

Highlights: You can enjoy the extraordinary views of Waimea Canyon that the Kukui Trail provides (in good weather) by going less than halfway down, to a pleasant viewpoint. There is a bench at a fine viewpoint between ¼ and ½ mile and another bench at a spectacular viewpoint at 1 mile. This trip goes to the 1-mile bench, but you may prefer to stop at the first bench.

Driving instructions: Follow the driving instructions for Trip 24.

Permit required: None, but sign in at the hunter's check station.

Description. Follow Trip 24 to the brown post. Continue ahead to the hunter's check station, where you'll sign in. Then continue southeast past the picnic pavilion and begin descending a ridge on switchbacks. *Koa*, silk oak, *ohia*, and lantana line the trail here, and they, in turn, are often covered with twining passionflower vines (see below). This pleasant, broken, dry-forest cover allows you fine views over the adjacent valleys as well as east into the great canyon. To the east-northeast, Waialae Falls makes its dramatic plunge over distant cliffs. Many of the distant valleys are filled with the light-green canopy of *kukui*, but the valley just south of the Kukui Trail is filled with silk oaks—stunning when dressed in their showy golden-orange blossoms. Watch carefully for roots and debris.

Along this trail, you'll find white PVC-pipe mileage markers at ¼-mile intervals. The first viewpoint bench is between the ¼- and ½-mile markers. Stop for a rest and an eyeful even if you plan to go on to the bench near the 1-mile mark.

Near the ¾-mile point, you cross a deeply eroded area where you have to tiptoe carefully over terrain that seems about to slide away. But you're soon over it safely and, a little past the 1-mile marker, you reach the second bench. This viewpoint has a more complete view than the

first bench. You're still high enough to enjoy the sweeping vistas over
Waimea Canyon, and, at the same time, you're far enough into it that
you can see some of the formations that rise from its floor.

Linger awhile, then retrace your steps. Don't forget to sign out at
the hunter's check station.

Edible passionfruit (*lilikoi*)....The passionflower vines you see along
the Kukui Trail (indeed, along the length of the Waimea River) produce
the edible passionfruit, the delicately-flavored *lilikoi*. (It's not the banana passionflower, also called banana poka, that you'll find smothering everything farther up in the mountains, although both are introduced
plants.) You should try the delicious *lilikoi* confections served around
the island before you try a real *lilikoi* so you'll know what it ought to
smell and taste like. The *lilikoi* fruit is ripe when it turns yellow to pur-
plish-brown and its skin is deeply wrinkled. The skin and the white inner rind are quite tough, so cut the fruit open and suck or spoon out the
contents. Unfortunately, its runny, seedy, yellowish contents look awful
despite that ethereal *lilikoi* scent and taste!

The "passion" in "passionflower" and "passionfruit" doesn't refer
to romantic passion. It refers to fancied resemblances in the
passionflower's appearance to instruments of the "passion of Christ"—
Christ's crucifixion.

A shelter within a shelter at Wiliwili Camp (Trip 26)

Trip 26. Kukui Trail to Wiliwili Camp

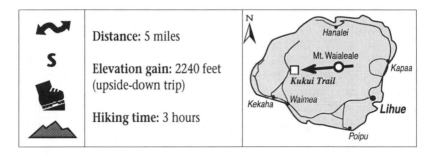

Distance: 5 miles

Elevation gain: 2240 feet
(upside-down trip)

Hiking time: 3 hours

Topos: *Waimea Canyon*

Trail map: At the end of Trip 24.

Highlights: You'll enjoy the excellent canyon views on the upper part of this trail. From Wiliwili Camp, backpackers have some interesting dayhiking options.

Driving instructions: Follow the driving instructions of Trip 24.

Permit required:

Dayhike: As for Trip 25. If you plan to hike south down the Waimea River beyond Waialae Stream, get one of the permits from the self-issue dispensing box for the Mokihana Ridge Game Management Area at the hunter's check station when you sign in.

Backpack: You must apply to the Division of Forestry and Wildlife in Lihue for permission to camp in Waimea Canyon (see "Getting Permits"). See below for special regulations for Waimea Canyon (Puu Ka Pele Forest Reserve). You'll need one of the self-issue permits for the Mokihana Ridge Game Management Area if you plan to dayhike south of Waialae Stream.

Description. Follow Trip 25 to the 1-mile bench. After taking in the view, you go ¼ mile farther and then reach a bare area where erosion has made the trail indistinct. Proceed downhill toward hill 2009 to a saddle and turn left, where you'll find the trail discernable again. (The trail does not go up hill 2009.) You make a switchback, pass some *pukiawe* and *aalii*, and soon reach a steep, long, bare slope of colorful soil that trends north-northwest toward Poo Kaeha, the prominent butte down in the canyon and to the north. Swamp mahogany and a telephone line border this slope. You're treated to constantly changing, breathtaking views as you carefully descend 540 feet on this slope by following the occasional duck and a beaten path that switchbacks across the slope to the forested edge of the next segment. If you haven't put on your mosquito repellent yet, do so before plunging into the forest!

The trail bears east (right) into the forest and begins a steep, switchbacking descent under a dense cover of *kukui*, silk oak, and swamp mahogany. You emerge past some sisal plants at forested Wiliwili Camp 2½ miles from the trailhead, where a striking dark-red cliff looms on the other side of the river. Look for the bright red, navy-bean-like seeds of the *wiliwili* tree here. The trees are covered with wood rose and blue morning glory, and the dense understory is full of weeds with very sticky seeds. Wiliwili Camp has a pavilion, table, pit toilet, and room to pitch a tent. The river is a few steps away on the other side of the trail that runs along the canyon floor past Wiliwili Camp; that trail is the remnant of a road.

If Wiliwili Camp does not suit you, other tent sites may be hard to locate in all the vegetation. You may prefer to continue another ½ mile north and across the Waimea River to Kaluahaulu Camp if you are confident about toting a full pack across the "cliff" section described in Trip 28 and if the river is low. I don't recommend backpacking into Koaie Canyon (see Trip 28). (Local pronunciation of "Koaie" is "KWY-uh.")

Backpackers will find that there are at least three good dayhiking possibilities from Wiliwili Camp; Trips 27, 28, and 29 describe them. The inner-canyon views from Wiliwili Camp are unremarkable, so dayhikers may want to walk upriver ½ mile to enjoy some colorful inner-canyon views by following Trip 28 to the river crossing for the Koaie Canyon trail. Very sturdy dayhikers may want to combine this trip with Trip 27 and go all the way downriver to Waimea town if the water is low and they can arrange the necessary shuttle.

Retrace your steps when you're ready to leave.

Waimea Canyon (Puu Ka Pele Forest Reserve) Camping Regulations....Current policy limits your stay in Waimea Canyon to 4 overnights in any 30-day period. Pack out all your trash. You may not stay more than 2 consecutive nights at any one campsite. Open fires are not allowed, so bring and use a backpacker's stove. The use of the shelters (pavilions) at the four established campsites (Wiliwili and Kaluahaulu in Waimea Canyon itself, Hipalau and Lonomea in Koaie Canyon) is on a first-come, first-served basis. You may not camp downriver south of Waialae Stream.

Trip 27. Waimea River Adventure

or **E to S**	**Distance:** Up to 15 miles as out-and-back side trip; 10 miles as shuttle trip **Elevation gain:** 1320 feet as out-and-back side trip; 160 feet as shuttle trip **Hiking time:** Up to 10 hours as side trip; 6 hours as shuttle trip	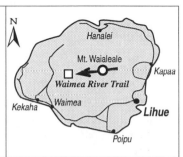

Topos: *Waimea Canyon, Kekaha, Hanapepe*

Trail map: Starts on the map at the end of Trip 24; continues and ends on the maps in this trip.

Highlights: The fun of walking on generally easy footing down much of the the Waimea River, from the lower end of the Kukui Trail to Waimea town; some fine inner-canyon scenery; the wonderful, herbal scent of the dry-country vegetation along the southern part of the trail. Do not take this trip if the river is high or if it's raining (in the latter case, the river can rise abruptly).

Driving instructions: Not applicable unless you do this as a shuttle trip from the Kukui Trail trailhead. In that case, follow the driving instructions of Trip 24. See below for directions on reversing this trip to walk upriver from Waimea town.

Permit required: As for Trip 26, be sure you have secured your self-issue permit at the hunter's check station up near the trailhead if you intend hiking downriver into the Mokihana Ridge Game Management Area.

Description. If you are doing this as a shuttle trip, start by following Trips 24, 25, and 26 from the Kukui Trailhead to Wiliwili Camp.

From Wiliwili Camp, walk the few steps to the road/trail along the river and turn south (right) on it. The road soon peters out, leaving you to traverse below some cliffs for a short distance, then becomes followable again. Where the road forks, follow the right fork into the forest, where it becomes a footpath. You pass along Hawaiian stonework walls and then cross a cliff above the river. After passing a ruined stock gate and a boundary sign, you're in the Mokihana Ridge Game Management Area on a negotiated right-of-way through private property. Be alert for hunting activity.

The footpath descends to meet the road again at an obscure junction. Now you enjoy a pleasant up-and-down stroll on the rocky old road under broken shade—*kukui,* swamp mahogany, silk oak, and monkeypod. The rugged, reddish faces of Waimea Canyon's cliffs can be glimpsed through the trees. You cross a stream where a few taro plants grow, after which the road crosses the river but you don't. You traverse the base of a cliff, cross a region of sand and boulders, cross the channel of Kekaha Ditch (which carries irrigation water from the Waimea River for sugarcane fields around Waimea town), and reach what seems to be a little settlement: fenced-off buildings, plumeria trees, and signs saying HORSES & MULES KEEP OUT OF THIS AREA. You skirt the buildings, pass under a rickety suspension bridge that crosses the river to Mauka Powerhouse on the other side, pass a low dam, and reach your first river ford below Wiliwili Camp (or your last, if you're hiking upriver). From here to Waimea town, you may meet Kekaha Sugar Company vehicles on the road.

From map on page 100

WAIMEA CANYON TRAIL

Mauka Powerhouse

KEKAHA DITCH

WAIMEA CANYON TRAIL/ KEKAHA DITCH 4WD

1 mile

½

¼

0

Waimea River

Poolo- loole

KEKAHA DITCH

WAIMEA CANYON TRAIL/ KEKAHA DITCH 4WD

N

To map on page 107

After fording the river to the east bank, you may notice overflow water rushing down a sluice from Kekaha Ditch, which runs above the road here. At a large overflow stream, Java plum and mango trees close in over the road. Suddenly you come upon a clearing with banana trees, a taro patch, and stone walls. You pass through an old gate (please close it after you) as the forest closes in, and you soon ford the Waimea River again. Here on the west bank, you'll notice a profusion of spindly coffee shrubs as you continue on to the next ford.

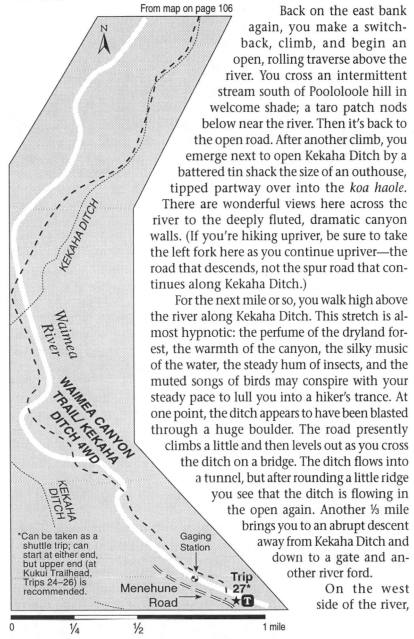

From map on page 106

N

KEKAHA DITCH

Waimea River

WAIMEA CANYON TRAIL/KEKAHA DITCH 4WD

KEKAHA DITCH

*Can be taken as a shuttle trip; can start at either end, but upper end (at Kukui Trailhead, Trips 24–26) is recommended.

Gaging Station

Trip 27*

Menehune Road

0   ¼   ½   1 mile

Back on the east bank again, you make a switchback, climb, and begin an open, rolling traverse above the river. You cross an intermittent stream south of Poololoole hill in welcome shade; a taro patch nods below near the river. Then it's back to the open road. After another climb, you emerge next to open Kekaha Ditch by a battered tin shack the size of an outhouse, tipped partway over into the *koa haole*. There are wonderful views here across the river to the deeply fluted, dramatic canyon walls. (If you're hiking upriver, be sure to take the left fork here as you continue upriver—the road that descends, not the spur road that continues along Kekaha Ditch.)

For the next mile or so, you walk high above the river along Kekaha Ditch. This stretch is almost hypnotic: the perfume of the dryland forest, the warmth of the canyon, the silky music of the water, the steady hum of insects, and the muted songs of birds may conspire with your steady pace to lull you into a hiker's trance. At one point, the ditch appears to have been blasted through a huge boulder. The road presently climbs a little and then levels out as you cross the ditch on a bridge. The ditch flows into a tunnel, but after rounding a little ridge you see that the ditch is flowing in the open again. Another ⅓ mile brings you to an abrupt descent away from Kekaha Ditch and down to a gate and another river ford.

On the west side of the river,

you continue south on the road, crossing some huge black pipes, through which the ditch now runs, on a wooden structure. One fourth mile from the ford, you encounter a channel and pick your way along either side of it. (If you're walking upriver, you may mistake this for the fifth ford, but it's not. Stay on the west side of the river and cross the pipes to reach the real fifth ford.) Back on the road again, you reach the next ford near a striking monolith on the canyon wall. Three more fords remain in this last mile under swamp mahogany, *koa haole*, and an occasional *kukui* tree. You pass through a gate (please close it) and make your next ford at a very scenic spot near which a frail wooden suspension bridge crosses the river (don't attempt the bridge!) The next-to-last ford comes up in ⅓ mile. Between it and the last ford, you pass through a gate (please close it) and reach the hunter's check station. Sign out here and deposit your permit stub. You make your final ford to Waimea town under big swamp mahogany trees and emerge on Menehune Road near some homes. Retrace your steps if you're dayhiking from Wiliwili Camp. If you're doing this as a shuttle, it should be only a few steps from here to your shuttle ride.

Hiking upriver from Waimea town.... This is a delightful trip from either end no matter how far you go. If you'd prefer to hike upriver from Waimea town, follow the driving instructions of Trip 22 from Lihue to Waimea town. Instead of stopping at Ft. Elizabeth, cross the Waimea River and, in a few blocks, turn inland on obscure Menehune Road, which runs between the police station and the shopping center with the Big Save store. Follow this road past the ruins of Menehune Ditch and the picturesque, rickety "swinging bridge," almost to the road's end, 2 miles. You can't park at the very end of the road, where it dips down to the first ford of the river, so find a place where you can park off the pavement without blocking anyone's garage or driveway.

Follow the road across the river—your first of eight or so fords. You must not hike this if the water is high. How high is "high"? If it's foaming along carrying debris with it, stay out. You may find local people at the trailhead who can advise you on the river's height. Or you may carefully wade in and try it. If it's raining in the mountains, the water may rise, and flash floods will be possible, so it would be a good idea to postpone this hike.

Shortly after the first ford, you come to the Mokihana Ridge Game Management Area hunter's check station. Issue yourself a permit and sign in here at this mailbox. Continue, reversing the directions of the main trip description, above.

Trip 28. Koaie Canyon Side Trip

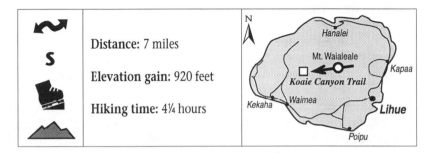

Distance: 7 miles

Elevation gain: 920 feet

Hiking time: 4¼ hours

Topos: *Waimea Canyon*

Trail map: Starts on the map at the end of Trip 24; ends on the map at the end of this trip.

Highlights: Good inner-canyon views from points along the Waimea River in the first ½ mile; a visit to a remote side-canyon of Waimea Canyon.

Driving instructions: Not applicable.

Permit required: As for Trip 26.

Description. Walk the few steps from Wiliwili Camp to the road/trail along the river and turn north (left) on it. You shortly cross the bed of a large intermittent stream and climb steeply to what seems to be a T-junction. Bear east (right) here and follow the road back down toward the river, where it and you bear north again. Where the road appears to cross the river, you don't. Continue north on that same side across a little stream. The route bears northwest as you traverse a narrow, spring-dampened, rocky track on the face of a low cliff above the river. The cliff face dries out in a few yards, but you'll have to look for good handholds and footholds. Soon you reach a point where the track descends across a pile of rocks to a sandy bank, beyond which you pick up the old road and continue north again. The road dips abruptly to a signed river ford ½ mile from Wiliwili Camp; ford the river here.

You pick up the road on the other side, in deep forest at first, and pass the site of pleasant Kaluahaulu Camp (pavilion, table, pit toilet). Continuing north, the road is at times overgrown with young sisal plants and presently appears to be about to cross a large stream. Before it does so, you should look carefully for Division of Forestry and Wildlife plastic ribbons (tags) marking the beginning of a track that leaves the east (right) side of the road going uphill. This is the beginning of the Koaie Canyon Trail, and it is apt to be extremely overgrown with lantana, grasses, cayenne vervain, sisal, and a variety of sticky-seeded weeds. This trail would probably have to be brushed out with a bulldozer every few months in order to be kept open. It's slower going from here on. Be sure to watch your step carefully, as the dense growth sometimes conceals places where the narrow track has sheared away on the downhill side.

The Koaie Canyon Trail stays well above the stream most of the time on these overgrown slopes under broken forest cover. Growth is heavy enough to interfere with canyon views; stop and enjoy those views when you have a chance to. The track generally climbs, with an occasional plunge into deep forests of *kukui* and swamp mahogany, where you will need to follow colored plastic tags. At 2 miles from Wiliwili Camp, you pass through an old Hawaiian stone wall; you'll see these walls periodically from now on. You reach quiet Hipalau Camp (pavilion, table) shortly after passing through that first wall.

After Hipalau Camp, the track gets rougher, and you'll need a spider stick. There may be very impressive spider "eyries" in the immense sisals you must brush through. The track spends more time in the forest now and crosses some minor landslides. At 3 miles (2½ miles into Koaie Canyon), you cross a tributary of Koaie Stream and soon pass through a dense growth of coffee plants. Tranquil Lonomea Camp (pavilion, table) is less than ½ mile farther on, and you'll want to stop there for a rest.

Return the way you came. You should allow some time back at Wiliwili Camp to pick seeds off yourself and your gear.

Why the Waimea River periodically flows red.... The Waimea River periodically flows "red," but legend says it did not always do so. Once upon a time, the river always flowed clear. In those days, a reckless, cruel man named Mano lived high in Koiae Canyon in a cave behind a waterfall. He came down from Koaie Canyon to trifle with and then abandon the young women of the settled areas around the river. One day he heard about the beautiful daughter of the chief of the people who lived around the mouth of the great river. Komaliu was not only lovely but intelligent and industrious, single-mindedly attending to the welfare of her community. Many great chiefs had sought her as a wife, but she had refused all offers of marriage. Mano found a way to present himself to her father as a chief worthy of her. He succeeded in making her father like him very much and believe his false stories of chiefhood.

Komaliu, however, saw through the façade to his cruel heart, was skeptical of his claims, and did not want to marry him. Her father was distressed by her refusal, so she agreed to reconsider if Mano's genealogical chant revealed his ancestry to be of suitable rank. Mano had no such genealogical chant and knew he was about to be unmasked. At the feast at which he was to have revealed his ancestry, Mano instead drugged the food.

When everyone else in the village fell asleep, Mano kidnapped Komaliu and carried her to his cave behind the waterfall. Komaliu woke to find Mano demanding that she marry him as the price for his leading her back home. She refused. Mano threatened to kill her, but still she refused. Mano slew her with his war club; as she died, her blood flowed into the waterfall and stained first Koaie Stream, then the river, red from bank to bank. Mano fled, knowing the river would broadcast his crime.

Everyone knew something terrible had happened when the cloudy reddish water reached the village. The chief traced the redness to its source and found Komaliu's body. Grieving, he ordered his people to hunt Mano down and kill him, named the waterfall Komaliu's Waterfall, and gave the river, the canyon, and the village the name Waimea in Komaliu's memory, for "Waimea" means "reddish water."

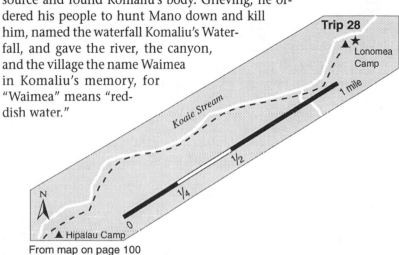

From map on page 100

At Lonomea Camp

Trip 29. Northern Dam Side Trip

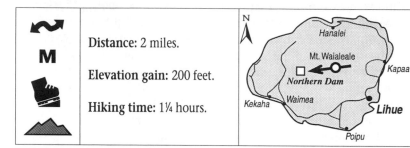

Distance: 2 miles.

Elevation gain: 200 feet.

Hiking time: 1¼ hours.

Topos: *Waimea Canyon*
Trail map: At the end of Trip 24.
Highlights: An interesting scramble on trails and ledges offers you fine inner-canyon views from its higher sections and brings you to the picturesque setting of the upper Kekaha Ditch dam in Waimea Canyon. Caution: This route is probably intended for dam maintenance, not for the average hiker. Some of the cliff-face sections are quite exposed, and you must use some none-too-sturdy planks to cross gaps in the route. Please be very careful.
Driving instructions: Not applicable.
Permit required: As for Trip 26.

Description. Follow Trip 28 to about 50 feet before the road begins to dip sharply toward the river (to the ford for Kaluahaulu Camp and Koaie Canyon). A broken post marks the approximate spot where you pick up a faint footpath on the west (your left). The footpath climbs up and over the cliff here. After descending, you briefly follow the cliff base, where there are bits of concrete among the stones, evidence of construction many years ago.

A stiff climb brings you to the next section of road/trail, and soon you're walking next to Kekaha Ditch, perhaps right on its edge, as here it is an open flume. Where the flume emerges from the rock, you pick up a path along the cliff face and then walk about 300 yards on a fragment of the old road. Test the plank "bridges" along this section to be sure they are sound and will bear your weight before you use them to cross.

Back on the cliff face again, you approach the upper dam and pass under the cable of a defunct aerial tram. Through a couple of large air vents in the cliff face, you can hear water for the ditch gurgling in the tunnel the dam initially diverts it into. You may descend to the boulder beach behind the dam on iron stairsteps set on rods driven into the cliff face (test them before you put your weight on them), or you may prefer to find your own way down the cliff. What a scenic spot for a dam! To the north, there's a shack with a no trespassing sign (and please don't trespass). On the opposite side of the pool behind the dam, water diverted from Koaie Stream flows out of another tunnel and into the pool.

Return the way you came.

Kekaha Ditch.... Kekaha Ditch brings water to the Kekaha Sugar Company's canefields, which spread all around the southwestern coast of Kauai. Kekaha Ditch begins in Waimea and Koaie canyons well above Wiliwili Camp. A dam on Koaie Stream diverts part of that stream's water into a tunnel that leads through a ridge to a pool behind a low dam on the Waimea River—the dam you visit on this side trip. This second dam diverts part of the collected water into a tunnel for Kekaha Ditch on the west wall of Waimea Canyon. The remainder of the water flows over the dam and on down the river. In some places, the ditch is a tunnel in the canyon wall; in others, it's an open flume. Trip 27 follows the river's course, and sometimes the ditch's, from Wiliwili Camp south to Waimea town.

Kekaha Ditch

Poo Kaeha as seen from up-river

Trip 30. Milolii Ridge

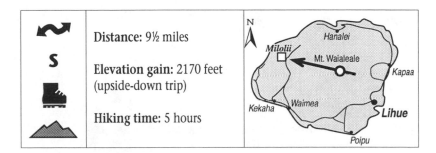

Distance: 9½ miles

Elevation gain: 2170 feet
(upside-down trip)

Hiking time: 5 hours

Topos: *Makaha Point*
Trail map: At the end of this trip.
Highlights: A pleasant hike on a 4WD road/trail, this also offers occasional fine views of the adjacent ridges and out over the ocean, some bird-watching opportunities, and a chance to peek into remote Milolii Valley.

Driving instructions: You'll be heading up the highway bordering Waimea Canyon, so let's start by repeating most of the driving instructions of Trip 24 to the Kukui Trailhead. There are two highways into Waimea Canyon, Highway 550 (Waimea Canyon Road) from Waimea and Highway 55 (Kokee Road) from Kekaha. You should be aware that different Kauai maps mark these highways differently, but on the ground, the highway from Kekaha is marked 55 and the highway out of Waimea is hardly marked at all. Highway 55 is easier to find because its junction with the road you'll take from Lihue, Highway 50, is better marked. Highway 550 is shorter, narrower, and steeper, but it's also more scenic.

To take Highway 550, drive south and west from Lihue on Highway 50 to Waimea town, 24 miles. Look for Waimea Baptist Church on the right (inland) side of the road as you're going through the town. Turn right onto the road that's on the west side of Waimea Baptist Church. That road is Highway 550 (Waimea Canyon Road). Follow it for 7 miles uphill to its junction with Highway 55. From here to its end at Puu o Kila (see Trip 43), the road is considered to be Highway 550.

To take Highway 55, drive south and west from Lihue on Highway 50 to Kekaha town, 27 miles. Turn right onto signed Highway 55 (Kokee Road) and follow it for 8 miles, through a gully and then uphill to its junction with Highway 550.

From the junction of Highways 55 and 550, now on Highway 550, continue driving up the road almost to the 14-mile marker. Look for Makaha Ridge Road going off to the west (left if you're driving uphill).

Turn onto that road, which sports several signs warning you that it's in marginal condition and dead-ends at a U.S. Navy facility. You, however, are going only ⅓ mile to its junction with Milolii Road, marked by a white PVC pipe that says MILOLII, which will be on your right as you descend Makaha Ridge Road. Park off the road and begin your hike here.

Permit required: None.

Description. Begin your trip by walking northeast and slightly uphill on Milolii Road. Follow the road as it curls around Kaunuohua Ridge, bobbing up and down through *koa* and *ohia* forest interspersed with an occasional strawberry guava shrub. At ½ mile, you glimpse the antenna towers of Kokee Tracking Station. Gradually, the road bears west, and strawberry guava comes to dominate the up-slope side of the road, blackberry the down-slope. In season, look for little, spherical, yellow strawberry guavas along here; they are simply delicious when ripe. The banks are steep and crumbly, so be careful when going after fruit.

At 1¼ mile, the road pitches downhill very steeply between deeply cut banks but soon levels out again. You cross the boundary of the Na Pali-Kona Forest Re-

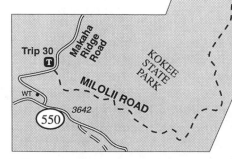

(Antennas; Makaha Ridge view)

(Milolii Beach/ Valley view)

Paaiki Valley

MILOLII ROAD

MILOLII RIDGE

3059
Picnic Area

serve just before the 1¾-mile marker. The guava shrubs retreat, and the koa trees reassert themselves as the handsome native sedge, *uki*, joins the understory. The forest thins in this area, permitting fine views, particularly to the west across adjacent Makaha Ridge to "mysterious" Niihau.

A picnic shelter just north of the road a little past the 2½-mile marker provides a welcome place to rest and some respite from either the rain or the sun, depending on the weather. You'll see not only *koa* and *ohia* here but also *pukiawe*, swamp mahogany, and *uki uki* (not a sedge but a lily). As you leave the picnic shelter, you pass some old gateposts and a low, rusty stake labeled START (it's so obscure you may not even notice it). The topo indicates that beyond here, the light-duty road you've been on becomes a 4WD trail, but you'll hardly notice any difference. It plunges precipitously down through a road cut whose colorful layers on the up-hill side tell a story in reds, oranges, tans, and browns of repeated epi-sodes of volcanism and erosion.

After leveling off, you make a brief climb and notice that the road is marbled with the wonderful soil colors of Kauai. The long-needled pines growing along the road seem strangely out of place here. Your next plunge down through the volcanic layer-cake of Milolii Ridge begins with ocean views and ends in a forest of silk oak, *koa*, and pines. Even a few delicate *iliau* decorate the road bank here, while lantana, *aalii*, cayenne vervain, and grasses form the understory. Keep your ears and eyes open for na-tive birds (particularly the red *apapane* and the greenish *amakihi*) from here on. Be sure to glance out underneath the trees to see glimpses of the ocean and of adjacent, jagged ridges. You started your hike in the forests of Kokee, but now you've walked out to the southern end of the Na Pali Coast, as those ridges attest. Sightseeing helicopters zoom over-head frequently as they head out over Milolii Ridge for their runs up the Na Pali Coast.

Near its end, the road becomes quite overgrown and forks. The right fork is the more interesting. It descends northwest ⅓ mile over a couple of bare areas and ends at a tiny grove of wind-battered pines near the edge of a cliff. The windswept cliff edge provides an opportunity to look down at the beach and a little of the floor of Milolii Valley, which is accessible only by boat. Across the valley, near the back, you may see a waterfall. Milolii Valley was once inhabited; see Trip 35. Please be very careful, as the cliffs are fragile, and it is 1600 nonstop, fatal feet down if you should fall. Back at the road fork, the left fork leads a short distance to a couple of sets of microwave antennas and a view of the Navy facility on Makaha Ridge.

When you're ready, return the way you came.

Trip 31. Halemanu Valley Road to Cliff Trail

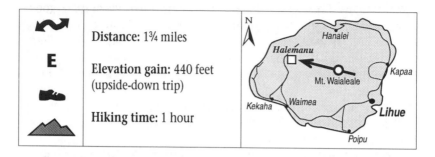

Distance: 1¾ miles

E

Elevation gain: 440 feet
(upside-down trip)

Hiking time: 1 hour

N

Hanalei
Halemanu
Kapaa
Mt. Waialeale
Kekaha Waimea
Lihue
Poipu

Topos: Optional: *Haena*

Trail map: At the end of this trip.

Highlights: This walk takes you a little way into a lovely, forested valley and then to a spectacular overlook of Waimea Canyon. It's the one for you if you don't have much time in Kokee State Park but would enjoy a short hike that would give you a taste of the forest and a view of the canyon completely different from any highway view.

Driving instructions: As described in Trip 30's driving instructions, take Highway 55 or Highway 550 from Waimea or Kekaha town to the highways' junction above Waimea Canyon. Continue up the hill toward Kokee State Park, bypassing Mahaka Ridge Road. A little past the 14-mile marker, but before you reach a signed turnoff left into Kokee State Park's main visitor area, you'll spot signed Halemanu Valley Road, which will be on your right as you're driving up toward Kokee. Halemanu Valley Road is in no condition for passenger cars to drive on, so park off the road and start your hike here.

Permit required: None.

Description. You begin your hike by descending moderately north-northwest between banks of glory-bush (the one with the showy, single, purple flowers) and thickets of blackberry. At ⅓ mile, a bank of ginger flourishes on your left along with *koa* and *ohia*. Halemanu Stream bubbles along the valley floor, crossing your path under the road. Look for the pretty red *apapane* bird here. Near the ½-mile point, you encounter sugi cedars, mountain *naupaka*, lantana, fuchsia, and even some little plum trees.

In a little over ½ mile, you reach the marked junction of Halemanu Valley Road with the road that leads off to the Cliff, Canyon, and Black Pipe trails. Go south (right) on this obvious old road. It ends at a wide spot where there's another marked junction: the Canyon and Black Pipe trails diverge from the Cliff Trail here. Take the Cliff Trail—the right fork—south, climbing a little, and then leveling out, to a sublime view down Waimea Canyon all the way to the ocean (if visibility is good). The canyon wall drops away abruptly at your feet; fortunately, a long railing allows plenty of room for you to enjoy this view safely. Below you, you may notice a nearby, bare knob on the east side of the canyon, possibly with a hiker or two on it; it's part of the Canyon Trail. At the far end of the railing, avoid a precipitous trail-of-use that descends to "views" not worth bothering with. There's no picnic shelter out here, but who can think of food when enjoying a spectacle such as this!

Retrace your steps when you can tear yourself away from this sight.

Mountain roads and mountain trails.... Most of the mountain roads in the Kokee area are not fit for passenger cars, yet you need to use them to get to several mountain trails. The obvious solution is to incorporate those roads into your hikes, as trips in this book do. That's good news, not bad news, because those mountain roads are beautiful in their own right and deserve to be savored at the hiker's pace. You do need to be alert for the occasional vehicle; traffic is lighter on weekdays.

There's an advantage for birdwatchers in hiking a mountain road: birds normally hard to see in the dense forest canopy will occasionally fly across the open space created by the road, giving you a better chance to see them. And mountain roads have some real advantages over the trails as hiking routes when the weather is bad: they are easier to follow

Magnificent view of Waimea Canyon from the end of the Cliff Trail

when visibility is low, and you don't have to push your way through sopping wet vegetation.

However, the hard-packed surfaces of mountain roads can be very slippery when wet. After a good rain and some 4WD traffic, the surface of a Kauai mountain road may be churned to mud resembling dark-red oatmeal. You'll have to pick your way around the mud and the puddles. Boots are better than tennis shoes on a wet mountain road.

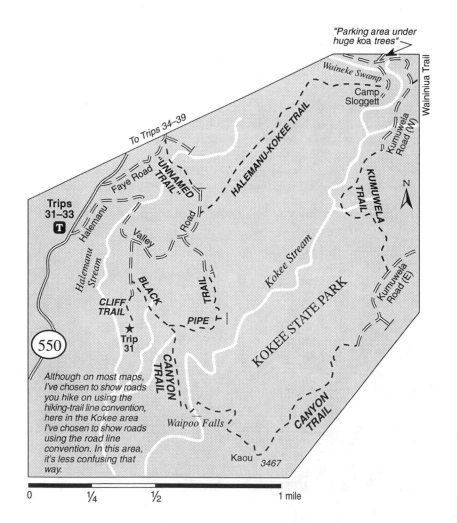

Trip 32. Cliff and Black Pipe Trails

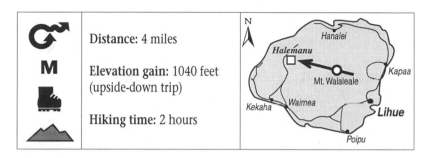

Distance: 4 miles

Elevation gain: 1040 feet
(upside-down trip)

Hiking time: 2 hours

Topos: *Makaha Point, Haena, Waimea Canyon*
Trail map: At the end of Trip 31.
Highlights: After taking in the wonderful views from the end of the Cliff Trail, you continue your scenic forest walk on the Black Pipe Trail, taking in more good canyon views along the way.
Driving instructions: Follow the driving instructions of Trip 31.
Permit required: None.

Description. Follow the hiking directions of Trip 31 to the Cliff Trail overlook. After enjoying that view, retrace your steps to the Cliff-Canyon-Black Pipe junction and turn right (southeast) onto the Canyon and Black Pipe trails, which descend very steeply, switchbacking, and pass through a hedge of ginger. Nawaimaka Stream rushes below on your right as your trail rolls gently up and down, bearing generally southward above the stream's little ravine. Excellent views of Waimea Canyon open up to the west (right).

In ⅓ mile from the Cliff-Canyon-Black Pipe junction, you reach a fork where the Canyon Trail departs southward (right). Continue eastward (left) on the Black Pipe Trail in dryland forest of *koa, ohia, pukiawe,* and silk oak. The yellow flowers of a species of *Bidens* brighten the understory here. Watch out for a spot where, near the head of a ravine, ginger may grow over the trail so heavily you can't see your feet as you push through it! A short, steep climb brings you to more canyon views. Forested Kumuwela Ridge rises in the foreground, Kokee Stream flows below you, and that bare knob on the Canyon Trail stands out prominently to the south of you.

Round the ridge you go now, down into the forest, through blackberry, lantana, and then a little meadow. At an unmarked fork not quite a mile from the Cliff-Canyon-Black Pipe junction, you go north (left and upward) on switchbacks, meeting an old road under *koa* and spicy-smelling eucalyptus by a sign that says BLACK PIPE TRAIL. You bear west (left) on the road, which immediately makes a switchback, descends and then rises around a ravine, and passes under flowery arches and immense swamp mahogany trees. In ¼ mile, you reach a junction with Halemanu Valley Road, where you turn west (left) past some plum trees.

Another ¼ mile brings you back to your junction with the road that leads off to the Cliff-Canyon-Black Pipe junction. Go northwest (right) here and reluctantly retrace your steps up Halemanu Valley Road to your car.

Trip 33. Canyon Trail Adventure

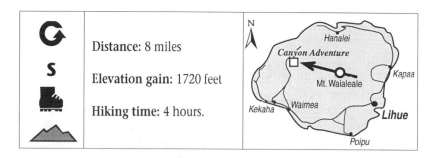

Distance: 8 miles

Elevation gain: 1720 feet

Hiking time: 4 hours.

Topos: *Makaha Point, Haena, Waimea Canyon*
Trail map: At the end of Trip 31.
Highlights: This long loop trip combines Halemanu Valley Road, the Cliff and Canyon trails, Kumuwela Road, and the Kumuwela and Halemanu-Kokee trails to offer you a wide variety of forest experiences and dazzling canyon vistas. There's even an opportunity to splash in a couple of cascades at the head of Waipoo Falls.
Driving instructions: Follow the driving instructions of Trip 31.
Permit required: None.

Description. Follow the hiking description of Trip 32 to the Black Pipe-Canyon junction. At that junction, turn south (right) and descend steep "stairsteps" in the trail. A few gentle switchbacks through the forest and a rise bring you to a breathtaking canyon traverse. From here, you wind down through volcanic boulders to a saddle just below that bare knob that's so prominent from the Cliff and Black Pipe trails. The trail ascends the knob rather steeply, and the views from the top of the knob are unbeatable. On the canyon face of the knob, a few determined *ohia* trees cling to earth and to life. Below you in the canyon, helicopters may seem to outnumber the white-tailed tropicbirds that float on the air currents. To the southeast, you'll notice some ornate formations, including arches, on the end of an adjacent ridge—surely ephemeral features in soil as soft as this is.

The descent from the top of the knob on the eroded trail calls for some caution, as the soil is very loose and the footing consequently poor. But you're soon safely down in a ravine brilliant with lantana, blackberry, and banana passionflower, where, ½ mile from the Black Pipe-Canyon junction, you reach a T-junction. A sign for WAIPOO FALLS here points you left to FALL 1, the upper cascade; right to FALL 2, the lower cascade; and right to the KUMUWELA TRAIL. You don't have to visit either cascade, as the Canyon Trail crosses Kokee Stream just above Fall 2, but most people will want to. Each is just a minute or two off the Canyon Trail. Getting to Fall 1, where there is a pool you can paddle in, requires some bouldering. Getting to Fall 2, where you can sit under the cascades, requires you to descend a little cliff where care in hand and foot placement is necessary. Below Fall 2 is the really long waterfall that is so prominent from many of the highway lookouts after a good rain. With caution, you can look partway down its chasm from Fall 2; you may see feral goats along the slopes there.

Back on the Canyon Trail, you boulder-hop Kokee Stream above Fall 2 and climb a grassy slope up to broken forest cover. A segment of meadow brings you back to the canyon's edge and sensational canyon views. The trail presently attacks a steep, barren slope where the tread is so deeply eroded you may find it easier to walk on its edges. There are a couple of tracks here that lead out to airy canyon overlooks, but the main trail zigzags through dryland forest up to a splendid, open viewpoint, this time across Poomau Canyon to Awini Falls. If it's been raining, you're sure to see other, intermittent falls on the distant wall. It's a great place for lunch.

A few steps away from this viewpoint, your trail bears left (northeast) into the forest, where a very short trail of use takes off to your right for a view of the great canyon. The main trail dips into a grassy valley, then climbs steeply on switchbacks under swamp mahogany, traverses forest and meadow with an occasional canyon view, and meets Kumuwela Road 2 miles from the Black Pipe-Canyon junction. This is the end of the Canyon Trail but not of your adventures on this hike.

Turn north (left) onto Kumuwela Road, whose complications are discussed below. Walk past the junction on the right—it's with the Ditch Trail (see Appendix B) but may be unsigned—to the signed junction with the Kumuwela Trail, ⅓ mile from the end of the Canyon Trail.

Turn northwest (left) onto the Kumuwela Trail for a lovely, woodsy, but often very steep descent from Kumuwela Ridge to an unnamed tributary of Kokee Stream. Be alert for obstacles hidden by the dense growth around the trail and for thorny blackberry vines that reach out over the trail at eye level. You cross an intermittent stream and pass through a dense stand of karakanut trees which are the result of aerial reseeding done in the 1930s. Now you bear north and uphill for a short distance, then descend gently past a slope covered with a native, pink-flowered wild begonia, the showy and beautiful *akaakaawa*, as well as ginger, fern, reeds, fragrant Japanese honeysuckle, and fuchsia. The sight of blooming *akaakaawa* alone is enough to justify a visit to this trail! One more down-and-up segment brings you to the northern end of the Kumuwela

Trail and to the other section of Kumuwela Road. Here, on your left, a piece of private property sports several NO TRESPASSING signs (ah, that aloha spirit!). You can take a hint, so you turn right (east) here, cross Maluapopoki Stream where it flows under the road amidst hydrangea bushes, and stay on forested Kumuwela Road, avoiding all temptation to swerve onto someone's private drive.

Soon you pass the unmarked northern end of the Waininiua Trail and presently cross Elekeninui Stream on a bridge. The road veers west under sugi cedars to a junction you may ignore (it's with a spur road to Mohihi Road) and almost immediately reaches another junction, this time with a spur road south to Camp Sloggett. This double junction, under a pair of huge *koa* trees, serves as a parking area for those who can drive partway down Kumuwela Road before starting their walks.

You turn south (left) down the spur road toward Camp Sloggett, cross the stream again, and walk a few yards down the road. Just before you'd reach a couple of buildings, you turn sharply west (right) onto signed TRAIL 7—the Halemanu-Kokee Trail (or, according to some signs, the Kokee-Halemanu Trail). The trail starts here at its northeastern end with a moderate climb past some air plants into a koa forest, makes a switchback, and then settles down to a tranquil 1¼-mile ramble along a grassy, moderately forested ridge with occasional views out over the surrounding forest canopy. At its southwest end, this pleasant trail abruptly descends a grassy slope to meet Halemanu Valley Road.

Back on Halemanu Valley Road, you turn south (left), ignore an unmarked side road that comes in from the left, and walk ⅓ mile to the Cliff-Canyon-Black Pipe junction. From here, you retrace your steps just over ½ mile on Halemanu Valley Road to your car to end a long but beautiful and very satisfying hike.

Kumuwela Road.... There are at least two discontinuous sections of the Kokee mountain road named Kumuwela Road. One section connects the east end of the Canyon Trail and the south end of the Kumuwela Trail; it eventually comes out at Mohihi Road near the Berry Flat Trail. It's Kumuwela Road (E) on the map. You use a segment of that section to go from the Canyon Trail to the Kumuwela Trail. The other section begins across the highway from Kokee Lodge, has a spur that goes to Mohihi Road, and ends at the north end of the Kumuwela Trail. It's Kumuwela Road (W) on the map. You use that section to get from the north end of the Kumuwela Trail to the Halemanu-Kokee Trail. Although the road and trail situation in the Kokee region looks terribly confusing on a map, it is fairly straightforward when you are out there hiking.

Trip 34. Nualolo Trail

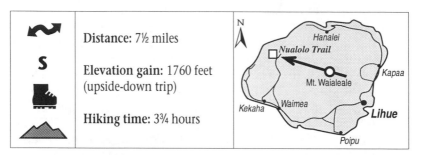

Distance: 7½ miles

Elevation gain: 1760 feet
(upside-down trip)

Hiking time: 3¾ hours

Topos: *Haena, Makaha Point*

Trail map: At the end of this trip.

Highlights: The dizzying views of Nualolo Beach and remote Nualolo Valley are your rewards for this trip.

Driving instructions: As described in Trip 30's driving instructions, take Highway 55 or Highway 550 from Waimea or Kekaha town to the highways' junction above Waimea Canyon. Continue up the hill toward Kokee State Park, bypassing Mahaka Ridge and Halemanu Valley roads. Continue up the highway 1⅓ miles past Halemanu Valley Road to the marked turnoff for Kokee State Park Headquarters, a short paved road that leads off to the west (left) between Kokee Ranger Station and a broad meadow and into the parking lots for Kokee Lodge and Kokee Museum. Park here to begin your hike. The trailhead for the Nualolo Trail is so close to Kokee Lodge and Kokee Museum that you may as well park there.

Permit required: None.

Description. Walk back down the road past Kokee Ranger Station, where you may want to sign in at the check station on the front porch. The station is seldom staffed, but there is a bulletin board where notices about trail closures, etc., may be posted. Turn south (right) at the highway and walk a very few steps to the Nualolo Trail, which leaves from the north (right) side of the highway. You walk uphill past some *ape*, *koa*, and elderberry, and immediately start switchbacking uphill moderately to steeply. Soon you're contouring around a slope under eucalyptus, *koa*, and karakanut interspersed with the occasional mountain *naupaka* and *manono*. You top the ridge near the ¼-mile point and soon begin a steep descent that can be very slippery when wet. As you near ½ mile, the trail levels out amid *ohia*, *koa*, ferns, and a great deal of karakanut—at times it may seem that the trail has been hacked through karakanut thickets. Listen and watch for birds in the *ohia* and *koa* canopy; you're almost certain to hear the rusty-hinge call of the red *iiwi*, perhaps even to see the bird.

The trail's pattern is to drop steeply, level out, perhaps climb a little, and then repeat the process by dropping again. Around the 1-mile point, you dip through a pair of grassy swales separated by an avenue of ferns. Beyond here, you'll find *pukiawe* to please your eye and *mokihana* to tease your nose. Nearing the 2-mile point, there's a marked change to a drier climate, and the appearance of the scrubbier *koa* and *ohia* reflects that fact. Out to sea, there's a view of Niihau and the uninhabited islet of Lehua. You bear north at 2 miles, cross a narrow saddle, and enjoy good views until you begin descending through a series of deep, steep, clay "slots." You cross another narrow saddle, ascend steeply but briefly, and soon traverse a narrow ridge with good views through the vegetation.

At 3 miles, you reach a junction with the Anaki Hunter's Route and bear right in order to continue on the Nualolo Trail. Just after this, there's an appallingly steep slot to descend before you reach the next junction, this one with the Nualolo Cliff Trail, which connects with the Awaawapuhi Trail (see Trip 36). From here, it's a ¾-mile round trip out to windy Lolo Vista Point, and the narrow, crumbly track out to it is almost continuously exposed above steep cliffs. Please do not attempt it if it's wet. The views from Lolo Vista Point *are* breathtaking, but you can get fine views around the junction without all that exposure.

Return the way you came when you've had your fill of these wonderful views.

Rainy-day choices.... The Nualolo Trail contains a number of very steep places and a few very exposed places. Since these are dangerous when the trail is wet, please don't take this trip on a rainy day. You wouldn't get any views for all your trouble, anyway. If you want to walk out toward the coast on a rainy day, the Awaawapuhi Trail (Trip 35) is a better choice and offers the bonus of its marked plants. It is shorter, less precipitous, and less overgrown. However, it won't offer views on a rainy day, either. Another rainy-day possibility is Milolii Ridge (Trip 30) if you're up to it. It loses so much elevation that it's possible to literally walk out from under the rain—but no guarantees. It's very steep in places, but none of them expose you to a fatal fall. However, it would be unwise to go down to the overlook of Milolii Valley if it were raining; that might expose you to a fatal fall.

If you're really anxious to see Nualolo Valley but the weather is unsettled (occasional rain and fog), your best bet is to get an early start

(7 AM, for example) and to take the
Awaawapuhi Trail. The rain and
fog may not start until
midmorning, so you will have
a good chance of getting to
the viewpoints at the end of
the trail at a safe pace before the fog closes in.

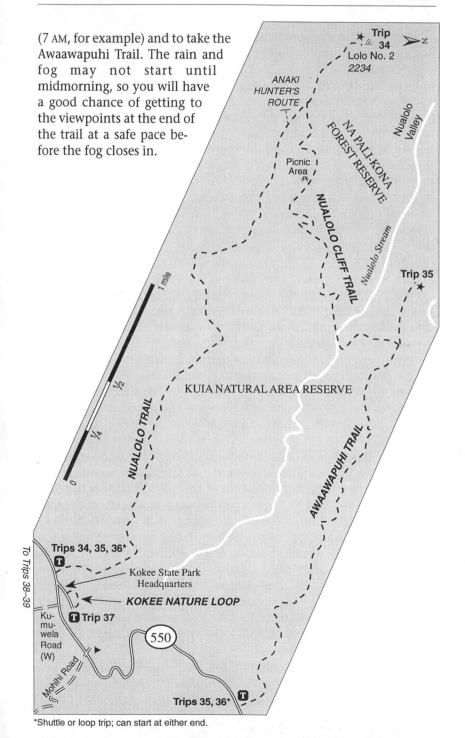

*Shuttle or loop trip; can start at either end.

Trip 35. Awaawapuhi Trail

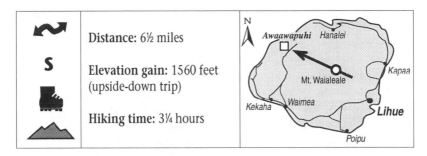

Distance: 6½ miles

Elevation gain: 1560 feet
(upside-down trip)

Hiking time: 3¼ hours

Topos: *Haena, Makaha Point*
Trail map: At the end of Trip 34.

Highlights: Occasional good views along and some spectacular views from the end of this gently-graded trail make it well worth your time. For those who have obtained the pamphlet that is the guide to its marked plants (" 'Awa'awa'puhi Botanical Trail Guide," available at Kokee Museum; see Bibliography), it also offers an exceptional opportunity to see and identify native and introduced plants in a natural setting. Allow plenty of extra time to stop and read about the marked plants; however, if you're trying to beat the rain out to the viewpoints, save the plant-identification for the way back.

I've put this trip right after the Nualolo Trail because near their seaward ends, atop the cliffs of the Na Pali Coast, the Nualolo and Awaawapuhi trails are connected by the Nualolo Cliff Trail to make a wonderful shuttle or loop trip.That's the next trip in this book.

Driving instructions: Follow the driving instructions of Trip 34 but don't turn left at Kokee State Park Headquarters. Instead, continue up the highway to the Awaawapuhi Trail trailhead just before the 17-mile marker. There's a large parking lot on the left side of the highway here, and the trail begins on the left side of the lot as you stand with your back to the highway.

Permit required: None.

Description. From the trailhead, you ascend very briefly and then descend through *ohia*, blackberry, banana passionflower, and orange-flowered ginger. The first half of the Awaawapuhi Trail is unremarkable except for the marked plants. Around the ½-mile point, you encounter switchbacks where the footing may be very poor when the trail is wet. Between 1¼ and 1½ miles, the forest changes from wet to dry, although little pockets of wet forest exist in sheltered nooks beyond here.

It's near 1¾ miles that you have your first good viewpoint: an overlook of the densely forested upper reaches of Awaawapuhi Valley across to adjacent Honopu Ridge to the north. The slope beneath your feet is deeply eroded, so be careful and don't go beyond the edge here. An exposed slope, eroded on its downhill side, lets you look south over forested upper Nualolo Valley near the 2-mile point. Overlooks and views to the sea present themselves occasionally now, and soon you're at the junction with the Nualolo Cliff Trail. Continue ahead (west; right) as indicated by the sign to the end of the Awaawapuhi Trail.

The view of Nualolo Valley from the end of the Awaawapuhi Trail is spectacular! The steep, almost bare, fantastically eroded pali of the lower valleys, exquisite in themselves, are a startling contrast to their forest-filled upper regions. Wild goats are likely to be clinging to the precipitous slopes here. The view of Awaawapuhi Valley, with its stream meandering down its velvety green floor, is even more striking, and you'll also enjoy the sight of the *pali* stretching away toward the sea. Linger to enjoy this area if the weather is good; it's a nice spot for a picnic. Be sure to stay behind the railings; some people who've gone beyond them hoping for better views have fallen to their deaths.

Return the way you came when ready.

Na Pali Coast valleys and Kokee....Many of the deep valleys whose green chasms you see from the trails leading west from Kokee State Park are inaccessible to the hiker. Once upon a time, there were trails from Kokee to Nualolo and also to Milolii. Today, those trails have vanished, and Honopu, Awaawapuhi, Nualolo, and Milolii valleys are accessible only by boat. At Honopu and Awaawapuhi, it's actually only the beach that's accessible, as the valley floors hang high above the ocean.

Yet Awaawapuhi, Nualolo, and Milolii supported small communities of Hawaiians, who found in them all the necessities of life, until the early years of the twentieth century, when they were abandoned. (Honopu apparently wasn't settled; it's too small to support a community.)

Milolii was readily accessible by canoe; today, it's a state park where boaters may camp. Fishing from the beach and farming in the valley made the community self-sufficient. Nualolo consists of two parts, a beach called Nualolo Kai and a valley called Nualolo Aina, separated from Nualolo Kai by the cliff at Alapii Point. As at Milolii, there was fishing at the beach and farming in the valley. Canoes could land at Nualolo Kai then as boaters may today (it's now Nualolo State Park; no camping). Travel between Nualolo Kai and Nualolo Aina required the Hawaiians to climb over the cliff at Alapii Point, and they maintained a ladder there to help them get over it. The ladder disintegrated after Nualolo was abandoned, and travel between Nualolo Kai and Nualolo Aina is almost impossible now. Awaawapuhi, being a hanging valley, is virtually inaccessible from the sea. The Hawaiians traveled between Nualolo Aina and Awaawapuhi over the ridges and along perilous cliff-face trails. Access to Honopu was by a similar, difficult route.

Why did anyone settle in this isolated region in the first place? As the native population grew, it simply expanded into whatever suitable unsettled areas were still available. Life in those isolated but self-sufficient valleys was the same as everywhere else on Kauai. That changed when life in Hawaii changed gradually but decisively throughout the 1800s and early 1900s. Western religion and schooling replaced native culture, the native population was ravaged by foreign diseases, and foreign ventures displaced native communities. Life in the remote Na Pali Coast valleys ceased to be economically and culturally self-sustaining, and their human populations abandoned them in favor of the advantages of the communities on Kauai's north and south shores.

On the Awaawapuhi Trail

Trip 36. Nualolo-Awaawapuhi Adventure

Distance: 9¼ miles as a shuttle; 10¾ miles as a loop

Elevation gain: 2980 feet (upside-down trip)

Hiking time: 5 hours

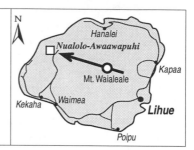

Topos: *Haena, Makaha Point*

Trail map: At the end of Trip 34.

Highlights: You're treated to more of those wonderful views of the Na Pali Coast that you enjoyed on Trips 34 and 35.

Driving instructions: If you're setting up a shuttle, follow the driving instructions of Trip 35 in order to leave your shuttle car at the Awaawapuhi Trail, then drive 1½ miles back down Highway 550 to park at Kokee State Park Headquarters near the start of the Nualolo Trail. If you're doing this as a loop, just follow the driving instructions of Trip 34 to Kokee State Park Headquarters and the Nualolo Trail.

Permit required: None.

Description. Follow Trip 34 to the junction of the Nualolo and Nualolo Cliff trails, from which you may elect to go out to Lolo Vista Point. Upon returning to the junction, you turn east (left) onto the Nualolo Cliff Trail and—surprise!—find yourself briefly in dense forest. Crossing a bare section gives you an opportunity to enjoy some spectacular scenery; then you're back in dense forest. Just as you emerge from the forest, the trail makes a steep switchback and carries you up to a grassy ridge. Helicopters darting in and out of the remote Na Pali Coast valleys at your feet seem determined to plaster themselves onto the cliffs! There's a picnic shelter on this ridge.

A few yards from the picnic shelter, the trail brings you to the edge of a cliff where there are marvelous Na Pali Coast views framed by wind-blasted *ohia* trees. There's a wonderfully scenic, open stretch ahead of you for a short distance, but soon you're back in the forest. You encounter some switchbacks and work your way around a gully with only an occasional glimpse of the *pali* below. After crossing an intermittent stream, you wind through a deep gully lined with ferns, lantana, and blackberry. Ignore the dangerous tracks that lead away from the main trail around here.

As you enter the next valley, the cascading stream in its depths catches your eye. Nearing it, you climb over a little cliff and cross Nualolo Stream just below that picturesque, mossy little waterfall. *Akaakaawa* clings to the face of the cliffs around the fall, its pale-pink bells bowed down by spray. It's a place worth pausing to savor.

You soon meet the Awaawapuhi Trail and turn west (left) to descend to the lookout at the end of the trail, as described in Trip 35.

Now reverse the hike description of Trip 35 to reach your shuttle car at the trailhead of the Awaawapuhi Trail. I think closing the loop on foot is a bad idea, because between the Awaawapuhi and Nualolo trailheads, the highway is barely wide enough for two cars to pass and is steep and winding in some places. Many tourists drive it much faster than it's designed for. The shoulder is generally narrow and unpleasant for walking, especially in the rain, because of the long, dense grasses. Shrubbery or the shoulder's shrinking to zero occasionally forces you to cross or to detour onto the roadway as you walk. If you must close the loop on the highway, it's 1½ miles downhill from the Awaawapuhi Trail to your car at Kokee State Park Headquarters.

A breathtaking view down fluted green cliffs into the depths of Nualolo Valley

Trip 37. Kokee Nature Loop

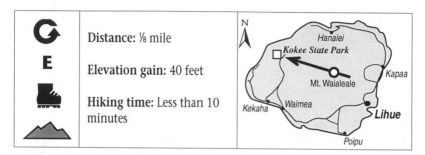

Distance: ⅛ mile

Elevation gain: 40 feet

Hiking time: Less than 10 minutes

Topos: Optional: *Haena*
Trail map: At the end of Trip 34.
Highlights: A convenient opportunity to stretch your legs after the long drive up the hill to Kokee State Park or in between visits to Kokee Lodge and Kokee Museum; a close-up look at two of Kauai's worst pest plants. Kokee Museum is a gem; you'll find a visit to it very rewarding.
Driving instructions: Follow the driving instructions of Trip 34.
Permit required: None.

Description. The beginning of the nature loop may be unsigned. Signed or not, it's behind the handsome stone picnic pavilion about 300 feet beyond Kokee Museum. A short climb brings you to an unmarked junction, where you go left along a grassy track (right will take you smack into impenetrable, prickly blackberry thickets). Along this trail, few plants are currently marked, and, sadly, many plants are being smothered by those aggressive introduced vines, the banana passionflower (sometimes called "banana poka") and the blackberry. Banana passionflower drapes itself over trees. Its large, hanging flowers start out as green tubes, then abruptly flare out into wide-open pink petals from which a cluster of white stamens juts; it has solitary, dangling yellow fruit that slightly resembles a small banana in shape and color. Blackberry has white, five-petalled flowers about an inch wide which resemble single white roses (they're relatives of the rose). It has the usual blackberry-raspberry type of fruit, and it forms dense, thorny thickets. On this slope, banana passionflower and blackberry clothe the other plants so thickly that it's hard to tell what else might be there. Making an easy traverse across the slope, you climb over a pipeline to reach a switchback that brings you safely downhill, just behind Kokee Museum. Stroll along the edge of the meadow behind the museum to return to your starting point.

As you stroll back, you can take in the real show here: the flock of strutting, gabbling, scolding, clucking jungle fowl (moa). The gaudy roosters have patches of bright red, orange, gold, and iridescent blue feathers. Their tailfeathers include two which are extra-long—just meant to be flaunted, and these showoffs know it! The striped and speckled hens in their superior camouflage may be leading a fluffy chick or two in and out through the parked cars. Please be careful of them: there aren't many jungle fowl left any more. They are the descendants of the fowl the Polynesians brought with them when they colonized Hawaii, and this is one of the few places where they still thrive. You can buy feed for them at Kokee Lodge, and the mad scramble that ensues when you toss the feed to them is the best show in town. They patrol the meadow, crowing constantly and loudly, policing each other vigilantly. You'll even see them perched in the trees. A poster at Kokee Lodge says they're monogamous, but you wouldn't know it from the highjinks in the meadow.

Kanaloa-huluhulu, the hairy giant....I've seen at least two versions of the legend that explains why, in this region of forest and bog, there is a large open meadow here at Kokee. One is on a poster in Kokee Lodge; here's a short version of the other one.

Word came to the king of Kauai's constable, Kaua-hoa, that things were not well in the mountains. Travelers were being waylaid and slain in the center of Kokee, where many trails intersected. It was a boggy place, heavily overgrown, where a person unfamiliar with the trails could easily get lost. Travelers had to go slowly there, so they were easy prey for the villain, who was said to be a giant living in a small grove of *lehua* trees in the bog.

Kaua-hoa took food and weapons and went to Kokee. He made no attempt to conceal his presence, as he wanted to lure the giant out into the open. Soon Kaua-hoa came to the bog and the *lehua* grove. A man covered with long, matted hair sprang out from the *lehua* trees and tried to block Kaua-hoa's way, claiming that no one could use the trails without his permission. The hairy man was not much taller than Kaua-hoa, but he was a giant in breadth and musculature. His arms were very long, and his hands reached to his knees. His name was Kanaloa, he said.

"The trails were built for everyone to use, not for an ugly, hairy fool to usurp," Kaua-hoa told Kanaloa. Kaua-hoa taunted Kanaloa, calling him "Kanaloa-huluhulu," the very hairy one. Kanaloa-huluhulu swung his club at Kaua-hoa, but the giant's arms were so long that it took him a long time to swing the club, and Kaua-hoa had little trouble dodging the blows. As the two fought, they trampled many plants and broke down many trees. Birds fled from the noise and destruction.

At last, Kaua-hoa brought the giant down and cut off his head. Leaving Kanaloa-huluhulu's body in the bog, Kaua-hoa took the head to Kilohana and threw it down the cliffs to be lost in the trees and rocks

thousands of feet below. You see, a giant does not die just because someone cuts off his head. A giant does not die until sunset, and he will not
die at all if he can find his head and put it back on his body. So Kanaloa-
huluhulu soon got up and began feeling around for his head. In his
frantic search, he tore up the *lehua* trees and crushed all the remaining
shrubs. He stamped the bog so hard as he ran back and forth seeking his
head that the ground became firm and dry. At sunset, he fell down dead
at last.

The place, which is now the meadow at Kokee State Park Headquarters, is called "Kanaloa-huluhulu" because some people believe that
Kanaloa-huluhulu's ghost haunts it, still searching for his head.

Trip 38. Halemanu-Kokee Walk

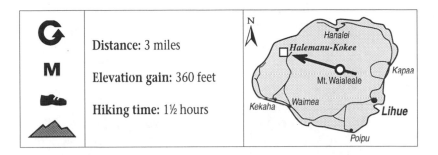

Distance: 3 miles

Elevation gain: 360 feet

Hiking time: 1½ hours

Topos: *Haena*

Trail map: At the end of this trip.

Highlights: This leisurely hike samples a lovely combination of forest roads and trails in Kokee State Park. Like to sleep in? If so, this is the trip for you! The Unnamed Trail on the first part of this loop is very wet in the morning. You'll be soaked to the skin almost immediately unless you let the sunshine dry it. An 11 A.M. start sounds about right.

Driving instructions: Follow the driving instructions of Trip 34. The hike as described starts here. (Alternatively, if your car can handle it, you may prefer to drive the short distance down Kumuwela Road to the marked parking area under the huge koa trees at the junction of Kumuwela Road and the spur road to Camp Sloggett. You'll start your hike there.)

Permit required: None.

Description. Walk back to the highway, turn right, and walk carefully down it (southwest) ⅓ mile to the marked north end of Faye (FY-uh) Road. Take Faye Road south down into a beautiful little valley; you'll wish that one of the vacation homes along here were yours. The fragrance of the many blooming plants along Faye Road is delightful. In ⅓ mile on Faye Road, you reach a T-junction from which a spur road goes southeast to a couple of homes and Faye Road swings southwest to return to the highway. It looks as if you're at a dead end. Surprise: the unmarked Unnamed Trail lies straight ahead of you through deep grass and between a couple of clumps of ginger. Head for that first clump of ginger; behind it you'll find what you can't see from Faye Road: the trail sign.

The Unnamed Trail bears left around the ginger. Luscious birdsong complements the scents and sights of ginger, nasturtium, Japanese honeysuckle, banana passionflower, and fuchsia along here. You pass under large evergreens and through tall grasses, and cross a little stream while pushing your way through ginger plants growing right over the trail! Now you make a couple of switchbacks up a slope and pursue a narrow track eastward through tall hedges of Japanese honeysuckle, blackberry, and glory-bush. The vegetation opens up a little as you approach an unnamed spur road ⅓ mile from the start of the Unnamed Trail (1 mile from your start at Kokee). To your left, a chain blocks off the road and a sign announces U.S. PROPERTY NO TRESPASSING. You bear right and in just a few yards meet Halemanu Valley Road.

A simple gate you can climb over or move aside (please replace) separates the unnamed spur road from Halemanu Valley Road. Once over or through the gate, you bear south (right) on Halemanu Valley Road past some huge evergreens. It's barely ⅛ mile more to the Halemanu-Kokee Trail from here. Look to your left for that trail's sign. Follow the trail uphill through deep, soft grass into the moderate forest cover described in Trip 33. Reverse the hike description of Trip 33 from here to the Kumuwela Road-Camp Sloggett spur road junction at the parking area under the huge *koa* trees. (If you left your car here, your version of this hike starts and ends here.)

Turn west (left) onto pretty Kumuwela Road and walk west, then northwest, toward the highway, which is ⅓ mile from here. You soon pass a big angel's-trumpet tree on your left, which intermittently bursts into bloom with huge white, trumpet-shaped flowers. As you continue, be alert for the sight of tall reeds and the murmur of running water on your left. These are your only clues that you're passing little Waineke Swamp. You'll notice elderberry trees along here in addition to the many other introduced plants. Ignore the side road to the long building on your left just before the highway.

Back at the highway, you may decide to return to your car on the road, or you may cross the highway and pick up a trail-of-use through the grass and down the bluff to Kanaloa-huluhulu Meadow, which you'll cross to return to your car. If you got a suitably late start, it must be just about time for a picnic lunch at the pavilion next to the museum or for lunch at the Lodge. You've earned it!

Angel's-trumpet tree.... This introduced tree, which looks so exotic when in bloom, is a datura and a relative of the low, grayish jimsonweed that's a common roadside plant in dry places along the mainland Pacific Coast. The blossoms of the angel's-trumpet tree hang downward, while the smaller trumpet flowers of the jimsonweed open upward. Both plants are poisonous in spite of their lovely flowers.

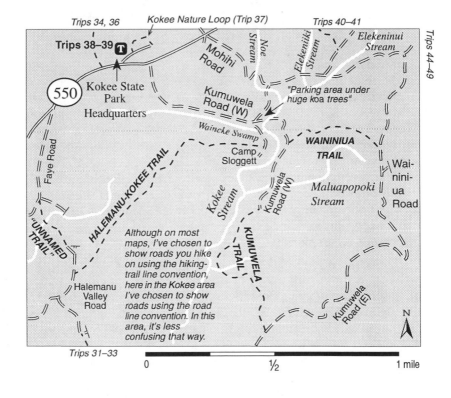

Trips 34, 36   Kokee Nature Loop (Trip 37)   Trips 40–41

Trips 38–39

Kokee State Park Headquarters
550

Mohihi Road
Noe Stream
Elekeniiki Stream
Elekeninui Stream

Kumuwela Road (W)

"Parking area under huge koa trees"

Waincke Swamp

Faye Road

HALEMANU-KOKEE TRAIL

Camp Sloggett

WAININIUA TRAIL

Waini- ua Road

Kokee Stream

Kumuwela Road (W)

Maluapopoki Stream

"UNNAMED TRAIL"

KUMUWELA TRAIL

Halemanu Valley Road

Although on most maps, I've chosen to show roads you hike on using the hiking-trail line convention, here in the Kokee area I've chosen to show roads using the road line convention. In this area, it's less confusing that way.

Kumuwela Road (E)

N

Trips 31–33

0   ½   1 mile

Trips 44–49

Trip 39. Kumuwela-Waininiua Semiloop

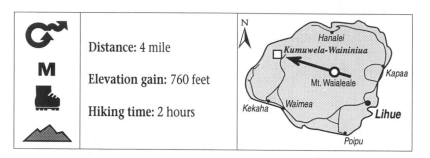

Distance: 4 mile

Elevation gain: 760 feet

Hiking time: 2 hours

Topos: *Haena*
Trail map: At the end of Trip 38.
Highlights: Birdwatching along the eastern section of Kumuwela Road—plan your timing for this hike so that you can take an hour or so to relax at one of the grassy spots along the road, have lunch, and watch birds flying across Kumuwela Road.
Driving instructions: Follow the driving instructions of Trip 37. The hike description below assumes you'll start from Kanaloa-huluhulu Meadow (Kokee Lodge and Museum). (You may also start from the parking area under the huge koa trees on Kumuwela Road if your car can get to it. That would cut ⅔ mile off this trip.)
Permit required: None.

Description. Walk back to the highway, carefully cross it, and walk a few steps north to the start of Kumuwela Road (or cross Kanaloa-huluhulu Meadow and follow the trail-of-use up the bluff, then cross the highway to Kumuwela Road). Stroll down scenic Kumuwela Road past a spur road to a long building and past little Waineke Swamp to the parking area under the huge *koa* trees. There's a riot of colorful introduced flowers to admire along this section of Kumuwela Road. As you continue on Kumuwela Road past the parking area under the huge *koa* trees, you'll be looking for the start of the Waininiua Trail. As of this writing, it's unmarked, so here's how to find it. The Waininiua Trail will be on your left (east) ⅔ mile down Kumuwela Road from the highway, *after* you cross Elekeninui Stream and *before* the road drops to cross Maluapopoki Stream. It looks like an old road going off to the southeast. A fragment of an illegible sign is nailed to an *ohia* tree about 50 feet up the trail. (It's easy to mistake someone's private driveway for this trail.)

The Waininiua Trail climbs slightly, almost immediately doubles back on itself, and then begins curving gently around the ravine of

Maluapopoki Stream under fairly heavy *koa* and *ohia* forest cover. The grade steepens a little, then flattens as you reach thickets of strawberry guava. Soon you notice swamp mahogany in the forest cover and air plants in the understory. You may encounter strawberry plants—yes, *fragaria*—in the understory a little beyond here. In 1¼ miles from your start, the trail winds downhill to meet the eastern section of Kumuwela Road. Glory be, there's a sign for the Waininiua Trail on this end!

Turn southeast (right) here and follow Kumuwela Road through silk oak, *ohia*, and ferny-leafed *koa* trees. Stay on Kumuwela Road at the junction with Waininiua Road. Patches of meadow occasionally break the forest at the edge of Kumuwela Road, and the road's openness contrasts nicely with the closed-in feeling you may have gotten from the Waininiua Trail. When you find a patch of short grass along the road, make yourself comfortable and look for birds, especially *apapane* and *elepaio*, flitting through the lofty *ohia* and *koa* trees.

At 2 miles from the start, you reach a junction with the Kumuwela Trail. Turn northwest (right) onto it. From here, follow Trip 37 down the Kumuwela Trail and up Kumuwela Road to the start of the Waininiua Trail. Retrace your steps up Kumuwela Road from the start of the Waininiua Trail to your car at Kanaloa-huluhulu Meadow to finish your hike (or at the parking area on Kumuwela Road, if that's where you left it).

Watching the *elepaio*....The charming, 5½-inch *elepaio* is readily identified by the jaunty angle at which it cocks its tail: about 45° above its fluffy rump. The Kauai *elepaio* is greenish; you may also see the *elepaio* of the other islands, such as the chestnut *elepaio* of Hawaii. The curious *elepaio* often flies down to have a closer look at people. If the *elepaio* doesn't volunteer to come close to you, try "pishing" at it: make a soft, toneless "psh-psh-psh" sound. You're likely to attract it to a twig near you and to find yourself being examined closely, first by one bright black eye, then the other. Say, who's doing the watching around here?!

Trip 40. Puu Kaohelo-"Mystery Trail" Loop

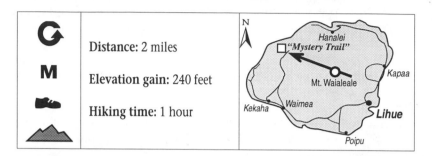

Distance: 2 miles

Elevation gain: 240 feet

Hiking time: 1 hour

Topos: *Haena*
Trail map: At the end of this trip.
Highlights: Besides being pretty and full of flowers, this forest walk delivers a little surprise: strawberry plants! There's no guarantee they'll have any edible fruit for you, but it's nevertheless pleasant to come across them.
Driving instructions: Follow the driving instructions of Trip 34 but stay on the highway at the turnoff for Kokee State Park Headquarters. Continue a short distance up the highway and turn left into the parking lot for Kokee Campground. Park and start your hike here.
Permit required: None.
Description. Walk back to the highway and carefully cross it to the start of Mohihi Road, which is slightly off to your left. (Mohihi Road is also known as the Camp 10 Road and the Mohihi-Camp 10 Road.) Ignore the private driveway and the water-tank road. Walk down beautiful Mohihi Road—it's my favorite of all the Kokee forest roads—under handsome shade trees and past banks lavishly blooming with introduced plants, especially the cascading daisy fleabane and that showy shade-lover, impatiens. You notice that the ditch on the north side of the road is ablaze with impatiens—a spectacle you couldn't see from a car. You cross Noe Stream on a bridge, pass a fenced-off meadow with handsome private vacation homes, cross Elekeniiki Stream, and reach a signed junction with the road that leads to the Puu Kaohelo Trail, ⅔ mile from the highway.
Turn north (left) onto the road to Puu Kaohelo and follow it past ginger, Japanese honeysuckle, and ferny-leafed *koa*. Just beyond a gated driveway on your left, a sign directs you to turn left (northwest) onto the Puu Kaohelo Trail. Follow the trail uphill through honeysuckle and blackberry, *koa*, *uluhe*, strawberry guava, and *ohia*. There may be a lot of

downed wood along this stretch, so watch your step. Look for strawberry plants along this trail, under some strawberry guavas. A false trail on your left leads to a view of the splendidly-overgrown ravine of Elekeniiki Stream. The Puu Kaohelo trail arrives at an unmarked fork at ½ mile along the trail. The right (east) fork is the continuation of the Puu Kaohelo Trail. But you take the left fork north; this is what I've dubbed the "Mystery Trail" (see below). It's unmaintained, so please be cautious.

A few yards down the Mystery Trail, there's an *ohia* tree that appears to have stilts instead of ordinary roots, and you can walk right through them. Soon you bear west above the flowery ravine of Elekeniiki Stream and walk through strawberry, daisy fleabane, blackberry, honeysuckle, and a vervain with triple spikes of pale blue flowers. You round the head of the ravine, climb a little as you bear west, and pass some mountain *naupaka*. The trail carries you southeast through a lush garden of fern, strawberry, and daisy fleabane, and then southwest through some *uki uki*. Nearing 1 mile from the start of the Puu Kaohelo Trail, you plunge briefly back into the forest and emerge at a construction site—or maybe, by the time you hike this trail, the construction will have been completed—near an old water tank. Look for the orange-flowered spikes of montbretia here. Walk through this area, past the tank, to pick up a road that you follow for about 100 yards to the highway Turn left (south) here on the highway's shoulder and carefully walk down the shoulder a short distance to close the loop at the start of Mohihi Road, almost opposite the lot where you parked your car.

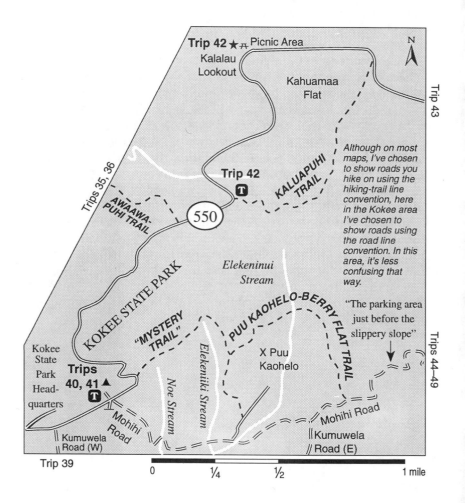

Trip 42 ★ 🪑 Picnic Area

Kalalau
Lookout

Kahuamaa
Flat

N

Trip 43

Trips 35, 36

Trip 42

550

AWAAWA-
PUHI TRAIL

KALUAPUHI
TRAIL

*Although on most
maps, I've chosen
to show roads you
hike on using the
hiking-trail line
convention, here
in the Kokee area
I've chosen to
show roads using
the road line
convention. In this
area, it's less
confusing that
way.*

*Elekeninui
Stream*

KOKEE STATE PARK

"MYSTERY
TRAIL"

PUU KAOHELO-BERRY FLAT TRAIL

"The parking area
just before the
slippery slope"

Trips 44–49

X Puu
Kaohelo

Kokee
State
Park
Head-
quarters

Trips
40, 41 ▲

Elekeniiki Stream

Noe Stream

Mohihi
Road

Mohihi Road

Kumuwela
Road (W)

Kumuwela
Road (E)

Trip 39

0   ¼   ½   1 mile

Trip 41. Puu Kaohelo-Berry Flat Semiloop

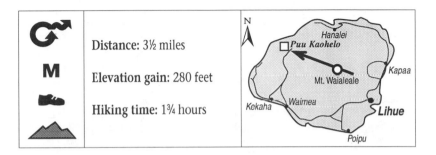

Distance: 3½ miles

Elevation gain: 280 feet

Hiking time: 1¾ hours

Topos: *Haena*
Trail map: At the end of Trip 42.
Highlights: Both of these are forest trails, but there's an interesting contrast between the Puu Kaohelo Trail and the Berry Flat Trail, as you'll see.
Driving instructions: Follow the driving instructions of Trip 40.
Permit required: None.

Description. Follow Trip 40 to the unmarked fork that is the junction with the Mystery Trail. Take the right fork east, descending a little as you pass through *koa* and ginger. You cross a boggy spot and resume climbing through some jungle-movie scenery (the normal forest cover here is augmented by rope-like vines that remind you of Tarzan shows). Presently you cross a couple of streamlets on logs.

Evergreens—sugi cedar and redwood—suddenly intrude on the native forest ¾ mile from the start of the Puu Kaohelo Trail. A few more yards bring you to a junction where a trail sign points you back down the Puu Kaohelo Trail, ahead to a dead end, and right to the Berry Flat Trail. Don't bother with the dead end, unless you find a quarter mile of dense strawberry guava irresistible. Bear right onto the Berry Flat Trail, make a switchback, descend to cross a stream on logs, and then stroll along under sugi cedar, redwood, swamp mahogany, and a few *ohia* trees. You feel as if you were on a path in a mainland mountain forest; it's a marked contrast with the jungle-movie feeling of the Puu Kaohelo Trail. Near the trail's end, there are some mountain *naupaka*, *uki uki*, and a few strawberry and blackberry plants (the only berries along the Berry Flat Trail). The trail dips and rises, then ends at Mohihi Road.

Turn west (right) onto Mohihi Road and follow it past its junction with the eastern section of Kumuwela Road. You meet the spur road to the Puu Kaohelo Trail in just over ½ mile. From here, retrace your steps to your car.

Trip 42. Kaluapuhi Trail to Kalalau Lookout

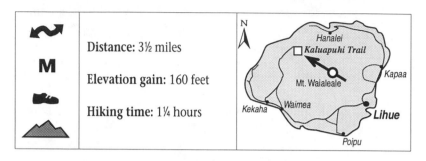

Distance: 3½ miles

Elevation gain: 160 feet

Hiking time: 1¼ hours

Topos: *Haena*
Trail map: At the end of Trip 40.
Highlights: The pleasant upland forest of the Kaluapuhi Trail is an interesting contrast to the rugged Na Pali Coast valley, Kalalau Valley, which you see from the Kalalau Lookout.

Driving instructions: Follow the driving instructions of Trip 35 past the Awaawapuhi Trail and the 17-mile marker on the highway. Look for the sign for the Kaluapuhi Trail on the east side of the highway not far beyond the 17-mile marker. There's just room for one car to park off the road here.

Permit required: None.

Description. You leave the trailhead going north and uphill, leveling off almost immediately amid tangles of *uluhe*. You soon bear east through open forest dominated by *ohia* and mountain *naupaka*. To the north (left) lies the ravine where Awaawapuhi Valley's stream originates. As the trail winds around the ravine, you brush past *uluhe* and ginger— unfortunately not the fragrant native ginger, *awapuhi*, from which Awaawapuhi takes its name. Strawberry guava thickets appear and the forest cover becomes more dense as you dip into a little side ravine. Banana passionflower and blackberry are busy smothering other plants, and daisy fleabane with its small white flowers forms showy mounds along the trail or cascades down the sides of the ravine.

You meet the "tail of the trail" at a T-junction in a little more than ½ mile. The "tail," which is the south (right) fork here, is not worth bothering with. You turn north (left) on the main trail. You wind through Metheley plum, *ohia*, *uluhe*, and the occasional *olapa* tree as you bear northward. As you near the north end of this trail, you notice strawberry plants trailing on the ground in a few places, pass a couple of spindly evergreen trees, and emerge where the trail meets the road between the Kalalau and Puu o Kila lookouts. Note this unmarked junction for your return.

Turn west (left) onto the road's shoulder and carefully walk along it for ¾ mile to the Kalalau Lookout (water, restrooms). It's on the ocean side of the road, and a path to it leaves the road just past the signed bus parking area. The views down into dramatic Kalalau Valley from here are wonderful when the weather permits, and it's a very pleasant spot to rest and picnic. Ideally, the weather should be clear and sunny for you to get the best views. If it's just cloudy (rather than raining), the clouds may clear once in a while to give you a glimpse of Kalalau Valley. Kalalau Valley was once accessible by trail from Kokee, but that trail has long since disappeared. Please do not try to hike down from here. If you're anxious to see the valley close up, take the Kalalau Trail from Kee Beach as described in Trip 56 and visit the valley from Kalalau Beach as described in Trip 57.

When you're ready, return the way you came.

Koolau the leper.....One of the most famous stories about Kalalau Valley is that of Koolau, a victim of Hansen's Disease, popularly called leprosy. Some time in the mid-1800s, Hansen's Disease appeared in Hawaii. Hansen's Disease is contagious but only through long and continued exposure. Unfortunately, native Hawaiian family life provided an excellent opportunity to spread the disease: the common poi bowl, the common sleeping mats.

Anyone suspected of having Hansen's Disease was seized, separated forever from the uninfected, shipped in cages to an isolated peninsula on Molokai, thrown overboard to drown or swim to shore, and abandoned to the horrors of the disease and the depredations of fellow victims until death. Father Damien brought love and care to the unfortunate victims in the 1870s, but the prospect of exile for life still made people resist transport to Molokai.

Koolau, his son (who also had the disease), and his wife, Piilani (who was not infected), were among a band of lepers and their families who fled to Kalalau Valley in 1892 in order to escape banishment to Molokai. In 1893, the authorities caught everyone else, but Koolau and his family shot it out with them and escaped. They hid in Kalalau Valley until, two years later, Koolau and his son died. Piilani returned to civilization alone with her tragic story.

About the Alakai Swamp. . . .

Five of the next seven trips—Trips 43–46 and 49—skirt or enter Kauai's Alakai Swamp, one of the few areas in Hawaii where you can still find plenty of native Hawaiian plants and animals. Most of these hikes are off Mohihi Road, which you first encountered on Trips 40 and 41 and which leads out of Kokee State Park to camping areas and trailheads on the edge of the Alakai Swamp.

The Alakai Swamp is ecologically extremely vulnerable, and we who enter it have special responsibilities. The swamp is home—their last refuge—to many rare, native Hawaiian plants and animals. Please be exceptionally careful. Make sure you carry no alien plant or animal species into the swamp; clean your boots and clothing well before hiking here. Take nothing from the swamp except photos and the mud that sticks to you. Stay on the trail—on the boardwalk if one is available. *The survival of the swamp and its rare species depends on you!*

The Division of Land and Natural Resources has built raised, wooden boardwalks into the Alakai Swamp along some of the worst parts of the two major hiking routes, the Pihea and the Alakai Swamp trails. For much of their length, those trails were formerly hard to follow, difficult, and dangerous. Now, the walkways provide safe, easy-to-follow routes for hikers and protect rare species from trampling by hiking boots. The Pihea Trail boardwalk is largely completed, but the Alakai Swamp Trail boardwalk awaits completion by volunteers. Check on the boardwalks' status with the Division of Land and Natural Resources, Department of Forestry and Wildlife, Kauai District (see "Getting Permits" in this book).

Off the major trails and boardwalks, most of the Alakai Swamp is very rugged: steep ridges separated by narrow valleys, plateaus covered by deep bogs, all raked by nearly constant, cold rain, fog, and howling wind in an eternal twilight. Deep in the swamp, route-finding is difficult because it's impossible to maintain a trail and because visibility is so poor it's impossible to navigate with map and compass or even by following colored plastic tags. There are no vistas, you can't stride along, and you're in danger of getting lost or falling into a bog you can't get out of. The trips in this book that take you into the Alakai Swamp don't go into its worst bogs. I wouldn't send *you* out into *them*.

If you are still determined to explore the Alakai Swamp off the better trails and the boardwalks, please go with a highly experienced guide whose Alakai Swamp credentials you check out and find impeccable.

Trip 43. Pihea Trail

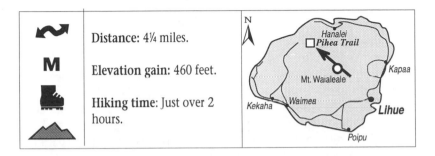

Distance: 4¼ miles.

Elevation gain: 460 feet.

Hiking time: Just over 2 hours.

Topos: *Haena*

Trail map: At the end of this trip.

Highlights: Here, on the edge of the Alakai Swamp, you are alternately treated to the *possibility* of heart-stopping views into Kalalau Valley and vistas over the rugged, forested swamp itself. The weather here is "swamp weather," however, so you may have to content yourself with misty views, if any. This is the only trail into the Alakai Swamp that starts from a major road, and the scar left by an attempt to build a road into it provides you with an easier foray into the swamp than any other trip in this book. Shortly after the road cut ends, a raised, wooden walkway begins, carrying you over the swampiest parts of this trail.

Driving instructions: Continue up Highway 550 past Kokee State Park Headquarters and the turnoff to the Kalalau Lookout to the end of the pothole-filled road at the Puu o Kila Lookout. Park here and walk up to the lookout itself for spectacular Na Pali Coast views, weather permitting. The trail starts from the parking lot.

Permit required: None.

Description. Leave the parking lot on the clay surface of the old road cut (see below). You descend moderately and then level out in the midst of *ohia* trees and shrubs. In places the swamp has almost completely reclaimed the road cut, reducing it to a narrow footpath; in others, the cut still remains fairly wide. Watch out for stretches that are deeply eroded and offer only poor footing. Some of the *ohia* trees along the way are so stunted they are shrub-sized, one of *ohia*'s typical adaptations to this very wet environment.

As you go, look for the many places where you can stop to see Kalalau Valley on the north or the Alakai Swamp on the south. Even if it's not clear, it's worth your while to wait a bit and see if the clouds part or the rain stops. The view of Kalalau Valley from Puu o Kila and from this trail is even more breathtaking than that from the Kalalau Lookout, and no place along the highway gives you a chance like this to look out over the swamp.

At the end of the old road cut, there's a trail junction: left to the point marked "Pihea 4284" on the topo ("Pihea Vista"); right to continue on the Pihea Trail.

The scramble to Pihea Vista isn't worth the trouble unless the weather is dry and clear. The distance and elevation figures for this hike don't include going to Pihea Vista. If you wish to go to Pihea Vista, take the left fork at the junction. Soon you confront a steep, muddy scramble of almost 80 feet upward, mostly hand-over-hand, using roots, tree limbs, and anything else you can hang onto. Test all hand- and footholds, as this route takes a serious beating from hikers. At Pihea Vista, you'll find a brass benchmark sticking out of a tiny plateau that's been trampled bare. The view from here must be astonishing if and when it's ever clear! Don't hesitate to use the "fanny belay" (sit down and scoot on your rear end) in order to get safely back down.

To continue on the Pihea Trail from the junction, turn right if you *didn't* go to Pihea Vista or left if you've just come from Pihea Vista—east-southeast in either case. You shortly pick up the raised, wooden walkway, which is complete except for a few gaps from here to the junction with the Alakai Swamp Trail. Native plants you'll see along this stretch include the native sedge, *uki*; the familiar, red-flowered *ohia*; a variety of ferns; the long-leafed, orange-berried *painiu*, which usually grows on tree limbs and trunks; the handsome *lapalapa* and *olapa* trees with their fluttering leaves; *maile* vines, and *mokihana* shrubs with their anise-scented berries. You meet the Alakai Swamp Trail a mile from the Pihea Vista junction. Retrace your steps from here.

Optionally, you can continue on the Pihea Trail to Kawaikoi Camp on Mohihi Road and then retrace your steps. The remainder of the Pihea Trail, from this junction to Kawaikoi Camp, is described in reverse as the first leg of Trip 44, from Kawaikoi Camp to the Pihea-Alakai Swamp trails' junction. This will add 3⅓ miles of very scenic trail, 480 feet of elevation gain, and 1⅔ hours not shown in the icon box for *this* trip.

The road cut.... The road cut along the first part of the Pihea Trail is the result of an attempt to build a road between Kokee and Haena, part of which would have crossed the Alakai Swamp — and would have been an ecological disaster. But the County Board of Supervisors favored it, money was allocated, and construction began in the 1950s. They succeeded in pushing the road a short way into the Alakai Swamp, as you've seen. Then the swamp, with its incredible muck and rainfall, had the final say. Construction bogged down in the mud, the money was gone, and everyone had to agree that there was no possible way to push the road any farther. A wonderful anecdote tells of a bulldozer temporarily abandoned at the end of the cut when work stopped. When its owners returned to retrieve it, it was gone: the swamp had swallowed it whole.

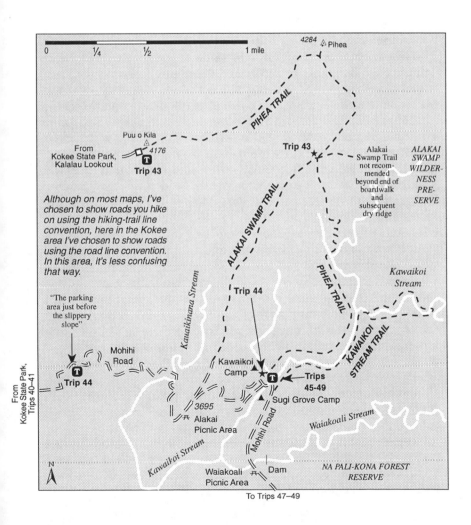

To Trips 47–49

Trip 44. Kawaikoi-Sugi Grove Backpack

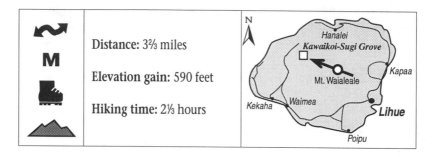

Distance: 3⅔ miles

Elevation gain: 590 feet

Hiking time: 2⅓ hours

Topos: *Haena*
Trail map: At the end of Trip 43.
Highlights: Backpacking down Mohihi Road and staying at Kawaikoi Camp or Sugi Grove Camp offers you relatively easy access to some spectacular mountain trails. Kawaikoi Camp is a beautiful little meadow dotted with plum trees and boasting a pair of pavilions and a pit toilet. The southern end of the Pihea Trail is at Kawaikoi Camp. Sugi Grove Camp is ⅒ mile farther down the road across Kawaikoi Stream, with similar amenities, this time in a grove of sugi cedars. The Kawaikoi Stream Trail starts just across the road from Sugi Grove Camp. (At one time there was a third campground at the far end of Mohihi Road, the notorious Camp 10, but it's only a picnic area now. It's said to have been "the coldest and wettest habitation on Kauai.")

Driving instructions: Follow the driving instructions of Trip 42 to Mohihi Road and, if the road is dry and firm, turn east (right) onto Mohihi Road. With care and a dry road, you may be able to drive 1½ miles down Mohihi Road to a point where a sign warns you that from here on, it's 4WD ONLY and it's SLIPPERY WHEN WET. You can park just before that sign under the trees in an informal parking area on the north side of the road. The description below assumes that you will start your trip from that point, *"the parking area just before the slippery slope."* When wet, the slope beyond here is so slippery that cars without four-wheel drive have to be towed out.

To avoid driving on Mohihi Road at all, park at Kokee Lodge/Museum or Kokee Campground and start your trip from there. From there, it's 6⅔ miles round trip, total elevation gain of 990 feet.

Permit required: You must apply to the Division of Forestry and Wildlife, Kauai District, for a permit to camp at either Kawaikoi Camp or Sugi Grove Camp. See "Getting permits and permission" in this book. See also the regulations, below.

Description. From the parking area just before the slippery slope, you walk downhill and soon cross a tributary of Kauaikinana Stream on a bridge beneath which the stream drops in showy cascades. You round a ridge in a pretty valley and presently cross the main channel of Kauaikinana Stream. Now you begin climbing toward Alakai Picnic Area; the mud and ruts at a switchback just after another tributary should convince you of your wisdom in not trying to drive down here. You round a ridge and, as a delightful scene opens up before you, arrive at the picnic area and the boundary of the Na Pali-Kona Forest Reserve. There's a view over Poomau Canyon from the picnic area. The beginning of the Alakai Swamp Trail lies across Mohihi Road from the picnic area and up a spur road.

Back on the road, it's only ¾ mile from here to Kawaikoi Camp, and you soon begin a gentle descent to it. When you see stands of sugi cedar on a ridge ahead of you, you'll know you're almost there. You may want to get a look at Kawaikoi Stream to decide whether you want to cross it to Sugi Grove Camp before you decide at which camp to stay. Bear in mind that anything substantial that gets wet during that stream crossing, such as your boots, is unlikely to dry out during your stay here. And don't cross it if it's running high!

You are on the edge of the Alakai Swamp here, and you can expect rain nightly and probably sometime during the day, too. A rainproof tent is essential. The combination of rain and wind, together with relatively low temperatures, can make this area quite chilly at night. But if you're prepared, a stay here is very enjoyable. There's something special about sipping your evening tea as you watch the last of the sunshine from the west create rainbows in the showers sweeping across the ridges to the east. You may find yourself sharing the campground with people, mostly hunters, who have come down in 4WD vehicles, but most drivers seem to prefer to daytrip.

Na Pali-Kona Forest Reserve Campground Regulations.... You can ask for a permit that will allow you to camp at either Kawaikoi Camp or Sugi Grove Camp, so that you can decide which you prefer when you actually get there. Current regulations state that open fires are not allowed. The shelters (pavilions) are available on a first-come, first-served basis. You must get your water from the stream and purify it.

Trip 45. Pihea-Alakai Side Trip

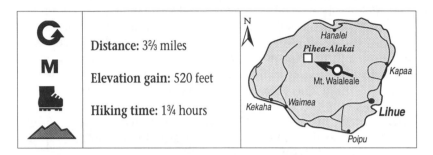

Distance: 3⅔ miles

Elevation gain: 520 feet

Hiking time: 1¾ hours

Topos: *Haena*

Trail map: At the end of Trip 43.

Highlights: This trip treats you to the beauty of Kawaikoi Stream, birdwatching opportunities from an excellent perch, and a taste of the famous Alakai Swamp. It's one of my all-time favorites.

Driving instructions: Not applicable.

Permit required: None.

Description. This hike starts from the south end of the Pihea Trail, which is on the north-northeast edge of Kawaikoi Camp. Look for an opening in the shrubbery, under ohia, marked by a stake that says END. You cross an unnamed tributary of Kawaikoi Stream on a footbridge, pass through some strawberry guavas, and emerge on the streambank amid *lapalapa, uluhe,* and bird's-nest fern. Honeysuckle and blackberry crowd the steep bank where you make a couple of switchbacks across a tributary. Streamlets cross your fern-lined path, too many to count when it's rainy. You presently find yourself strolling through a charming natural archway of trees; look for *uki uki* and soft green mounds of delicate mosses here. The understory yields briefly to a soggy little meadow, but soon you're back on the grassy track.

As you approach the ½-mile point, you can see the tread of the Kawaikoi Stream Trail across the water. Soon you reach a junction where, if you wish and if Kawaikoi Stream is not too high, you can switchback down to the stream, ford it, and pick up the Kawaikoi Stream Trail. But this trip continues on the Pihea Trail; see Trip 46 for the Kawaikoi Stream Trail. The native Hawaiian raspberry, the nearly thornless *akala*, has succumbed to grazing animals in most places and become rare. But a little past the ½-mile point, you'll see a few of these lovely plants. Look for their broad, bright-green leaves and pink blossoms. Their large red berries have little flavor; you'll get more enjoyment from a good photo of them than from tasting them! Also look for the thick, ridged leaves and flower- and berry-clusters of the *puaha-nui* (also called *kanawao*) in this area. It's related to the ornamental hydrangea. *Manono* grows here, too, with its clusters of tiny, pendent, greenish flowers. Be on the lookout for a bizarre fungus: a low, salmon-colored, hollow-centered, two-inch disk from which radiate seven or so short "arms" that terminate in pairs of peach-colored "fingers." Surely it's not alive (but it is)!

A streamside picnic shelter welcomes you at ¾ mile. Beyond it, you cross a tributary on logs and begin to climb above a branch of Kawaikoi Stream almost imperceptibly. You pass under an overhang of *uluhe* and descend back to streamside with the help of a couple of short, steep trail sections. Near the one-mile point, you begin climbing steeply on grassy switchbacks. Look for a large shrub with oval leaves and squarish green berries along here: the anise-scented *mokihana* of Kauai. If your eyes don't spot it, your nose surely will! The switchbacks at last bring you to the top of a ridge and to a damp little bench that offers some exceptional birdwatching opportunities. The ridge drops very steeply away in front of this bench, allowing you to look down into the forest canopy of the stream valley. It's a great place to see birds ordinarily hidden by the canopy when you try to look up into it. Near the bench, awkward shrubs lift branches studded with misshapen berries: *alani*, a relative of the *mokihana*.

Leaving the bench, you enter the Alakai Swamp and travel along a ridgetop on a track surrounded by rain-forest growth. From here to Mohihi Road, the going can be very swampy. The Division of Land and Natural Resources has built wooden walkways over the worst parts of the established routes through the Alakai Swamp; it won't be long now before you pick up the walkway. Where old trees have fallen over, the upturned disks of their roots, cemented with mud, make circular "walls" on one side of you, and watery mud fills the hollows their roots left behind. It's just over 2 miles from Kawaikoi Camp on the Pihea Trail to the junction with the Alakai Swamp Trail. Turn southwest (left) onto the Alakai Swamp Trail here. The character of the forest and the trail change markedly. Under the dense forest cover, walkways carry you over ankle- to calf-deep bogs through which hikers formerly had to splash their muddy way. These rain-forest bogs soon give way to a strange meadow where stunted shrubs form isolated islands in what's essentially one huge bog. Fallen telephone poles, artifacts of a World War II communications project, lie abandoned here.

Astonishingly, you come out of the telephone-pole bog to find yourself on what looks like a tidy country lane. Evergreens and *ohia* border the path; *uluhe* forms neat hedges. It's an old road that descends gently then makes a steep up-and-down across a narrow saddle, a little past which you reach the check station at the beginning of the Alakai Swamp Trail. The trailhead is set back from Mohihi Road, so continue across the grassy flat past a rain gauge to meet the road in ⅙ more mile.

The Alakai Picnic Area is just across the road, and you may want to stroll over to take a breather there and get out of the rain before closing the loop. If the weather is clear, there's a fine view over Poomau Canyon from the far edge of the picnic area. When you're ready, take Mohihi Road east to Kawaikoi Camp as described in Trip 44 to close the loop.

Kawaikoi Stream's lush, idyllic setting near Kawaikoi and Sugi Grove camps

Trip 46. Kawaikoi Stream Trail

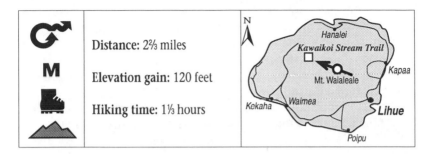

Distance: 2⅔ miles

Elevation gain: 120 feet

Hiking time: 1⅓ hours

Topos: *Haena*

Trail map: At the end of Trip 43.

Highlights: Division of Forestry and Wildlife literature describes this as ". . .likely the most scenic mountain stream side trail in Hawaii. . . ." That's an understatement: this may be one of the most scenic streamside trails *anywhere*. There's also a variety of interesting plants, especially native ones, to delight the amateur botanist. It's another of my all-time favorite hikes.

Driving instructions: Not applicable.

Permit required: None.

Description. From your campsite at Kawaikoi Camp, return to Mohihi Road and turn east (left) toward Kawaikoi Stream. Ford the stream if the water is low; postpone this trip if it's not! Follow the road a few more paces to the turnoff to Sugi Grove Camp on your right and to the trailhead on your left. You turn sharply northwest (left) onto the trail and climb a little through a cedar grove that also boasts a few redwoods, cross a swampy segment, and come out above Kawaikoi Stream.

You walk north on a bark- and twig-strewn track, now in the evergreens' shade, now between hummocks of velvety chartreuse moss, now over springy grass in the open sun. Japanese honeysuckle perfumes the air; look for tree ferns where a spring gushes over the trail. The trail soon brings you down to the water's edge, where you wander into an exquisite picture: tall *ohia* trees rise gracefully above a broad stream that drifts through a valley between banks of lush greenery, the whole scene framed by wooded slopes and bright blue sky.

The trail forks at ¾ mile amid *ohia* and ginger. This is the beginning of the loop portion, and you bear southeast (right) on the fork that stays high. You climb briefly and walk along ferny banks, past *manono* and daisy fleabane. At the 1-mile mark, you stroll through the broken shade of *ohia* and strawberry guava, listening for the aptly described "rusty hinge" call of the red *iiwi* bird: *chirp, chirp, skweeeeerk!* Watch your footing where you hop across a little stream; it's boggy here, and you're in a branch of the Alakai Swamp. The ground becomes curiously spongy and hollow-sounding underfoot, and there are more superb stream views on your left. *Puaha-nui (kanawao), olapa, pukiawe,* and *mokihana,* which you may recognize by its faint anise scent, grow along this segment together with many other shrubs and vines that will send you rummaging through your pack for your plant guides.

Near 1¼ miles, you make a short, steep descent past a lovely overlook of the stream to a fork. The west (left) fork is the main trail; the east (right) fork is a short trail-of-use to another stream overlook. The main trail makes a sharp turn to a spot where you boulder-hop Kawaikoi Stream to the opposite bank. Muddy and dry trail sections now alternate; sometimes you walk gingerly on logs over mud, sometimes stride briskly along leaf-littered trail. Too soon, you ford Kawaikoi Stream again, walk up the bank on the other side, and close the loop portion of this trip. From here, you reluctantly retrace your steps to Kawaikoi Camp.

Another view of beautiful Kawaikoi Stream

Trip 47. Poomau Canyon Lookout Side Trip

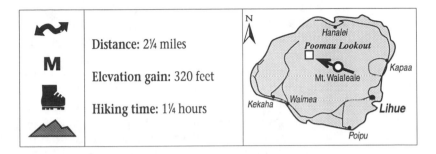

Distance: 2¼ miles

Elevation gain: 320 feet

Hiking time: 1¼ hours

Topos: *Haena*

Trail map: Starts on the map at the end of Trip 43; ends on the map at the end of this trip.

Highlights: This almost-easy trip brings you to a magnificent view of one of Waimea Canyon's largest tributaries, Poomau Canyon.

Driving instructions: Not applicable.

Permit required: None.

Description. Follow Trip 46 down Mohihi Road, past the Kawaikoi Stream Trail, and between dense groves of sugi cedar. Mohihi Road turns south here as you pass Waiakoali Picnic Area, and cross Waiakoali Stream. Beyond Mohihi Ditch (an irrigation ditch not shown on the map) and private Mohihi Ditch Trail (a 4WD road; no trespassing), you reach the Poomau Canyon Lookout Trail under a lone sugi cedar on the west side of the road.

Turn west (right) onto the trail. In a hundred yards, you cross Mohihi Ditch on a bridge, cross Mohihi Ditch Trail, and bear uphill through *koa*, strawberry guava, and *ohia*. The trail curves and then descends on a track where your nose may detect *mokihana* before your eyes do. The trail makes a few switchbacks and emerges at an *ohia*-shaded bump that offers you a dizzying view of Poomau Canyon. Below you, white-tailed tropicbirds soar in the canyon's awesome depths. Distant Poomau Stream winds toward Waimea Canyon under light-green *kukui*. Unnamed ridges, elaborately shaped by erosion, extend into the canyon. To the southwest is a striking butte, point 2150 on the topo. Ahead of you on this slope, avoid a narrow trail-of-use that descends precipitously on poor footing to views that are no better than the ones you're already enjoying.

Retrace your steps when you're ready.

Waimea Canyon.... Waimea Canyon's features are so reminiscent of the Grand Canyon of the Colorado in Arizona that Waimea Canyon is often referred to as "the Grand Canyon of the Pacific." It's tempting to assume both canyons were shaped by the same forces, but it's believed Kauai isn't old enough for the processes that formed the Grand Canyon to have cut a canyon as deep and convoluted as Waimea Canyon.

Arizona's Grand Canyon is the result of millions of years of combined river-cutting and land-mass rising. The Colorado flows through that area today pretty much as it did millions of years ago when the land buckled and began to rise into the mountains and plateaus we now admire. As the land slowly rose, the persistent Colorado kept pace, cutting its channel deeper into the rising land to maintain its course.

Initially, the Waimea, Poomau, and Koaie streams flowed from the summit of Kauai's shield volcano separately, radiating outward toward the sea. However, the volcano's flank collapsed between Hanapepe and Waimea, and the stress of that collapse caused faults and slumping along the line of what we now know as Waimea Canyon. That diverted the flow of the three streams into one river whose cutting power combined with the existing weaknesses and slumping to slice through the volcano's flank and form spectacular Waimea Canyon relatively quickly.

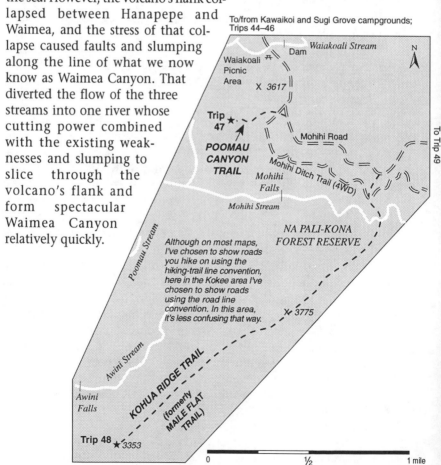

To/from Kawaikoi and Sugi Grove campgrounds; Trips 44–46

Waiakoali Stream

N

Dam

Waiakoali Picnic Area

X 3617

Trip 47

POOMAU CANYON TRAIL

Mohihi Road

Mohihi Ditch Trail (4WD)

To Trip 49

Mohihi Falls

Mohihi Stream

NA PALI-KONA FOREST RESERVE

Poomau Stream

Although on most maps, I've chosen to show roads you hike on using the hiking-trail line convention, here in the Kokee area I've chosen to show roads using the road line convention. In this area, it's less confusing that way.

X 3775

Awini Stream

KOHUA RIDGE TRAIL

(formerly MAILE FLAT TRAIL)

Awini Falls

Trip 48 ★ 3353

0   ½   1 mile

Trip 48. Kohua Ridge Side Trip

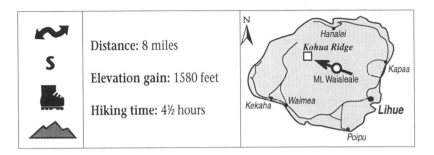

Distance: 8 miles

Elevation gain: 1580 feet

Hiking time: 4½ hours

Topos: *Haena, Waimea Canyon*
Trail map: Starts on the map at the end of Trip 43; ends on the map at the end of Trip 47.
Highlights: The superb views over Waimea Canyon from the end of Kohua Ridge are as dizzying as those over Poomau Canyon (Trip 47) but are far more sweeping. On the way, you get heart-stopping views of the depths of the adjacent valleys.
Driving instructions: Not applicable.
Permit required: None.

Description. Follow Trip 47 past the Poomau Canyon Trail. Continue south and then east on Mohihi Road for ¾ mile more to the Kohua Ridge Trail; it's on the south side of the road. Turn south (right) onto the trail and walk south, then southwest, on what seems to be an old road. You pass through strawberry guava thickets and descend steeply to cross Mohihi Ditch on a bridge, cross Mohihi Ditch Trail, and pick up the Kohua Ridge Trail on the other side of the road.
You continue descending, sometimes very steeply, under *koa* trees, past the ¼-mile marker. Watch for the trail to veer left very abruptly, bringing you to a point where, if the water is not running high, you can boulder-hop across Mohihi Stream. (If the water is running high, please don't try to cross.) A rest stop in this forested stream valley may reward you with the sight of an *iiwi* or an *apapane*.
From the streambank, you climb an extremely steep, slippery clay "slot" southward up the side of Kohua Ridge. The grade eases around ½ mile, then gets its second wind and attacks the ridge very steeply again, bringing you out onto a narrow *ohia*- and *koa*-clad saddle. The trail turns southwest (right) here; note this point for your return, as it is easy to overshoot it.
You begin a long, up-and-down walk along the forested top of Kohua

Ridge. Occasional breaks in the vegetation afford you spectacular views over Koiae Canyon to the south. Near the 1-mile point, you drop and then climb as you cross an extremely narrow saddle. Soon you're walking between dense hedges of blackberry and lantana. There may be quite a bit of downed wood along this stretch. Now it's up and down through *koa, pukiawe,* and *ohia,* with fluffy mounds of gray lichens dotting the soil. *Mokihana* may attract your olfactory attention along here. You brush through a patch of *uki uki* to reach an open area where you can look all the way down-canyon to the sea, if the weather permits.

Around the 1¾ mile point, you descend briefly through black boulders, then descend very steeply, and gradually ascend to another viewpoint. This last section of trail has near-vertical views down into Koaie Canyon or Awini Stream's canyon, depending on which side of Kohua Ridge you're on at the moment. You pass through an eroded area where *iliau* grow. Amid silk oaks, *aalii,* and tough grasses, you make another steep descent and ascent that bring you to an open space near the 2½-mile marker. A hundred feet beyond it, there's a railing marked KOHUA TRAIL VISTA END—and if you venture beyond the railing, it certainly will be *your* end. The panorama from here is incredible. You can see all the way to the ocean, of course. Below you and to the left (southwest) is Poo Kaeha, which figures so prominently as you descend the Kukui Trail. Above and left of it is the red slash of the eroded middle section of that trail. In front of you across the canyon is Puu Ka Pele; perhaps a day or two ago, you stopped there and gazed across Waimea Canyon, wondering what lay on distant Kohua Ridge. Poomau Canyon opens up on your right. You're just below point 3353 on Kohua Ridge, and what a treat it is! It's hard to leave this lookout before you've used up all the film in your camera. When you have, return the way you came.

Looking for the Kohua Ridge Trail on the topos?....Most of it isn't there. Only the eastern fragment is, though it's marked "Maile Flat Trail." You can approximate the rest of its route by drawing a line from the end of the "Maile Flat Trail" over the ridgeline southwestward to point 3353.

Trip 49. Mohihi-Waialae Side Trip

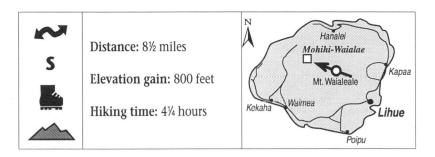

	Distance: 8½ miles	N
S	Elevation gain: 800 feet	Hanalei / Mohihi-Waialae / Mt. Waialeale / Kapaa / Kekaha / Waimea / Lihue / Poipu
	Hiking time: 4¼ hours	

Topos: *Haena, Waimea Canyon*

Trail map: Starts on the map at the end of Trip 43; continues on the map at the end of Trip 47; ends on the map at the end of this trip.

Highlights: On a fairly clear day, you'll get some fine views from the ridgetop this hike takes you to. If it's rained very recently, the views will include some lovely, remote waterfalls.

Driving instructions: Not applicable.

Permit required: None, but be sure to sign in at the check station at the Mohihi-Waialae Route's trailhead.

Description. Follow Trip 48 past the Kohua Ridge Trail and continue east on Mohihi Road, which is especially pretty from here to its end. The road dips a little through a forest of *koa* and *ohia*, and you shortly reach an unmarked fork not shown on the map. Bear left on the north-northeast fork, which is Mohihi Road (the east—right—fork, which seems to be a sort of 4WD trail-of-use, leads down to Mohihi Ditch and Mohihi Ditch Trail). You level out soon near a gully that contains a number of almost-tree-size, palm-like plants—some of the amazing lobeliods of Hawaii.

Now the road wanders through a delightful mix of forest and meadow until it bears southeast as it passes a picnic shelter under sugi cedars. A sign here points you down the road to the Mohihi-Waialae Route (some sources consider the route to start here). You descend steeply into the forest, cross Mohihi Ditch on a footbridge, and meet Mohihi Ditch Road at the boundary of the Alakai Swamp Wilderness Preserve. There's another picnic shelter here near the check station at the trailhead where you sign in.

You pick up the track of the Mohihi-Waialae Route next to the check station and drop steeply through sugi cedars on switchbacks to Mohihi Stream. If the water isn't too high, ford Mohihi Stream here and start toward a gauging-station shed. Don't pass that shed! The Mohihi-Waialae Route turns right (east) and almost disappears into the glory-bushes just before the shed. Turn right here and push the glory-bush branches aside to find the track.

On this track, you climb very steeply through *ohia, uluhe,* and *olapa,* level out briefly only to descend steeply, cross a small saddle, and ascend again, this time under sugi cedars. The climb steepens as the cedars give way to *ohia,* fern, and blackberry. You level out at a spot where you can look back at the roadend far below to the north-northwest.

Now you begin an up-and-down ridgetop trek with occasional wonderful views out over the surrounding landscape, especially south over Koaie Canyon. A light rain can add to your enjoyment by providing rainbows and filling the waterfalls.

Almost 1¼ miles from the trailhead, you come across a rickety bench; it offers you an opportunity for a rest and some excellent views southwest. On your way again, you may have occasion to reflect on the strange world of this Alakai Swamp ridgetop. It's not dense rain forest or boggy swamp yet. Instead, it may seem as if the sun roasts you while the rain bastes you and the wind tries to push your cooked remains off the ridge. *Ohia, mokihana, uki, lapa, olapa,* ferns, and *maile* appear along the track. Grotesque sedges and mosses spring from the boles of living trees, a strong clue that the boggy swamp is at hand.

You pass below a rain gauge and soon reach a junction where a false trail leads downhill to the left. You're in a rain-forest bog now, and plastic-ribbon tags mark the correct route (ahead). But this hike ends here near the rain gauge, so it's time for you to turn around and retrace your steps.

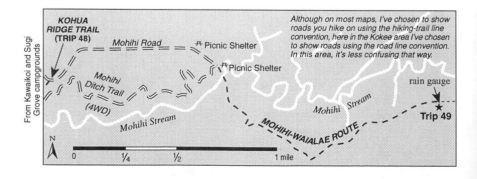

A picnic shelter at Kawaikoi Camp (Trip 44)

Mohihi Stream, set in steep rainforest ridges

About Kee Beach, the Kalalau Trail, and the Na Pali Coast...

At Kauai's extreme northwest end, you'll find beatiful Kee Beach and the world-famous Na Pali Coast. Kee Beach is literally at the end of the road (Highway 560). The Na Pali Coast is accessible only by boat (the old Hawaiians' preferred way of getting to it) and on foot along the famed Kalalau Trail; the trailhead is at Kee Beach.

This book begins its exploration of the area with an easy stroll at Kee Beach (Trip 50). It then divides the Kalalau Trail into several dayhikes and backpacks—Trips 51–57. Here's a not-to-scale overview, below:

Some of the dayhikes are possible only as side trips from camping areas you must backpack to. Permits are required to camp along the Kalalau Trail, where there are normally 3 legal camping areas, which are, in the order you'd reach them as you hiked away from Kee Beach, Hanakapiai, Hanakoa,* and Kalalau. Stays are limited to no more than 5 nights, with no more than one consecutive overnight at Hanakapiai and Hanakoa.

Permits also are required for dayhikes beyond Hanakapiai.

The Na Pali Coast's Kalalau Trail is sometimes touted as one of the world's most beautiful hikes, but I disagree. Those wishing to see the Na Pali Coast as it's typically shown in calendars, travelogues, and coffee-table books may find that helicopter or boat trips are better at providing the experience and scenery they expect. Being *on* the Na Pali Coast's Kalalau Trail is a very different experience, often far from idyllic. It's the difference between looking at a beautiful animal from a distance and being a flea on that animal.

Although the views from the Kalalau Trail can be outstanding, I think the trail is the most arduous one I have yet *backpacked*. Because of its difficulty, I strongly recommend you *not* take beginning backpackers on the Kalalau Trail. Most of the information you'll receive in advance does not address its difficulty. But the reality is:

• The general condition of the trail is poor compared to *maintained*

---

*Note that as of 1996, Hanakoa is closed to camping until the Division of State Parks can build a restroom there. It's an improvement worth waiting for.

trails in California, which is my principal point of reference. I believe this reflects the rapid rate of erosion and the fragility of the soil, not a lack of maintenance. *Boots are a must!*

- The narrow tread of the trail—where your feet go—is often full of rubble that rolls around under your feet.
- The terrain it crosses is not solid rock but softer, crumbling material—consolidated ash or clinker, perhaps—which provides poor footing on steep slopes.
- A little rain may turn the trail to slippery clay. A lot of rain may turn the trail into a sluice. This is more of a problem between Kee Beach and Hanakoa Valley, a stretch that's mostly rainforest. It's generally drier beyond Hanakoa.
- The trail is often very narrow, sometimes because the downhill side has sheared away, with a steep slope up on one side and a steep drop down on the other. There is little margin for error.
- The trail is rarely level, often climbing or descending steeply. That's not a problem by itself, but it makes the going more difficult on top of the problems above.
- The stream crossings may be very difficult, especially with a heavy pack. Allow plenty of time for them. *If the water is high or if it's raining inland, don't try to cross. Wait until the stream subsides, or until it stops raining* and *the stream subsides.*
- The camping areas are filthy, overused, crowded, and bug- and toad-infested. Camping at Hanakapiai and Hanakoa (if and when it's re-opened) may be chilly because very damp; camping at Kalalau may be very hot.

For all the trouble of walking the Kalalau Trail, you'd expect to be rewarded with an up-close and personal experience of the wild, *genuine* Hawaii—but no. Because of human disturbance, there are almost no native Hawaiian plants and birds left along the Kalalau Trail—or on most of the Na Pali Coast. (The Kokee area offers Kauai's visitors their best opportunity to see native Hawaiian plants and birds, especially on Trips 43–49.)

The Na Pali Coast was once notorious for its resident population of hippies and their ultra-casual, clothing-optional lifestyle. Those days are over. Nudity has always been illegal at all Hawaiian beaches. Expect to find a resident caretaker in the Kalalau area who will keep an eye on visitors and educate them about the environment, history, and proper care of this ecologically sensitive region.

Call me an iconoclast, but I regard *backpacking* the Kalalau Trail, which can take several days, as a poor use of the limited time most visitors probably have on Kauai. There is so much more to Kauai than the Na Pali Coast and the Kalalau Trail! If you want to experience the Na Pali Coast on foot, you're better off dayhiking it (Trips 51–54).

Trip 50. Kee Beach Stroll

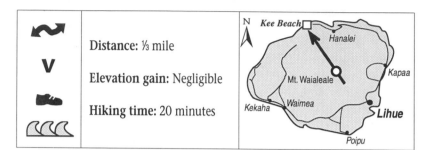

Distance: ⅓ mile

Elevation gain: Negligible

Hiking time: 20 minutes

Topos: Optional: *Haena*
Trail maps: At the end of this trip.
Highlights: Kee Beach, locally known as "Bali Hai," is an elegant little crescent of golden sand in a picture-perfect tropical setting. You can get a good view of the Na Pali Coast by walking out on the rocks on the "stroll" portion of this trip if the surf permits. If you're here at sunset, you may see the phenomenon known as "the green flash" (more below).
Driving instructions: From Lihue, drive north and then west on Highway 56 literally to the end of the road, which has become Highway 560 by then, 41 miles. The parking area is small. Your chances of finding a spot here are better if you arrive early. (On the other hand, you may want to come late and watch sunset from this west-facing beach.)
Permit required: None.

Description. Kee Beach has a little coral reef, and, if the sea is not too rough, you may want to try swimming here. Or you can just relax and picnic. Tropical almond, ironwood, and *kukui* trees form a backdrop for the beach. There are restrooms and a drinking fountain in the trees, abreast of the parking lot, and on your right as you face the ocean. You'll have lots of company here.
Stroll to Na Pali Coast view. To see the Na Pali Coast from Kee Beach, wait for low tide so you can walk out on the rocks a short distance. Be sure the surf is fairly tame before you walk that far out (⅙ mile). Always keep an eye on the surf! Look for a little path by a low wall on your left as you approach the beach from the parking area. You follow it over roots and under an arch of tropical almond trees and coconut palms. Veer to the right at a fork. From the *de facto* end of the path, continue out on the rocks if the surf permits. You won't have to go more than 50 feet before you can look to your left and see the rugged cliffs of the Na Pali Coast stretching for miles southwest into the sea haze. The

view is framed by the tropical vegetation surrounding the adjacent home, making it all the more striking. A rocky use-trail leads left and up from the end of the path to fine ocean views and an ancient hula platform, the site of one of the most revered *hula halau* (hula schools) in old Hawaii.

Green flash. The point where the sun sets isn't always visible from Kee Beach. In winter, it sets too far to the south. Otherwise, if you're here at sunset, plop yourself down in the sand at a spot where you'll have an unobstructed view toward where the sun will sink into the ocean. The green flash is a very real phenomenon (though my father did not believe that; see **The Tanqueray Flash**, below.) Sunlight must travel through many more miles of air just before the sun rises or just after it sets than when it's well above the horizon. The atmosphere acts as a prism, separating the light into rainbow colors. For various reasons, the emerald-green of the rainbow tends to come through most strongly: the green flash. It's usually very brief. These factors affect your chances of seeing the green flash:

• You need to have an unobstructed view of the point where the sun goes down into the sea.
• You can see the green flash only when there are no clouds at the point where the sun goes down. (Unfortunately, the sun's brightness may keep you from noticing very low clouds along the horizon until after it sets.)
• Your eyes must not be "exhausted" from staring at bright light.

You might try this technique to help you see the green flash when the other conditions are right:

• Don't look at the setting sun except very briefly, and only to determine when there's just a sliver of it left above the horizon.
• Avoid exhausting your eyes: don't look at any bright light, surface, or object.
• When there's just a sliver of the sun above the horizon, put your hand up in front of your face to shield your eyes from the remaining light, and turn toward the sun. *Keep that hand up so you don't look directly at the sun!* (Mom was right about this one.)
• Adjust your hand position so the tiniest bit of red light peeps around it. All you need to see is its *color*.
• Watch that bit of red light. Suddenly, it *may* turn rainbow-green. Drop your hand immediately! Where the sun went down, you'll see a brilliant green spot—the green flash.* Remember, don't drop your hand until (and if) the light turns green.

---

*The spot of green light, though very brilliant and obvious to your eyes, is too small for an ordinary camera to photograph. You'd need the help of a big telescope for that.

That technique worked for me. Don't worry too much about the green flash, though. Sunset can be spectacular here even if conditions aren't right for the green flash.

A little stormy? Perhaps it's stormy when you're at Kee Beach. A high surf makes it unwise to walk out to see the Na Pali Coast. Clouds obscure the horizon. However, if clouds don't completely cover the sky, you're likely to see a sunset that's far more spectacular than one where you can see the green flash. And the wind will not only push the surf up into mountainous waves, it will seize the foam from their crests and fling it far away, back out to sea, as wind blows the snow in long plumes from mountaintops. What a sight!

The Tanqueray Flash.... My father, as I said, did not believe in the green flash. Pop had his own theory about it. A famous *Los Angeles Times* columnist wrote about seeing the green flash. Pop sent his theory to the columnist: "The only green flash anyone's ever seen is through the bottom of a Tanqueray bottle." Pop got no reply. I lent Pop my copy of D. K. J. O'Connell's article on the green flash (see Bibliography), but I felt kind of bad about it: the Tanqueray theory had a certain charm. If you do see the green flash here and tell your mainland friends about it, be prepared to hear the Tanqueray theory from them!

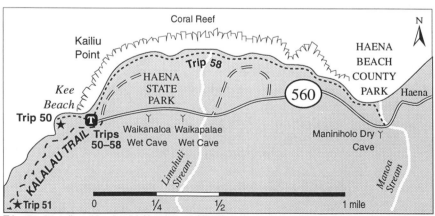

Trips 52–57; to/from Hanakapiai, Hanakoa, and Kalalau

Trip 51. Kee Beach to Viewpoint

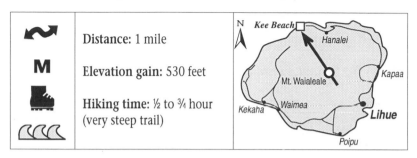

Distance: 1 mile

Elevation gain: 530 feet

Hiking time: ½ to ¾ hour
(very steep trail)

Topos: Optional: *Haena*
Trail maps: At the end of Trip 50.
Highlights: Excellent views of the Na Pali Coast and Kee Beach; a tropical setting that's so perfect it hardly seems that it can be real.
Driving instructions: Follow the driving directions for Trip 50. The Kalalau Trail starts on the south side of the parking area (left as you face the beach) by a little wooden shelter/bulletin board.
Permit required: None.

Description. Put on that mosquito repellent before starting out! The trail leaves the parking area under big tropical almond and *kukui* trees draped with pothos plants that have escaped from adjacent gardens.

You begin climbing steeply almost immediately. The trail is very rough: uneven rocks, sometimes wet and slippery. It's an accurate reflection of things to come, so watch your footing carefully. This is a very popular dayhike, and you're likely to have lots of company.

Lush tropical vegetation abounds here. *Hala* trees, *ti,* and beach *naupaka* are prominent. Your nose may detect the fragrance of sweet fern: a delicate, anise-like scent coming from big, chain-fern-like fronds. At first, the forest cover is so dense you really can't see anything except the greenery surrounding you. But starting at about ¼ mile, there are a number of points where you can stop to enjoy views of Kee Beach: the reef, the turquoise water, the shaggy ironwood trees, and the golden sand. This is what you came to Kauai for!

In only ½ mile you've climbed to a spectacular overlook of Kee Beach as well as an excellent viewpoint of the Na Pali Coast. Catch your breath and, after enjoying this aerial view of Kee Beach, look southwest along the Na Pali Coast. Immense cliffs drop hundreds, even thousands, of feet to the relentless, pounding sea. It seems impossible to count them all as they fade into the haze of salt spray. Maybe you hadn't planned to go any farther, but as you gaze into that blue distance, you might just change your mind. . . .

Trip 52. Kee Beach to Hanakapiai Beach

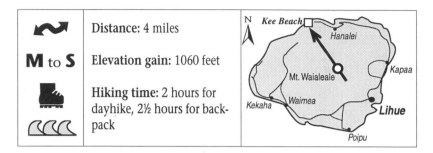

Distance: 4 miles	
M to **S**	**Elevation gain:** 1060 feet
	Hiking time: 2 hours for dayhike, 2½ hours for backpack

Topos: *Haena*

Trail maps: Starts on the map at the end of Trip 50; ends on the map at the end of this trip.

Highlights: Excellent views of the Na Pali Coast and Kee Beach; a visit to a tropical beach you can't drive to. Camping at Hanakapiai is restricted to one night (no two consecutive nights).

Driving instructions: Follow the driving instructions for Trip 50 to Kee Beach. It's okay to park here for a dayhike, but it's recommended that you *not* leave a car here overnight. There's apparently a lot of vandalism. That poses some problems. Perhaps you can arrange to have someone drop you off at Kee Beach. If that's not possible, you might try dropping your packs and most of the people in your party at the trailhead. Then drive the car back to an area where people may be around 24 hours a day, such as Haena Beach Park, and park it there. Walk back to the trailhead from there.

Permit required: You do not need a permit to *dayhike* to Hanakapiai. However, you do need a permit to stay there overnight, and you may camp there for only one night at a time. Apply to the Division of State Parks for your permit (see "Getting Permits" in this book).

Description. Follow the hiking description of Trip 51 to the ½-mile point. After catching your breath and enjoying the views here, you continue toward Hanakapiai. You'll continue to have plenty of company, as this is a very popular trip.

It's pretty steadily uphill until the 1-mile point, so give yourself a break and stop to enjoy the view every so often. Keep your eyes on the trail when you're moving, as the footing on this trail is always difficult. As you spend more time on the Kalalau Trail, you'll realize how fast the rate of erosion is on this crumbling volcanic terrain.

You've probably begun to notice the occasional metal stake with or

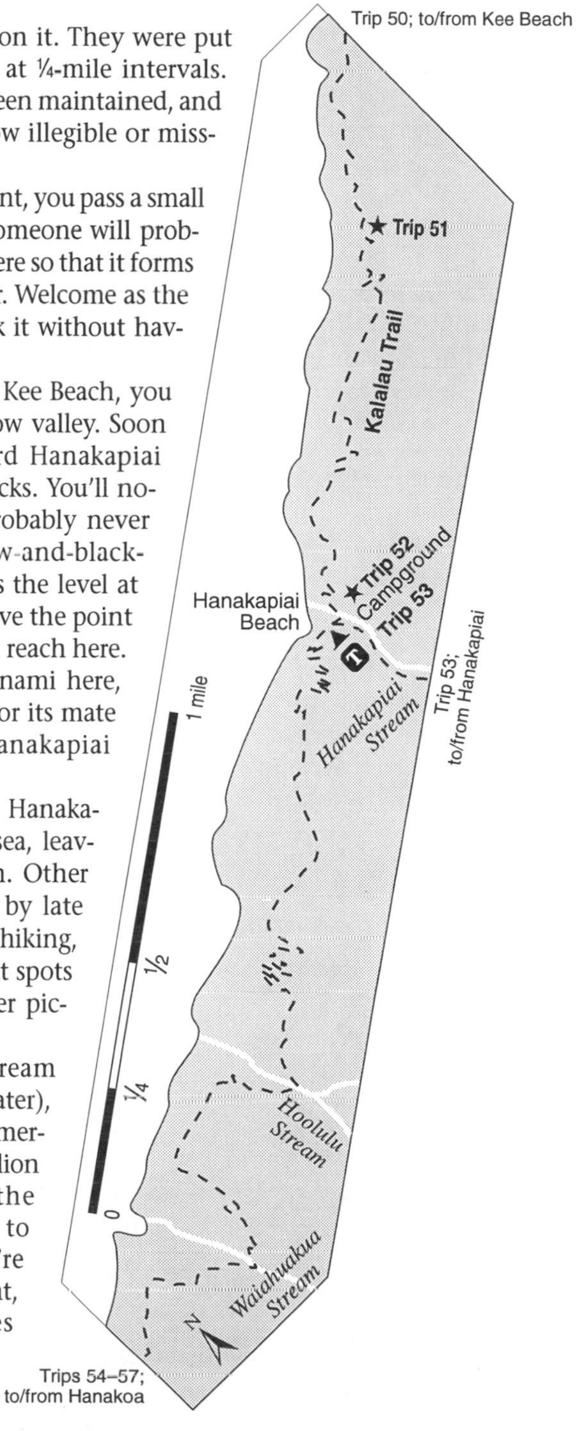

Trip 50; to/from Kee Beach

without mileage written on it. They were put in place many years ago at ¼-mile intervals. However, they have not been maintained, and a number of them are now illegible or missing.

Around the 1-mile point, you pass a small spring on the cliff face. Someone will probably have placed a *ti* leaf here so that it forms a little spigot for the water. Welcome as the water may be, don't drink it without having first treated it.

About 1½ miles from Kee Beach, you dip in and out of a shallow valley. Soon you're descending toward Hanakapiai Stream on steep switchbacks. You'll notice something you've probably never seen before: a big yellow-and-black-striped marker that shows the level at which you'll be safely above the point a tidal wave (tsunami) can reach here. If you're warned of a tsunami here, get up above this marker or its mate on the other side of Hanakapiai Stream.

Winter storms sweep Hanakapiai's sand beach out to sea, leaving only a boulder beach. Other currents return the sand by late summer. If you're just dayhiking, the boulders and some flat spots among the *hala* trees offer picnicking perches.

After fording the stream (very difficult at high water), you climb steeply past numerous trashcans under a pavilion to the junction with the Hanakapiai Valley Trail to Hanakapiai Falls. If you're planning to stay overnight, several overused sites huddle close together

★ Trip 51

Kalalau Trail

Hanakapiai Beach

★ Trip 52 Campground

Trip 53

Trip 53; to/from Hanakapiai

1 mile

½

¼

0

Hanakapiai Stream

Hoolulu Stream

Waiahuakua Stream

N

Trips 54–57; to/from Hanakoa

in the *hala* trees overlooking the ocean. Still, the view out toward the sea, fringed by *hala* leaves, is one of those "Gosh, I'm really in paradise!" views. There are pit toilets here; unfortunately, they've been vandalized. An adjacent trash pit is a smelly eyesore. Please don't add to it: pack out your own trash.

Fortunately, there's a second, somewhat more pleasant, camping area inland. To get to it, turn inland from here on the Hanakapiai Valley trail. A few steps will bring you to sites under guava trees. It is not nearly as far inland as shown on the topo; there is no camping permitted that far into the valley. Pitch that tent; it's often rainy at Hanakapiai. Wild offspring of domestic cats eke out a meager living here, so if you're staying overnight, hang your food.

Kee Beach as seen from the Kalalau Trail

Trip 53. Hanakapiai Falls Dayhike or Side Trip

S (dayhike)

M (side trip)

Distance: 8 miles from Kee Beach; 4 miles from Hanakapiai Beach

Elevation gain: 1820 feet from Kee Beach; 760 feet from Hanakapiai Beach

Hiking time: 5 to 6 hours for dayhike from Kee Beach; 3 to 4 hours for side trip from Hanakapiai Beach

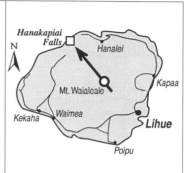

Topos: *Haena*

Trail maps: Dayhike starts on the map at the end of Trip 50 and continues on the map at the end of Trip 52; dayhike ends on, and side trip is on, the map at the end of this trip.

Highlights: Standing in the spray of a tropical waterfall that seems to cascade forever down impossibly steep slopes covered with dense green vegetation.

Driving instructions: Follow the driving instructions for Trip 50 to Kee Beach and the Kalalau Trail.

Permit required: As for Trip 52.

Description. Follow the hiking description of Trip 52 to Hanakapiai Beach, cross the stream, and pick up the Hanakapiai Valley Trail near the trash pit and toilets, if you're not already camped there. This is a very popular trip, even as a dayhike from Kee Beach, so you'll have lots of company on the ground. Less welcome will be the company in the air: helicopters full of sightseers taking the one-hour tour of this "little island" swarm in and out of the valley like mosquitoes. If you are camping at Hanakapiai, remember that you may stay there only one night, so you must combine this side trip with either your hike in or your hike out.

Much of the trail into Hanakapiai Valley can be like a cross-country route. Parts of it are heavily eroded, suggesting that it undergoes rapid change. Please use the following description with that in mind.

Follow the Hanakapiai Valley trail into the valley past the camping areas and on the west side of the stream. Look for a striking clump of giant bamboo; a spur trail leads left to a space underneath the bamboo where you'll find a picnic table and benches—a "bamboo pavilion." The main trail's condition depends on how recently it was maintained; if you should find it indistinguishable from the tropical forest at some points, look for little tags of colored plastic ribbon tied to the shrubbery to guide you. It's best to visually locate the next tag before you move out of sight of the previous tag. It's also a good idea to allow yourself plenty of time to get lost and then get found again. The route is apt to be very muddy as you go deeper into the valley.

You have three major stream crossings to make and numerous minor ones. The first main crossing occurs soon after the "bamboo pavilion" and is a double crossing (the stream divides and flows around an obstacle). Now on the east side of the stream, you'll probably notice ancient stone walls that mark terraces where taro once grew. In the nineteenth century, there was a coffee plantation in Hanakapiai, and coffee shrubs still abound here. Look for the slender gray branches; five-inch-long narrow, glossy, ruffled leaves; and either fragrant white flowers or bright red berries that enclose the seeds that become coffee beans.

Just before the second main crossing, the current route brings you to a little "high spot" where you have a very good view of the falls. The route gets even rougher after this spot, so if you're tired of scrambling through mud, enjoy this view and then turn around.

Beyond the viewpoint, you negotiate a short, steep descent where you may have to cling to the vegetation because there's nothing solid

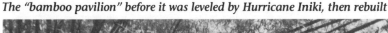

The "bamboo pavilion" before it was leveled by Hurricane Iniki, then rebuilt

Ed Schwartz

for your feet to hold onto. The second and third main crossings occur at about 1¾ miles, one right after the other around a beautiful big pool. You can circumvent the pool by making a wet Class-3 traverse on a narrow rock ledge on its west side. This pool probably offers safer swimming than does the pool at the base of the falls because of the rockfall hazard at the latter.

You approach the pool at the base of the falls on the east side of Hanakapiai Stream. It's a dramatic spectacle as the water plunges from more than 100 feet above into the big pool. Heavy spray from the falling water drenches the rocks, plants, and you. You're probably standing on the shattered rock that surrounds the base of the falls: rockfall is frequent here. It's hard to turn away from such a beautiful and awesome sight, but don't hang around too long and get beaned by falling boulders.

Retrace your steps when you're ready.

Waterfalls at work.....In Hawaii, the terrain tends to consist of alternating layers of resistant lava and less-resistant material such as consolidated ash or clinker. A stream wears through the softer layer faster and cascades over the harder layer. The force of the falling water wears away the rock at the base of the falls, forming a lovely pool. Undercut by that process, rock above the pool succumbs to gravity and falls away, shattering at the base of the falls. This process wears the stream's channel farther and farther back into the slope. Over eons, the stream cuts its gorge back toward its headwaters. Because harder and softer layers alternate, streams often form a chain of waterfalls on their long descent to the sea. A waterfall like Hanakapiai may be just one in the chain.

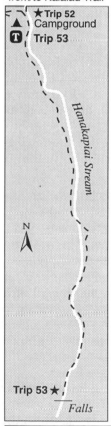

From Hanakapiai Beach; from/to Kalalau Trail

★ Trip 52
▲ Campground
🚻 Trip 53

Hanakapiai Stream

N

Trip 53 ★

Falls

0   ¼   ½   1 mile

Trip 54. Kee Beach to Hanakoa Valley Backpack

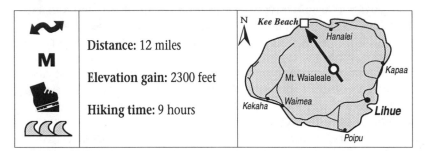

Distance: 12 miles

Elevation gain: 2300 feet

Hiking time: 9 hours

Topos: *Haena*

Trail maps: Begins on the map at the end of Trip 50; continues on the map at the end of Trip 52; ends on the map at the end of this trip.

Highlights: More fabulous scenery as you explore the famed Kalalau Trail.

If and when Hanakoa is open to camping again, backpackers can enjoy camping first near a tropical beach (Hanakapiai) and then in a lush tropical valley (Hanakoa) on ancient terraces under coffee shrubs. Camping at Hanakoa also offers you a chance to visit Hanakoa Falls. However, camping is limited to one night (no two consecutive nights at Hanakoa).

Driving instructions: As for Trip 50.

Permit required: Permits required for dayhiking this far as well as for camping at Hanakoa (see Trip 52).

Description:

Day 1 *(2 miles).* Follow Trip 52 from Kee Beach to Hanakapiai.

Day 2 *(4 miles).* Leaving Hanakapiai, the trail climbs steep switchbacks as it gains 800 feet. You pass a patch of immense sisals, relatives of the century plant that's grown as an ornamental in the Southwest on the mainland. The sisal leaf is a handsome medium green, unlike the century plant leaf, which is gray-green and often has a yellow border. Both plants' leaves are armed with a wicked terminal thorn. Watch out for that thorn on leaves that overhang the trail: it could wind up in your eye or ear. Sisal fibers were once prized for rope, and the sisal was introduced to the islands in the hope of starting a rope industry. You'll have a chance to test the fibers' strength if a sisal has fallen across the trail and you must circumvent it while hanging onto its leaves.

The trail crosses an intrusion of black rock along here. Water seeps from springs that emerge at its face, which is exposed on the side of the trail, and runs into a shallow pool formed in the same rock, which the trail traverses, before spilling down the slope. At the top of the switchbacks, you're at the highest point on the Kalalau Trail, 840 feet. Stop, rest, and enjoy the view.

Now you begin traversing the nose of the ridge that separates Hanakapiai and Hoolulu valleys, and the gradient is gentle for a while. You duck in and out of shallow gullies for almost ⅓ mile until you round the ridge. Pause here to enjoy the view into Hoolulu Valley; look for a big waterfall near the back of the valley on the west side. After this pleasant stop, you begin descending into Hoolulu Valley on steep switchbacks. Watch out for places where previous hikers have slipped and broken away the downhill edge of the narrow trail.

Hoolulu Valley includes several smaller sub-valleys, so that you bob in and out of little valleys while you're traversing it. Under groves of *kukui* trees you'll discover a kind of natural pavement of *kukui* shells pressed into the clay of the trail—pleasant footing for a change. You may meet some jungle-movie-quality centipedes here, six to seven inches long, rustling through the leaf litter. They're said to be non-poisonous but capable of inflicting painful bites with their jaws or pinches with their terminal pincers.

After crossing Hoolulu Stream, you climb a little and emerge on the nose of the ridge that separates Hoolulu and Waiahuakua valleys. Enjoy the view north to Kee Beach and south into Waiahuakua Valley, where you may spy a distant waterfall. The descent into Waiahuakua Valley is somewhat gentler than the one into Hoolulu Valley, and you're soon across the stream, through the valley, and out onto the ridge that separates Waiahuakua and Hanakoa valleys.

Now you climb as you dip in and out of gullies. But be sure to pause and take in the view south into Hanakoa Valley just before you descend into its densely-forested depths. Waterfalls course down the valley's steep green sides (I counted three "biggies.") Following this trip description, there's a description of a side trip to one of them.

As you approach Hanakoa Stream, the shrubbery seems to be coffee, coffee, coffee. At Hanakoa, you camp on a bench 440 feet above sea level and inland from the sea cliffs. Hanakoa Stream flows across this bench on its way to the cliffs, dividing it into two camping areas. Campsites under coffee shrubs dot both sides of the stream. On the east side, decaying Hanakoa Shack offers no practical shelter but plenty of graffiti to read. Hanakoa Stream is a difficult double crossing (the stream forks around a little barrier here).

You reach the sites on the west side of the stream after a rocky climb up the trail. They are somewhat larger and more pleasant than the ones on the east side. Each of these campsites occupies an ancient stone-walled terrace; the excellent condition of these terraces testifies to the skill and dedication of their builders. When they were used to grow taro, these valleys had to be kept free of the dense forest and were open, sunny places. It's only since they were abandoned that the rain forest has reclaimed them. The stone terraces are more obvious here in Hanakoa, I think, than anywhere else right along the trail. Admire their beauty and durability as you relax and enjoy your dinner. Keep the repellent handy; mosquitoes abound here.

Days 3 and 4 *(6 miles)*. Reverse the steps of Days 1 and 2.

Hanging valleys....Valleys like Hoolulu, Waiahuakua, and Hanakoa are "hanging valleys." There are no gently sloping areas where their streams meet the sea to form a beach. Instead, these valleys end abruptly at sea cliffs, and the stream tumbles steeply down to meet the ocean. How does that happen? It's the work of the waves that batter a coast like this, where the slope of the land is relatively steep. The moment that the new land rises above the ocean's surface, waves begin undercutting its edge. Then masses of undercut material fall away, leaving high cliffs. Most of the streams along this coast are relatively small and haven't had a chance to scour out a large valley that reaches the sea. The sea makes cliffs faster than the small streams carve their valleys, so the streams find only a cliff when they reach the edge of the land. You'll notice some beautiful little waterfalls where streams leap from the cliffs to the sea. It's

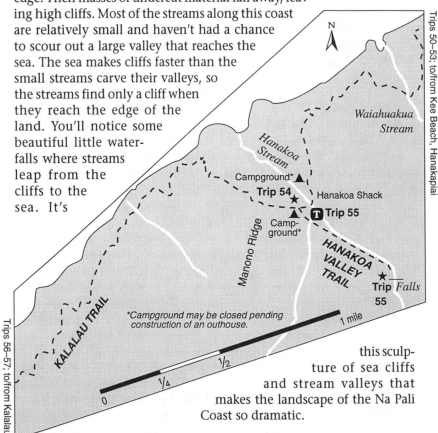

this sculpture of sea cliffs and stream valleys that makes the landscape of the Na Pali Coast so dramatic.

Trip 55. Hanakoa Falls Side Trip

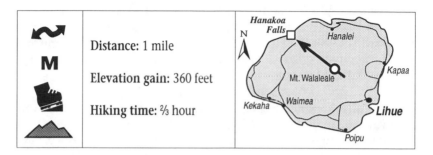

Distance: 1 mile

Elevation gain: 360 feet

Hiking time: ⅔ hour

Topos: *Haena*

Trail maps: At the end of Trip 54.

Highlights: A waterfall as beautiful as Hanakapiai Falls in a setting that's far more peaceful—you may have it all to yourself for a bit. If your itinerary forces you to choose between Hanakapiai and Hanakoa falls, and if you feel up to negotiating a trail that may be very rough, I say go to Hanakoa Falls.

Driving instructions: Not applicable.

Permit required: Permits required for dayhiking this far as well as for camping at Hanakoa (see Trip 52).

Description. This description assumes you're camped at Hanakoa. Remember, you can stay at Hanakoa only one night; you'll have to combine this side trip with your arrival at or departure from Hanakoa. If you get to Hanakoa Falls early, you may have it all to yourself until the helicopters start whining in and out of the valley, making you wonder if you've been transported in time and space to the set of *Apocalypse Now.*

A sign on the Kalalau Trail on the west side of Hanakoa Stream points you southeast to Hanakoa Falls and indicates it's only ⅓ mile (but it's farther). The trail to Hanakoa Falls crosses the first terrace on the west side and exits at its southeast corner. It's not at all obvious; you may think at first that it exits at the northwest corner, but that path just goes to more terraces.

Follow the beaten track or colored plastic ribbon tags across the west fork of Hanakoa Stream, where a marker says "¾." Terraces cover the valley floor here, a testimony to its productivity long ago. As you near the east fork, the track makes a switchback before emerging on the west bank of the east fork. You traverse the bank to the foot of the falls. There are some spots where erosion has cut a little gully across the trail. Watch out when you quickly grab at the vegetation when you slip; you

may come up with a handful of thorny thimbleberry, one of many introduced plants that's become a pest. (This is *rubus rosaefolius,* not the
thimbleberry of the mainland Pacific coast states, which is *rubus
parviflorus.* The berry of the Hawaiian thimbleberry is somewhat juicier
and more palatable than the mainland one, but that's not saying much.)

The going becomes rocky as you approach the falls, and you boulder-hop the last few yards to the lip of the pool. There's less freshly
broken rock around here than at Hanakapiai Falls, and the setting is
more lush. Pick a perch out of the range of falling rock and enjoy the
spectacle!

Too soon, the *whoppa whoppa whoppa* of helicopters fills the valley.
You have company now, so you may as well retrace your steps to your
campsite at Hanakoa.

Enjoying a tranquil visit to Hanakoa Falls

Trip 56. Kee Beach to Kalalau Beach Backpack

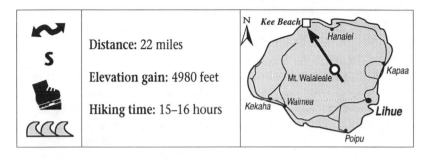

Distance: 22 miles

Elevation gain: 4980 feet

Hiking time: 15–16 hours

Topos: *Haena*

Trail maps: Starts on the map at the end of Trip 50; continues on the maps at the ends of Trips 52 and 54; ends on the map at the end of this trip.

Highlights: Sunshine, sunsets, and wonderful bird concerts.

Driving instructions: As for Trip 50.

Permit required: Permits required for dayhiking this far—assuming you can make this as a 22-mile dayhike!—as well as for camping at Kalalau (see Trip 52).

Description (moderate trip):

Days 1 and 2 *(6 miles).* Follow the hiking descriptions of Trips 52 and 54, first to Hanakapiai Beach and then to Hanakoa Valley.

Day 3 *(5 miles).* As you walk west out of Hanakoa Valley going uphill, you pass numerous terrace walls on the uphill side, overgrown with coffee. *Ti* dominates the downhill vegetation. The air continues warm and humid until you round the nose of the ridge that separates Hanakoa Valley from the next section of the Na Pali Coast to the southwest. This is Manono Ridge, and it blocks off much of the rainfall that makes the coast to the northeast so lush and humid; the coast is markedly drier from here on southwest.

You descend steep switchbacks past sisals into a dry gully on the west side of Manono Ridge. Emerging from the gully, you begin a precipitous traverse on loose conglomerate about 200 feet above the sea. Previously, there's been some vegetation to conceal the sheer drops, even if it was only a little grass. Here, nothing disguises the fact that you need to be extra careful. The unobstructed view of the ocean is breathtaking, literally, and the soil has an unusual gray-blue hue in some places. You're pretty obvious to the passengers in any tourist boats below; don't be surprised if they honk and wave at you.

From here to Kalalau, you'll see and hear terrain-damaging feral goats. Hunters help control their numbers; hunting is permitted here, so be sure to stick to the established trails.

The repeating pattern from here to Red Hill, a local name (not on the topo) for the steep west-trending slope that precedes Kalalau, is to traverse the nose of a ridge and then make steep descents into and ascents out of gullies. The first two gullies are dry, but later ones have small streams. Look for "onion" boulders (see below) on the dry ridges; at one point, you'll be climbing through some of them. One gully is particularly striking: it is filled with the gray-white trunks and branches of *kukui* trees that leaf out into their light-green crowns only above the gully. It's an eerie sight! Also look for *ape* plants, giant relatives of the *taro* plant. Look for the huge, slightly-crinkled, heart-shaped leaves of *ape* down in the gully among the tree trunks.

A final climb brings you to a little rest stop at the top of a steep red slope. The slope is Red Hill, and its crumbling soil is deeply gashed by erosion and offers very poor footing. The original route of the trail, where a mileage marker still sits, is now impassable because it's worn too deep. You need to pick your way down carefully, using one of the improvised routes, to the grassy area below, where you can again see the established trail.

It's not long before you're making your way through guava and Java

A view from the Kalalau Trail down a rugged coastal valley

plum trees and a yellow-flowered relative of cotton, *mao* or *huluhulu*. You're crossing the broad alluvial apron of Kalalau Valley at its seaward end. You descend briefly to Kalalau Stream; beyond the stream, you pass the trail to Kalalau Valley (no camping) and come out through guava and lantana onto the low bluffs above Kalalau Beach. What a welcome sight it is!

There are paths leading off through lantana and Indian pluchea into the trees on the inland side, and you can find good campsites there under *noni, kukui,* Java plum, and papaya trees. You may find goats grazing in the grassy area defined by stones, or you may sit there quietly and watch zebra doves and flocks of tiny finches searching for food. There are a pit toilet and a composting toilet near the east end of the camping zone and a pit toilet near the west end. The campsites become progressively more exposed and overused as you continue west.

Hoolea Falls at the west end of the beach cascades down a mossy groove that makes it a tempting place for a natural shower; unfortunately, hikers have been seriously injured by falling rock here. As always, never use soap in a stream, and treat all water before drinking it.

A walk to the west end of the beach allows you to wade a little in the surf if it's not too high, but swimming is very dangerous here. Look for dignified black birds with gray caps—black noddies *(noio)*—on the rocks near the end of the beach. Most of the sand is swept out to sea in the winter, leaving boulders at the east end and a narrow strip of sand at the west. In summer, a broad sand beach extends along the bluffs and past the sea caves. The cliffs are dangerous because of rockfall, so don't get too close to them. The rockslide at the far west end is said to be the remains of sea caves that collapsed in 1987.

This is the end of the Kalalau Trail. The cliffs of the Na Pali Coast are too sheer and too fragile to permit land travel southwest from here. The ancient Hawaiians used to travel this coast by canoe, not by trail, as long as the weather and sea conditions permitted. Today, modern tour boats take sightseers along the coast but are permitted to land at only a few places.

I hope you'll have at least one layover day here to dry out, sunbathe, visit Kalalau Valley (see side trip following), see a sunset and maybe the green flash, hear superb bird concerts, and watch an unbeatable display of stars (if the clouds and the moon permit). The white-rumped shama, or shama thrush, an introduced bird, is such a gifted singer that it's easy to forgive the introduction. Look for a medium-sized bird that's black above with chestnut breast, white rump, and white feathers under its long tail. Shamas flick their tails, so you may notice their white flashes. You're more likely to hear it than to see it. Its song is loud, rich, sweet, clear, and varied. It may not come around your campsite every day, but when it does, drop whatever you're doing and listen.

After dark, you may hear harmless big brown toads hopping through the leaf litter. They don't have the sense to stay out of your way, so try to stay out of theirs. Their skin secretes a poison, so wash your hands before touching your mouth, eyes, etc., if you handle a toad. Pests are few, but they move in fast: ants and cockroaches. Hang your food using rope or twine to which you've applied insect repellent; it's said to work for a while.

Days 4 through 6 *(11 miles).* Reverse the steps of Days 1 through 3.

"Onion" boulders.... There are good examples of boulders undergoing "spheroidal weathering" on some of the open slopes between Manono Ridge and Kalalau. An "onion" boulder consists of a rounded core surrounded by concentric shells of stone that turn out to be quite fragile. This is caused by a kind of chemical weathering in which water penetrates imperfections in the outer surface of the rock and reacts with the underlying rock to form a clay. The clay swells and forces the outer surface to separate from the inner surface. The undermined outer surface breaks away, and water attacks the new surface, repeating the cycle and resulting in the concentric shells, like the layers of an onion. The water penetrates more easily at edges and corners than on flat surfaces, so the process wears down sharp angles and produces a rounded core and shells.

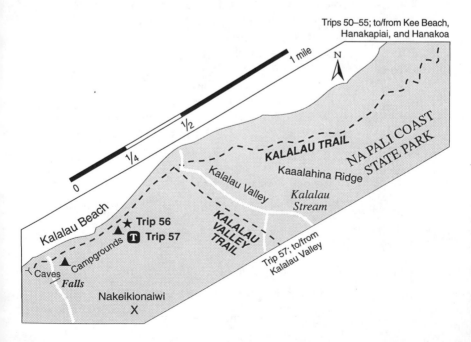

Trips 50–55; to/from Kee Beach, Hanakapiai, and Hanakoa

Trip 57. Kalalau Valley Side Trip

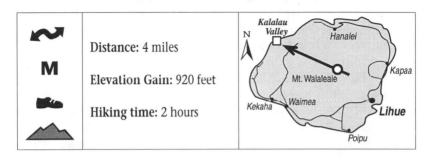

Distance: 4 miles

Elevation Gain: 920 feet

Hiking time: 2 hours

Topos: *Haena*

Trail maps: Begins on the map at the end of Trip 56; ends on the map at the end of this trip.

Highlights: A walk through a tropical valley to a large pool from whose clearing you can see the high, impossibly delicate spires that millions of years of erosion have carved from the adjacent ridges.

Driving instructions: Not applicable.

Permit required: Permit required to camp at Kalalau (see Trip 52). I'm assuming you won't want to dayhike all the way from Kee Beach into Kalalau Valley, but you'll need a dayhiking permit if you try to do so.

Description. This description assumes you're camped at Kalalau Beach. For this side trip, retrace your steps from your campsite at Kalalau Beach to the junction with the Kalalau Valley Trail. Turn right (inland) on the Kalalau Valley Trail and walk through lantana and Java plum. You soon reach a bare, steep, deeply eroded section which you scramble up as best you can.

Plunging back into forest again, you cross a small stream, follow the beaten track across ancient terraces, make your way up a steep gully, and pause at another open section to enjoy the view of the ridges around Kalalau Valley: Kaaalahina on the northeast and on the southwest the ridge on which Na-keiki-o-na-iwi, two prominent stone monoliths, sit. (See map for their location, called "Nakeikionaiwi" on the map and topo; see below for their story.) Terraces stretch in every direction under the trees; once, they were open, sunny places where taro grew. From here, the forest cover is dominated by guava trees. You'll recognize the presence of guava just by the fragrance of the fallen fruit. Look for the occasional mango tree, too, though it is rare to find any fruit left on them, I'm told.

You cross a tributary whose banks are fringed with wild ginger and then soon cross the main stream, where you may as well wade. The trail isn't obvious on the other side of the crossing. You pick it up in the dense ferns and follow it to a crossing of a very small tributary. The trail seems to fork here; take the right fork across the tributary, past some big sisals that you may need to hold onto because the trail is almost nonexistent here. In a few minutes you arrive at your destination, Big Pool. Water cascades from an upper pool over a rocky slide and into a large, guava-fringed pool where it's said that people used to gather to swim, sun, and gossip. The water may be quite cool. The open area around the pool allows more views of Na-keiki-o-na-iwi and the sculptured forms around them. It's a delightful, quiet place that's well worth the trouble to get to it even if you find the water too chilly to swim in. Stay awhile, then return the way you came.

Na-keiki-o-na-iwi....means "the children of the *iiwi* bird." I'll try to briefly retell my favorite version of this sad story.

Na-iwi, who was named for the *iiwi* bird, and his family were among the few Mu people who did not leave Kauai when the Menehunes left. Like the Menehunes, the Mu were nocturnal. Sunlight would turn them to stone. Na-iwi, his wife, and their children lived apart from all other people in a cave in the forests above Kalalau. Every day as they fell asleep in their cave, they could hear the people down in Kalalau working, talking, and playing together. Na-iwi's wife longed to work and talk with the women of Kalalau. One day she decided that sunlight couldn't possibly turn people to stone. She set off for Kalalau, and as she stepped into a clearing, the sunlight struck her, and she became stone.

Heartbroken, Na-iwi raised his son and daughter alone. He grew bananas in the mountains, and at night the children carried them down

Kalalau Beach

to Kalalau, where they would trade the bananas for fish and other sea delicacies. As his children grew, they heard the children of Kalalau laughing and playing in the sunshine and yearned to play with them. Na-iwi reminded them of their mother's fate, and his children realized that they would always be alone, for they thought the Kalalau children could play only in the sunlight.

One night, when the moon was very bright, Na-iwi's children went to Kalalau with their bananas and found the Kalalau children playing in the bright moonlight. Moonlight was no threat to Na-iwi's children! Soon, they were caught up in the laughter, friendship, and games they had dreamed of, and the night sped by. Too late, they tried to scale the steep ridges back to their cave, but daybreak caught them on the ridge and turned them to two stone monoliths before their anguished father's eyes.

Na-iwi grieved in the shadows till nightfall, then went to sit with them all that night. Near dawn, he went to the edge of the meadow where, years ago, his wife had turned to stone. He wept and spoke of his grief and loneliness until some of his sorrow washed away. Then, as sunlight touched the stone that had been his wife, he stepped out into the clearing to join her.

The stone spires called "Nakeikionaiwi" on the map were their children and rest today on the first ridge south of Kalalau Valley, near its west end.

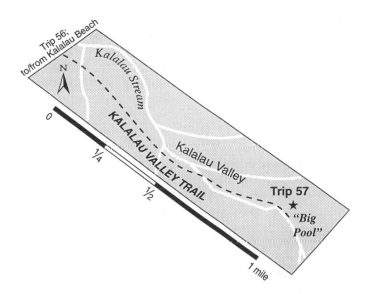

Trip 58. Kee Beach-Haena Beach Park Walk

 M

Distance: 2⅓ miles	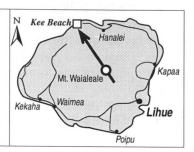
Elevation gain: 80 feet (to overlook of Waikapalae Wet Cave)	
Hiking time: 1¼ hours	

Topos: *Haena*

Trail maps: At the end of Trip 50.

Highlights: Tropical beach vistas, swimming at Kee Beach, and visits to mysterious caves highlight this short, scenic north-shore walk.

Driving instructions: Follow the directions of Trip 50.

Permit required: None.

Description. Begin your walk on the sand at Kee Beach and follow the beach away from the Na Pali Coast. (That means you'll be heading to your right as you face the ocean.) Inland, the beach is framed by a dense growth of ironwood, tropical almond, and *kukui* trees. Their debris—the elaborate little ironwood "cones," the big woody capsules of tropical almond, and the walnut-shell-like black capsules of *kukui*—litter the beach. Out to sea, huge blue swells race for the shore, only to break in a *boom!* of foam and spray on stony shelves far out in the water. It's a dazzling display of the power of one of Nature's principal agents of erosion here in Hawaii: the sea's relentless battering of the islands' edges. Be sure to look back from time to time to enjoy the views of the Na Pali Coast.

You begin to leave the crowd behind as you approach an unnamed stream that isn't on the topo and which may be intermittent. A short distance beyond the stream, there's a rocky section where you may prefer to detour into the trees in order to follow a trail-of-use through the pothos vines. Notice how the roots of the ironwood trees sometimes become tall and narrow as they snake through the sand here. Watch your footing on the dense mats of ironwood needles—they can be very slippery.

You presently ford pretty Limahuli Stream below some homes. The surf becomes more furious as you approach Haena Beach Park, which is a county park where camping is permitted. Altogether too soon, you cross a little stream and arrive at Haena Beach Park, 1⅓ miles from your start at Kee Beach, where you'll find water, restrooms, and, probably, lunch wagons in the parking lot. The sheer black cliffs, shiny with dripping water and lavishly decorated with tropical vegetation, make a perfect backdrop for this pretty beach. The surf here is usually too high for safe swimming, but you can rest at a table under the pavilion and watch the waves.

While you're enjoying the ocean view, you can decide whether you'll return on the beach the way you came or return on the road, visiting the three caves as you go. Even if you elect to return on the beach, you can easily visit Maniniholo Dry Cave: it's just across the road. This writeup assumes you'll return on the road and visit the caves.

However, the highway shoulders are narrow to nonexistent, so please be careful on the return via the caves. It's probably best to return the way you came if you have children along. That would make your hike a 2¾-mile, 1⅓-hour out-and-back trip.

Return on road. *Be alert* when walking on the road! It is narrow and winding and lacks easy-to-walk-on shoulders, and visitors sometimes drive too fast along it. (In general, I recommend that when *you* are walking on a road, you assume that everyone operating a vehicle on that road is deaf, blind, and insane.) It's 1 mile back to Kee Beach on the road, not including the short detours to the caves. The detours to the first and third caves, Maniniholo Dry Cave and Waikanaloa Wet Cave, are negligible.

Maniniholo Dry Cave beckons you just across the highway from Haena Beach Park. Maniniholo's floor is made of dry sand, and its ceiling becomes lower and lower as you continue toward the inky blackness at the back of the cave. You may have to get down on your hands and knees to avoid bumping your head on its ceiling. When you're well into its eerie darkness, turn around and look back out to the light streaming through the cave's dripping, fern-draped maw. Spooky! Maniniholo Cave is said to be a lava tube that eventually ends at an opening on the mountain above. Please don't try to find the opening yourself!

Back on the road, you walk carefully along the road, where you generally cannot stay on the preferred side—the one where you'd face oncoming traffic—for lack of a shoulder on that side. African tulip trees with their brilliant clusters of orange-red flowers, *hala*, and ironwood trees decorate the roadside, and huge pothos vines decorate the trees.

In ⅔ mile, you see an abandoned road that takes off steeply uphill on the south (inland) side of the road. This road leads very steeply up for about 100 yards to an overlook of Waikapalae Wet Cave. From that point, you may scramble down one of two extremely rough "paths" for a closer look at the shadowy pool of fresh water that fills the cave's floor. Don't be surprised if a spider has woven her web across the path so that you have to duck under it.

Upon your return to the road, a few more steps bring you to the ground-level entrance to Waikanaloa Wet Cave. Again, the floor of the cave is a shaded pool of fresh water, divided between at least two chambers that connect through the arch at the back of the chamber that you see from the road.

From Waikanaloa Wet Cave, it's just a few more steps back to the parking lot at Kee Beach.

Pele and Lohiau.....Legend says that the name "Haena," which means "the heat," refers to the passion of Pele, the volcano goddess, for the handsome Kauaian chief Lohiau who once dwelt here. Pele dug Waikanaloa and Waikapalae wet caves looking for a suitable home for herself and Lohiau, but all she found was cold, fresh water. (*Wai* means "fresh water.") A volcano goddess needs fire, not water! Disgusted, Pele left Kauai and Lohiau and finally found a home for herself in an active volcano, Kilauea on the Big Island of Hawaii. Now she longed to have Lohiau join her, so she sent her younger sister, Hiiaka, to Kauai to bring Lohiau to her. As often happens in these stories, not only was the journey full of adventures, but Hiiaka and Lohiau fell in love. Nevertheless, they continued back to Pele's home in Kilauea volcano. When Pele discovered their treachery, she buried Lohiau in lava. Hiiaka, grief-stricken, returned to Kauai alone. Pele's brothers restored Lohiau's life and took him back to Kauai, where he and Hiiaka were reunited and lived happily at Haena.

Trip 59. Lumahai Beach Walk

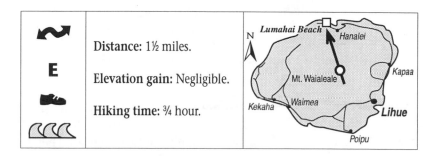

Distance: 1½ miles.

Elevation gain: Negligible.

Hiking time: ¾ hour.

Topos: Optional: *Hanalei*
Trail map: At the end of this trip.
Highlights: Hollywood made Lumahai Beach famous for its beauty (scenes for *South Pacific* were filmed here). When it's windy on the North Shore, go to see Lumahai Beach for its raging surf!
Driving instructions: Drive north from Lihue through Hanalei. At this point, Highway 56 has changed to Highway 560, and all the mileage-stake numbers have started over from zero. There may not be a sign on the highway for the "driveway" to Lumahai Beach. (The current on-highway sign is for an overlook east of this access.) After you pass the 5-mile marker *for Highway 560* and are nearing the 6-mile marker, look for a dirt driveway on the ocean side *just before* a two-lane bridge and the 6-mile marker. Turn in here and park wherever you can.
Permit required: None.
Description. The parking area is near the northwest end of the beach and the mouth of the Lumahai River. Begin by walking a few yards west to the riverbank and enjoying the peaceful view upriver and the contrasting view toward the sea, where the surf breaks on a line of black rocks. Remember that this is a walking and watching beach, not a swimming or surfing beach (extremely dangerous riptides, poor wave form).

Turn southeast along the beach and stroll toward the black cliff ½ mile away. Ironwood and *hau* form an idyllic tropical backdrop on your right while, if you're lucky enough to be there on a windy day, immense waves batter the sand. White wisps of foam run up the beach like fingers seeking to catch your feet and pull you into the sea. It's an exhilarating sight!

If the tide is in, or coming in, turn around at the cliff; don't tempt fate by wading into Lumahai's dangerous currents. You've seen the best of Lumahai. Otherwise, if there's plenty of beach available for getting

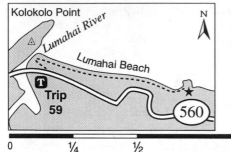

around the cliff, you may continue around to the smaller part of the beach (less than ¼ mile more). Don't let an incoming tide strand you here.

Retrace your steps to your car when you're ready.

Ironwood trees: no needles....Ironwood trees aren't conifers, and those needles aren't true needles at all. They're actually branchlets. Look closely at the joints on each branchlet, and you'll see tiny, brownish, tooth-like scales. These are said to be degenerate leaves, tissues of the kind that ought to develop into leaves but in this case fail to do so and instead become the scales you see.

Bibliography

"'Awa'awa'puhi Botanical Trail Guide." State of Hawaii, Department of Land and Natural Resources, Division of Forestry and Wildlife, 1988.

Day, A. Grove, and Carl Stroven, Eds., *A Hawaiian Reader*. Appleton-Century-Crofts, 1959. Reprint: Honolulu: Mutual Publishing Company, 1984.

Day, A. Grove, *Hawaii and Its People*. New York: Duell, Sloan and Pearce, 1955.

Department of Health, Kauai District Health Office, State of Hawaii, *Leptospirosis on Kauai*. Lihue: Kauai District Health Office, Health Promotion & Education Office & Epidemiology Branch, undated.

Doughty, Andrew, and Harriett Friedman, *Ultimate Kaua'i Guidebook*. 2nd ed. Lihue, HI: Wizard Publications, 1996.

East Kauai Soil and Water Conservation District Directors and Hawaii State Department of Land and Natural Resources Kauai District Division of Forestry, *A Trailside Guide to the Keahua Forestry Arboretum*. Directors of the East Kauai Soil and Water Conservation District, 1974.

Editors of *Sunset Magazine* and *Sunset* Books, *Sunset Western Garden Book*. 3rd ed. Menlo Park, California: Lane Magazine & Book Company, 1967.

Hargreaves, Dorothy, and Bob Hargreaves, *Hawaii Blossoms*. Kailua: Hargreaves Company.

———. *Tropical Trees of Hawaii*. Kailua: Hargreaves Company.

Hawai'i Audubon Society, *Hawaii's Birds*. 4th ed. Honolulu: Hawai'i Audubon Society, 1993.

Joesting, Edward, *Kauai, the Separate Kingdom*. Honolulu: University of Hawaii Press, 1984. Reprint: Honolulu: University of Hawaii Press, 1987.

Levi, Herbert W., and Lorna R. Levi, *Spiders and their Kin*. New York: Golden Press, 1987.

Macdonald, Gordon A., Agatin T. Abbott, and Frank L. Peterson, *Volcanoes in the Sea, the Geology of Hawaii*. 2nd ed. Honolulu: University of Hawaii Press, 1986.

Merlin, Mark David, *Hawaiian Coastal Plants and Scenic Shorelines*. 3rd printing. Honolulu: Oriental Publishing Co., 1986.

——. *Hawaiian Forest Plants*. 3rd ed. Honolulu: The Oriental Publishing Co., 1980.

O'Connell, D. K. J., S.J., "The Green Flash." *Light from the Sky*. San Francisco: W.H. Freeman and Company. (Reprinted from *Scientific American* (January 1960).)

Sohmer, S.H., and R. Gustafson, *Plants and Flowers of Hawai'i*. Honolulu: University of Hawaii Press, 1987.

Starbird, Ethel A., "Kauai, the Island That's Still Hawaii." *National Geographic* 152 (November 1977): 584-613.

Valier, Kathy, *The Kauai Guide to Hiking Trails Less Traveled with Camping Information*. Lihue: Magic Fishes Press, 1989.

——. *On the Na Pali Coast*. Honolulu: University of Hawaii Press, 1988.

Wenkam, Robert, *Kauai, Hawaii's Garden Island*. Deerfield, Illinois: Tradewinds Publishing, 1979. (Originally published as *Kauai and the Park Country of Hawaii*. San Francisco: Sierra Club, 1967. The 1967 original version contains (page 87) a quotation from an 1899 report of Hawaii's Minister of the Interior (Herberts):

> (On this land [Lihue Plantation] is an immense forest in excellent condition, fenced off from river to river, and any domestic animals found within the enclosure are shot. This plantation has also hundreds of acres of young and thrifty forest trees. . . .The result is that the Lihue Plantation has water to give away, while other parts of the island are short. It is an established fact that the destruction of forests in any country tends to diminish the supply of water. Let any one doubting this fact visit the Lihue Plantation and be convinced.)

Wichman, Frederick B., *Kauai Tales*. 3rd printing. Honolulu: Bamboo Ridge Press, 1985.

Winnett, Thomas, and Melanie Findling, *Backpacking Basics*. 4th ed. Berkeley: Wilderness Press, 1994.

Zim, Herbert S., Ph.D., and Lester Ingle, Ph.D., *Seashores*. New York: Simon and Schuster, 1955.

Zurich, David, *Hawaii, Naturally*. Berkeley: Wilderness Press, 1990.

Appendix A. Camping on Kauai

Backcountry camping accessible on foot. Backcountry camping that's accessible on foot is allowed in Waimea Canyon (Wiliwili and Kaluahaulu camps in Waimea Canyon proper, Hipalau and Lonomea camps in tributary Koaie Canyon), the Alakai Swamp (Koaie Camp), and on the Na Pali Coast (Hanakapiai Beach, Hanakoa Valley, and Kalalau Beach). See Trips 26–28, 52, 54, and 56 in this book.

Two scenic campgrounds in the Na Pali-Kona Forest Reserve east of Kokee State Park, Kawaikoi and Sugi Grove camps, are accessible only by a 4WD road, Mohihi Road. That makes them accessible only on foot for us tourists with rental passenger cars. See Trip 44 in this book.

Backcountry camping accessible by small boat. Milolii State Park offers camping but is accessible only by small boat, weather permitting. This "foot-oriented" book doesn't cover it. You can get more information by writing to the Division of State Parks; the address is in "Getting Permits or Permission." *On the Na Pali Coast* (see Bibliography) gives a delightful account of Milolii from the boater's point of view. (A second boat-accessible-only park, Nualolo Kai, is no longer open to camping.)

Car camping. Kauai offers lots of car camping—the kind of camping where you drive up, pay your bucks, pick a space, park your car, pitch your tent there, and live out of it. Or live out of your parked vehicle. For those of you who enjoy car camping, here is a list of the places you can car-camp in Kauai. Unless otherwise specified, only tent-camping is allowed. I have not verified anything about this information, which I am excerpting from agency literature. Campers must have permits, which you may obtain in advance by mail or in person if there is space available. Each agency has more rules for campers than I have room for here, so be sure to write ahead to get a permit application as well as a set of the agency's rules.

County Parks. You can apply for a permit to camp in a County Park in advance. Get your permit application from, and send your completed permit and payment to, County of Kauai, Department of Public Works, Division of Parks and Recreation, 4444 Rice Street, Moikeha Building, Suite 150, Lihue, HI 96766. When you apply, you must include the correct amount for your permit as a check or money order. Advance permits cost $3/person/night for adult (over 18) campers who are not residents of Hawaii; there is no charge for minors (under 18) or residents of Hawaii (you must provide proof of residency). Permits are not issued to minors. If you get a permit on demand from a Park Ranger, assuming there is space in the campground, the cost is $5/person/night. Stays are limited to 7 consecutive nights at any one campsite and to 60 days in one year-long period.

State Parks. Permits to camp in State Parks are issued Monday through Friday, 8 AM to 4 PM, at the Division of State Parks office in Lihue (see "Getting Permits" in this book). The person appearing to apply for the permit must provide proper identification for each person in the party who is 18 years old or older. "Proper identification" means a driver's license, passport, state I.D., or Social Security Card. You may also apply by mail at least seven days in advance of your proposed trip by writing to the Division of State Parks. When applying by mail, include a copy of the proper identification for each person in the party who is 18 years old or older and the names and ages of the minors (under 18) in the party. Submit a self-addressed, stamped size-10 envelope along with your request. Applications for the peak season (May–September) must be received at least 6 months in advance and will be issued pending space availability!

Name	Type	Nearest Town	Amenities; Restrictions
Haena Beach Park	County	Haena	Pavilion, toilets, showers, tables, grills; mobile campers allowed
Hanalei Beach Park	County	Hanalei	Toilets, tables, grills; open Fridays, Saturdays, and holidays only
Anini Beach Park	County	Kilauea	Pavilion, toilets, showers, grills, tables; swimming
Anahola Beach Park	County	Anahola	Toilets, showers, grills
Hanamaulu Beach Park	County	Hanamaulu	Pavilion, toilets, showers, grills, tables; mobile campers allowed
Niumalu Beach Park	County	Nawiliwili	Pavilion, toilets, showers, barbecue pits, tables; mobile campers allowed
Salt Pond Beach State Park	County	Hanapepe	Pavilion, toilets, showers, tables
Lucy Wright Park	County	Kekaha	Toilets, showers
Polihale State Park	State	Kekaha	Pavilion, toilets, showers, barbecue pits, tables; mobile campers allowed
Kokee State Park	State	Kekaha, Waimea	Restroom; mobile campers allowed

Cabins, tent-cabins. For camping in cabins in Kokee State Park, contact:

> Kokee Ventures
> P.O. Box 819
> Waimea, HI 96796
> (808) 335-6061

I understand these cabins are so popular that it's a good idea to apply as much as a year in advance of your visit!

For camping in cabins or furnished tents in the mountains west of Lihue, contact:

> Kahili Mountain Park, Inc.
> P.O. Box 298
> Koloa, Kauai, HI 96756.

Appendix B. Hikes You Won't Find Here and Why

You may have read articles on the following hikes, seen them mentioned in other books, or noticed them on topos. Here's why they're not in this book:

Hanalei

Hanalei Valley Trail. Closed.
Hanalei-Okolehao Route. Closed.

Kilauea Point National Wildlife Refuge

Reopened for short visits. Call the refuge at (808) 828-1413 for the latest information. Formerly Trip 4 in this book.

Lihue Area

Kalepa Ridge and Kilohana Crater dayhikes. The Lihue Plantation Company no longer issues permits to hike on their land. This means you can't hike to Kalepa Ridge and Kilohana Crater (formerly Trips 21–23) any more. The person I spoke with explained that the reason for this policy change was that the company's liability-insurance costs had become too high.

Kokee State Park

Ditch Trail. Reportedly terrific hiking when it's in good shape, but its hike-ability depends on how recently the trail has been maintained. Ask at park headquarters.

West of Kokee State Park

Honopu Trail. Closed since it was severely damaged by Hurricane Iwa in 1982. There are no plans to rebuild this trail.
Alakai Swamp Wilderness Preserve. The Alakai Swamp Wilderness Preserve protects most of the Alakai Swamp, and the Division of Forestry and Wildlife, which is responsible for the swamp, discourages entry into the Preserve. See "About the Alakai Swamp..." in this book.
Alakai Swamp Trail East of Junction with Pihea Trail. See "About the Alakai Swamp..." in this book.

Mohihi-Waialae Route Beyond "Rain Gauge." See Trip 49 in this book.
"Route to Mt. Waialeale." This shows up as a trail on at least a couple of tourist maps in spite of the fact that there is not and never has been a trail to Mt. Waialeale.

Waimea Canyon

The following trails were formerly closed due to hurricane damage. They are apparently open now, but they are largely hunters' routes, and I have not hiked them:

Kaluahaulu (or Kaluahaulu Waialae) Trail
Waialae Stream (to Poacher's Camp)
Puu Ki Waialae Trail

Appendix C. How I Got Distances, Elevations, Times, and Trail Maps

I estimated distances by time, knowing that I hike at 2 miles/hour and backpack at about 1⅓ miles/hour. I compared the distances I got by time with distance values from two other sources: distances I'd estimated by plotting the trail on graph paper and distances supplied by the agency in charge of that trail. When those distances were all close, I felt satisfied with the distance I'd estimated by time. I usually rounded the distances off to the nearest ¼ or ⅓ mile.

I determined elevation from my trail plots and with an altimeter, more often the former. Where I had altimeter data, I looked for close correspondence between those values, values I'd plotted, and any values supplied by the agency in charge of the trail.

Trail times are based on the time I actually spent *in motion* on the trail.

I made the trail maps by first scanning the topos into a computer. I put the resulting digitized topos that applied to a trip or set of trips in the "bottom layer" of an electronic drawing. I "traced" selected topo information from the bottom layer onto a "transparent" electronic upper layer. I left out the elevation contours because they would have taken me too long to draw and would have made these gray-scale maps far too busy. I added, deleted, or modified topo information that I knew had changed. I supplemented the digitized topos with maps from the Division of Forestry and Wildlife, Kauai District, which I also digitized and traced. My choices of conventions for trails, roads, boundaries, etc., primarily reflect the software's capabilities.

Index

Acknowledgments

For their encouragement, help, advice, endless patience, and financial support during both editions: my husband, Ed Schwartz, and Wilderness Press's president and editor-in-chief, Thomas Winnett. For their encouragement, help, and advice with this book's first edition: Barbara Dallavo and Christina Morey O'Keefe.

Kelly Poor and Dan Masaki shared their Kauai stories with me.

For sending useful information to and answering endless questions from a total stranger during the first edition's preparation: Division of Forestry and Wildlife, Kauai District (particularly Mr. Alvin Kyono and Mr. Thomas Telfer, who once answered and double-checked, respectively, a questionnaire from me which was six pages long); Division of State Parks, Kauai District; Hawaii Visitors Bureau.

Mr. Edwin Q. P. Pettys of the Division of Forestry and Wildlife was extremely helpful in 1993 when I updated this book in the wake of Hurricane Iniki (September 1992).

I am deeply indebted to readers who have written me with their compliments, criticisms, and new information. Until I became an author, I could imagine neither how important readers' inputs are nor how much I should enjoy receiving them. Keep up the good work, friends!

Andrew Doughty, co-author with Harriett Friedman of *The Ultimate Kauai Guidebook*, has been a generous source of last-minute details for this edition.

I hope I have accurately and adequately reflected the information these people, and many others, provided directly or indirectly. Any misunderstanding or errors are my responsibility.

——K.M.